Waking Up In
MEMPHIS

Printed in the United Kingdom by MPG Books Ltd, Bodmin

Published by Sanctuary Publishing Limited, Sanctuary House, 45–53
Sinclair Road, London W14 0NS, United Kingdom

www.sanctuarypublishing.com

ISBN: 1-86074-447-8

Waking Up In
MEMPHIS

Andria Lisle and Mike Evans

Sanctuary

Contents

Introduction

The Memphis Sound is legendary – but what has made Memphis the wellspring of so much good music? Theories abound, from the murky water in the Mississippi River to the hot temperatures and humidity in the air. But local musical icon Jim Dickinson got it just about right when he summed it up: 'Memphis music is about racial collision in both directions' – the impact of two cultures occupying the same space. Whether via broadcasting since the days of Dewey Phillips's pioneering *Red Hot And Blue* radio show, legendary record labels Sun and Stax, nightclubs from the Plantation Inn in the '40s and '50s to Wild Bill's in the here and now, or the actual musicians themselves, the evolution of Memphis music has been a direct result of integration.

Back when segregation was still the rule book for most ways of life in the South, in Memphis whites were recording blacks, learning to play from black musicians, impersonating blacks, and eventually performing alongside them. And it was a two-way street – black producers were coming to the fore, black radio stations impacted on white listeners (crucially on musicians and singers), and black musicians hitherto ignored found a crossover route to the broader white market.

The amazing richness of music and musical styles produced in this process can be appreciated just by reference to some of the names involved; Furry Lewis, Rufus Thomas, Ike Turner, Elvis Presley, Jerry Lee Lewis, Carla Thomas, Booker T, Sam and Dave, Otis Redding, The Box Tops, Isaac Hayes…the list goes on and on, right up to modern inheritors like The North Mississippi Allstars.

And behind this star-studded pageant over the years, there have always been equally important unsung heroes, musicians and songwriters, studio pioneers and evangelical journalists, who've been the backbone of the scene, sustaining its worth when times have been hard, believers all.

Now, after almost 50 years, the city has finally realised what a commodity this legacy of Memphis music can be. Today's politicians have embraced the notion, renovating Beale Street (now a worldwide tourist destination) and helping build the Museum of American Soul Music at the former site of the Stax recording studio. Internationally revered, today's Memphis music scene is a living testimony to its colour-blind originators.

So, what makes Memphis music so lasting? More specifically, going back in history, why did it become a centre for the blues? How did country and blues music merge to form rockabilly and rock 'n' roll? Was Elvis the first rock 'n' roller? What part did religion play in all this? How did a handful of open-minded blacks and whites revolutionise soul music in the 1960s? Lastly, how will these musical traditions so part of the Memphis fabric – blues, rockabilly, soul and rock 'n' roll – remain current in the 21st century?

In *Waking Up In Memphis*, Andria Lisle and Mike Evans look at this unique musical culture as it has manifested itself in the past and still does so today, by talking to people, listening to the music, and just experiencing Memphis. They come to it from very different perspectives: Andria Lisle lives and works as a journalist in Memphis, with a long and close association with many of the individuals concerned with the music past and present. Mike Evans is a writer based in London, England, who has become familiar with Memphis since the early '90s via several working visits, and has been a fan of its music for almost as long as he can remember. Together their contributions form an impressionistic, personalised picture which hopefully will convey to the reader something of the real flavour of that unique city and its musical heritage.

1 The Memphis Blues Again

THE MEMPHIS BLUES AGAIN
Andria Lisle

Memphis, my friend Robert Gordon says, can be easily mistaken for a town of doughnut shops and churches. Midtown, about 6km (4 miles) east of the city's downtown on the Mississippi River, certainly has its share of both. Though best known for its wide-ranging population of eccentrics and bohemians, midtown is also home to professionals, working-class families, and old-money cotton dynasties. Midtown architecture reflects this diversity: turn-of-the-century gothic mansions share the block with craftsman bungalows, shotgun shacks, columned buildings and Queen Anne-style cottages.

I've lived in Memphis for nearly half my life, moving from house to apartment to house, from one street to another, relocating seven times in a dozen years. I started out on Patterson Street, near the University of Memphis, in 1988, with seven room-mates. Our 100-year-old farmhouse was filthy, ramshackle and cheap. We modelled our set-up on a traditional punk-rock squat, although we all paid rent ($125 a month, I recall).

My current abode is much nicer than that dive on Patterson, which was demolished shortly after we all moved out. I have a small brick cottage that was built in the 1940s, conveniently located on Rembert Street just off Poplar Avenue, Memphis's main east–west drag. Two dogs and two cats share my space – five rooms and a big backyard. I have air conditioning (a necessity in this temperate climate), a remodelled bathroom and kitchen, and hundreds of books. What was once the dining room has been designated the record room; it's got floor-to-ceiling shelves groaning with vinyl LPs and compact discs.

The Hi-Tone Café, one of the best live venues in town, is located just around the corner, and rambling Overton Park – with the city's finest art museum and miles of woodland trails – is less than a block from my door.

My street is typical midtown – a hodgepodge of shotgun shacks and bungalows, with a few modern buildings where older homes once stood. Most folks moved in around World War II, though a few date back to the mid-1920s. There's a good mix of people in my neighbourhood – some own, while others (like me) rent; whites and blacks live side by side, as do students, professionals and the elderly. Most of us know each other's names.

Miss Lillian, an older black woman, lives halfway up the block in the tiny duplex with the perfect front yard. She spends most days on her knees in the flower garden, pausing only to greet the children and animals that inevitably wander by on their way to the park. 'What's up, honey chile?' she always asks, stopping to pat my dogs on their heads. When I have time, I ask Miss Lillian about particular people in the neighbourhood – she knows more than any newspaper and stays proudly up-to-date on all our comings and goings.

It's a musical neighbourhood – a classical guitarist and his artist wife live a few houses over, and a family of melodic Cubans owns the place across the street. A bassist, blues guitarist and drummer also make their homes on the block. When Jeff Buckley moved to Memphis in the spring of 1997 to record the follow-up to *Grace*, he rented the white frame house next door to mine. Down here, Jeff could definitely be himself, or be whichever self he wanted to be.

Memphis is an easy town to live in without too much money – much cheaper than New York. I think Jeff thought he could be here without bothering anybody, just sit at home and record if he had a mind to, but sometimes he'd just lie in the weeds that took over his front yard. Jeff never mowed his grass, so when he lay outside you couldn't even tell he was there. He would hide like that for days. We were friends, and then he died, just months after coming to town.

But there's another musician who once lived on my street – he moved in long before I was born – whose story fascinates me even more. He was a bluesman from the early 1900s, who went by the name of Nathan Beauregard. The late blues revivalist Bill Barth, who first came to Memphis in the 1960s, told of meeting Nathan when he was out canvassing for old records.

Barth included the story in *Confessions Of A Psychedelic Carpetbagger*. 'One day, I think it was a Sunday,' Barth wrote, 'I was working a nearby street asking if anyone had any old records, like Blind Lemon or Charley Patton, when someone invited me to take a look at a guitar they might want to sell. The house was small, and very dark inside, like walking into the gloom; midday Memphis burning outside the door though not a droplet of light could penetrate the shadows into the back of the inside room.'

Barth never bought the guitar – apparently, it wasn't actually for sale. But a few months later, he met the guitar's owner on my block, which he referred to as 'the type of street [that] people didn't live on for very long'.

'I got to the end of the row of gray shotgun shacks and was about to knock on the final door when I heard an old blues record coming from inside the house,' Barth wrote. 'I could not believe what I was hearing at first. I noticed my hand was frozen, still raised in a fist to knock on the door. I'd once heard of a [record] collector who had come across a house where an old lady was sitting and listening to her old blues records on her wind-up graphonola as the collector knocked on the door, and I flashed that this might be the same sort of thing. So I knocked.

'"Come on," the voice from inside beckoned. I opened the door and put a foot in the room, immediately looking for the graphonola, and noticing that there wasn't one. What there was instead was the old man whose guitar had been offered to me for sale two or three months earlier, only this time he was playing it. He had come out of retirement. "How ya doin?" Well, what could I say? "Sit down." I sat. We got acquainted, and he played some more. I was in heaven, or the blues version of it.'

The shotgun shacks Barth mentioned are across the street from my house. So named because of their floor plan – one room wide and three rooms deep, a bullet fired through the front door would exit the back door without piercing a single wall – they are practical structures built to precisely fit the narrow lots they occupy. Today, a college student lives in one, a landscaper in another, and black families occupy the rest. The only people who could pinpoint which house was Beauregard's are long gone – not even Miss Lillian can recall the veteran bluesman.

Nathan Beauregard was born in Ashland, Mississippi, in 1863. Blind since birth, he was a proficient guitarist by the time Theodore Roosevelt took his presidential oath. Nathan's repertoire drew on country dance tunes and string band numbers, as well as blues from Frank Stokes, Charley Patton, Gus Cannon and Son House. The material he played at the end of his life – including 'Nathan's Bumble Bee Blues' and 'Spoonful', his only two recordings I've managed to track down – was popular in the years between the world wars, during the first heyday of country blues.

In June 1969, when I was four months old, Nathan had already celebrated his 107th birthday. He performed at the Memphis Blues Festival that month, held in Overton Park just across Poplar Avenue. Nathan shared the stage with Furry Lewis, Sleepy John Estes, Fred McDowell, Johnny Woods, Napoleon Strickland and Othar Turner for the weekend event. Of all these country blues heavyweights, Nathan was the elder statesman, predating Furry, his closest rival, by 20 years.

At some point, the performers at the '69 festival were taken to Ardent Recording Studios on nearby Madison Avenue to lay down studio versions of their live sets. Those sessions have been reissued and repackaged in many formats, and I have two versions in my collection: a double LP called *Memphis Swamp Jam* on the Blue Thumb label, and the two-disc *Mississippi Delta Blues Jam In Memphis*, released on Arhoolie. For reasons I cannot quite justify, I prefer to listen to the dusty, scratched-up vinyl.

Listening to Beauregard's voice as he croaks out 'Nathan's Bumble Bee Blues' is nothing short of revelatory. 'I don't want no sugar, no sugar in my tea,' he sings, punctuating his own vocals with a slightly out-of-tune electric guitar. He answers his own rhyme in the next line, boasting, 'I got a long-haired woman sweet enough for me.' His voice is strong, even if his words are somewhat garbled – due, I believe, to a lack of teeth. Bill Barth called it 'high and lonesome, the kind [of voice] you once heard coming from the front porch and out on across the fields, in an earlier century'. An adaptation of Memphis Minnie's 'Bumble Bee', Nathan's 'Bumble Bee Blues' rambles on for ten and a half minutes, his guitar ringing and chiming along as he varies from 8- to 10- to 12-bar blues.

In his essay, Barth wrote that Nathan's hands were small and 'delicate, with strong nails'. Scrutinising the black-and-white portrait on the cover of *Memphis Swamp Jam*, I see a wizened old man in a clean white shirt, diminutive even next to Furry Lewis's narrow form. Nathan's heavy-lidded, unseeing eyes are half closed, and his left hand is casually draped over the neck of his guitar, again in contrast to Furry, who sits ramrod straight with a half smile on his sunny face. Nathan is the other side of the coin – small and sleepy and leathery, like an ancient lizard basking on a rock.

I enjoy looking at this picture as I listen to Nathan's two songs over and over again. It's hypnotising, a meditative exercise, and I like to think that I know Nathan Beauregard, that he's happy to have me on Rembert Street, playing these old blues. And I call to my dogs for a walk to the park, taking time at the bottom of my driveway to glance over at the row of shotgun shacks across the street. Often, I'll pause to wonder about this man, as old as country blues itself, who made his final home in midtown Memphis, Tennessee. Then the dogs strain at their leashes, and it's time to move on to Miss Lillian and the world beyond.

WC HANDY AND THE BEALE STREET BLUES
Mike Evans

Although born in Florence, Alabama, WC Handy, acknowledged in terms of songwriting, as the 'Father of the Blues', had a long working relationship with Memphis, and Beale Street in particular, where a statue of the first great African-American composer stands in a small park that bears his name.

Handy was not a blues performer, and it can be argued his songs were not strictly blues as such, but he was certainly the first formal songwriter to pick up on the black folk music with which he grew up, and the first to incorporate the flattened thirds and fifths that distinguish the blues idiom. Furthermore, a number of his songs, including 'Memphis Blues', 'Beale Street Blues', 'Careless Love' and most famously 'St Louis Blues', became classic items in the jazz and popular song repertoire of the 20th century.

William Christopher Handy was born on 16 November 1873. He grew up in a log cabin which had been built by his grandfather, a church minister; his father was also a preacher, and his strict religious upbringing discouraged any music of a secular nature. Despite this, legend has it he had a musical ear as a child and secretly saved enough money from odd jobs to buy a guitar he had seen in a local shop window; when he proudly brought it home, so the story goes, his father made him take it back and exchange it for a dictionary. He made another secret purchase when a young teenager, a cornet, taking lessons from fellow musicians in a barber shop – quite a common venue for musical activity at that time.

A musical career soon commenced when, not yet 20, he organised a quartet which was to perform at the prestigious Chicago Worlds Fair of 1893. Still teaching music for a living, he went on to join an outfit called Mahara's Minstrels for $6 a week, a three-year tour taking the troupe through Texas and Oklahoma, across the southeast through Tennessee and Georgia, and south to Florida and eventually to Cuba.

Marriage and the first of six children, however, led him to settle down, first in his hometown of Florence, Alabama, then in Clarksdale, Mississippi, where he directed a black band called the Knights Of Pythias from 1903. The band made the move to Memphis in 1909 and, from their initial HQ in Pee Wee's Saloon and then from their own office (both on Beale Street), Handy was to start writing the songs that were the first to be associated with the description 'blues'.

For some years he had been acutely aware of black gospel and folk music, wherein he recognised the roots of the blues; he was quoted in an interview thus: 'Each one of my blues is based on some old Negro song of the South... Something that sticks in my mind, that I hum to myself when I'm not thinking about it. Some old song that is a part of the memories of my childhood and of my race. I can tell you the exact song I used as a basis for any one of my blues.'

And it was in the musical hotbed of Memphis that this awareness was to come to fruition. Not long after settling in the city, he and the band were asked to play for the local political boss-man, Edward H Crump (whose immortality was guaranteed when, like Elvis many years later, he had a boulevard named after him). Handy had already written a song which was none too complimentary called 'Mr Crump', but some amendment to the lyrics quickly created an ideal anthem for the mayoral campaign. It was to evolve further when, in 1912, it became Handy's first big commercial hit as 'Memphis Blues'.

It was the first blues Handy ever wrote, and many considered it to be the first specifically published blues song in history, although due to Handy's initial problems in finding a publisher it actually appeared in print after 'Baby Seals Blues' by Artie Matthews, in the August of 1912 and Hart A Wand's 'Dallas Blues' in September. 'Memphis Blues' finally came out in early October after Handy decided to publish it himself.

Handy's partner in the publishing company was Harry Pace, and together they took on the task of getting the sheet music distributed to retailers, despite ingrained racial prejudice among many shops to stock 'coloured' songs and the unfamiliarity of the blues form. Whatever, 'Memphis Blues' was a huge hit across America, paving the way for his most celebrated composition, 'St Louis Blues', in 1914. 'St Louis Blues' was Handy's best-selling song and one of the most recorded in the history of popular music. Forty years after it was first published, it was still earning Handy annual royalties of nearly $25,000.

Among many other songs the prolific writer was composing and publishing, another Memphis-influenced piece was to be Handy's next big success in 1916, 'Beale Street Blues', with its immortal opening lines, 'If Beale Street could talk, if Beale Street could talk, married men would have to take their beds and walk'. Handy later described to an interviewer how the song was inspired by a fellow musician on Beale Street: 'As I was walking down Beale Street one night, my attention was caught by the sound of a piano. The insistent Negro rhythms were broken by a tinkle in the treble, then by a rumble in the bass; then they came together. I entered the cheap café and found a colored man at the piano, dog tired. He told me he had to play from seven at night until seven in the morning, and rested himself with alternate hands. He told me of his life, and it seemed to me that this poor, tired, happy-go-lucky musician represented his race. I set it down in notes, keeping faith with all that made the background of that poor piano thumper.'

Following these and other successes, the company moved to offices in New York in 1918, where hit followed hit including, most memorably, 'Careless Love' in 1921, 'Aunt Hagar's Blues (1922) and 'Hesitating Blues', with the classic nature of many of the compositions being confirmed by their adoption by the greatest names in jazz, blues and pop music, including Louis Armstrong, Billie Holiday, Fats Waller, Ray Charles and the great 'Queen of the Blues', Bessie Smith (whose celebrated 1925 recording of 'St Louis Blues' features the young Armstrong on cornet).

On his death from bronchial pneumonia in 1958, at the age of 84, Handy (who Hollywood had honoured with a biopic, *St Louis Blues*, starring Nat King Cole just the year before) was buried in New York, where 150,000 mourners lined the funeral route. His memory was later marked by the United States Postal Service with a commemorative stamp, as well as a statue in his birthplace acknowledging the most famous son of Florence, Alabama. More significantly, the Blues Foundation's annual equivalent of the Grammys are named after him, the WC Handy Awards. And in Memphis there is the statue, and the house (which was moved from another location) where he once resided and worked, both on the Beale Street his song helped immortalise.

THE LIFE AND TIMES OF REV GATEMOUTH MOORE
Andria Lisle

Judy Peiser's voice was incredulous. 'What do you mean, you've never heard of Gatemouth Moore?' she demanded. Judy, the Executive Director of the Center for Southern Folklore, was giving me a list of musicians who were scheduled to perform at that year's Music and Heritage Festival, and I apparently had asked her the wrong question. I'd heard of

Gatemouth Brown, the blues fiddle player, but Gatemouth Moore? Who in the world was he?

Judy walked over to the Center's gift shop and rooted around the selection of video tapes, eventually coming up with a copy of *Saturday Night, Sunday Morning: The Travels Of Gatemouth Moore*. She handed me the tape, and told me to go home and watch it immediately. 'I don't have anything to say to you until you watch this movie,' she told me, only half-joking. 'Now get home and watch it!'

I'd been doing volunteer work at the Center for Southern Folklore that summer – I had just lost a job, and had plenty of spare time. Booking the Music and Heritage Festival was a real blast – Judy's contacts on the local scene ran the gamut from Choctaw Indian dancers to boogie-woogie pianists and one-man bands. The festival in years past had also been a real eye-opener for me – the first place I saw Rufus Thomas, Othar Turner, and T-Model Ford – and, as a free event, it represented the pinnacle of Memphis music history.

That year, the Center could use a lot of help. In 1999, Performa Real Estate – which manages Beale Street – had decided not to renew the Center's lease, and evicted the non-profit in favour of a daiquiri bar called Wet Willie's. It was the Center's fifth home since opening its doors in 1972 and, by all accounts, its most profitable. For much of 2000, the Center was a nonentity, until real-estate magnate Jack Belz offered Judy space in his Peabody Place complex. The 3000 square feet of space are admittedly somewhat cavernous and mall-like, but Judy and her army of employees and volunteers have done what they can to make the room more homelike.

Dozens of quilts hang from the rafters, while folk art from the likes of New Orleans artist Dr Bob and Memphis native Tommy Foster adorn the stage, bar and gift shop. Regional music – everything from old-timey jazz to modern-day punk rock – blares from the loudspeakers situated around the building. A cafeteria-style restaurant, cybercafé and gallery space complete the picture.

But, entombed within the office and shopping complex, the Center for Southern Folklore gets only a small percentage of the walk-in business they were accustomed to on Beale Street. Curious tourists can no longer drop in from the sidewalk, lured inside by barrelhouse pianist Mose Vinson (until his recent demise, aged 85) or singer Joyce Cobb. They have to navigate their way past a grocery store, Time-Warner office and greeting card shop, before they can see the stage. It had been two years since the Center put together a festival, and Judy needed to throw a good party for her friends and fans.

I returned to the Center for Southern Folklore the next morning, full of questions. Where did Gatemouth live these days? Where was his church? And, most importantly, would he really perform at the festival this year? Of course, Judy – a tireless promoter of unsung Memphis music – had all the answers, and she supplied me with an address and phone number. 'Call him,' she said. 'He loves to talk.'

I didn't have any free time that week, but I cleared the next Monday afternoon, checking in with Gatemouth – the Rev AD Moore, officially – before heading south to Yazoo City to meet him. 'Too bad you didn't call me earlier,' he said over the phone, his laconic voice coming through loud and clear. 'I drove up to Memphis last month – presided over my daughter's wedding, down at the train station,' Gatemouth told me. 'Then I drove up to Chicago' ('*Chee-car-go*' was how he pronounced it) 'for a spell. I'll be back in Memphis for Judy's festival – you can count on that,' he said. 'But if you want to meet me sooner, come on down to Yazoo City.'

I didn't need any more of an invitation – after hanging up with Gatemouth, I called a friend, and quickly gassed up the car for the drive south. We consulted a road map, and decided to head down I-55 as far as Grenada, before cutting west down 49 towards Vicksburg. I loaded up the car with my collection of blues CDs, and we pulled out of Memphis by noon. It was a beautiful day – not too hot, considering it was already June – and we were only too happy to be on a little adventure.

Some three hours later, we pulled up to the African Methodist Episcopal Church on Lintonia Avenue, and there he was, parked out front in a shiny black Cadillac. The tinted window rolled down as I got close, and a black cowboy hat tipped in my direction. Then Gatemouth – a tall, brown-skinned man wearing a dark turtle-neck sweater and a black sharkskin suit – climbed out of the vehicle. His sunglasses and shiny gold cross flickered in the sunlight as he held out both arms to greet me. 'Welcome to Yazoo, baby,' he told me, enveloping me in his strong arms. 'I'm Reverend Gatemouth Moore.'

My companion and I stand open-mouthed. There's no way that this man is Rev Moore – this guy looks to be in his 50s but, according to Judy, Gatemouth is 88 years old. This must be his son, or a nephew... But no, the Reverend tells us, chuckling, 'I am the one and only Gatemouth. What you see is what you get, children. Now come on in and tell Daddy Gate what y'all want to know, and I'll do my best to answer your questions.' And with that, he unlocks the church office's door with a flourish, and beckons us inside.

Gatemouth is an old pro with the media and, even before I can pull it out of my backpack, he asks me about my tape recorder. 'You better get this down, baby, because I'm only telling this once,' he says, his twinkling eyes downplaying his stern demeanour. He waits patiently for me to get set up, then leans back, his hat off and his eyes closed, and starts talking.

'I was a boy soprano in Topeka, Kansas, from the time I was about nine years old,' Gatemouth says. 'I was born there, in November 1913. And until I was 15 years old, I won every amateur contest they had at school, singing songs like "My Yiddish Mama" and "Irish Eyes". I went to a white school there – didn't even know I was black, for a long time. My mama was the washerwoman for some millionaire white folks, and I lived in their house. I was their baby – they took me everywhere, and all my little playmates were white too. Then when I was 12, they started talking about giving me a bar mitzvah, and my mama brought me on home.

'When I was a young man, must've been 17 years old,' Gatemouth remembers, 'my aunt died in Kansas City, Missouri. This was my first chance to get over there. I headed straight over to 18th and Vine to a club called the Cherry Blossom, where I sang with Benny Moten's band. Count Basie was in that group too. That's where I got my first chance on stage.'

Soon after, Gatemouth joined the Beckman and Garrity Carnival, singing with a quartet called The Four Sharps. He performed at state fairs across the South, then, after the carnival closed, joined the famed FS Wolcott's Rabbit Foot Minstrels, at the height of the Depression. 'We wintered in Port Gibson, Mississippi, just down the road from here,' Gatemouth recalls. 'But I left the show in Clarksdale – I got stranded on the corner of Fourth and Issaquena Street, in the heart of the "New World". I stayed in Clarksdale for a year,' he laughs, shaking his head.

'One day, I was hanging out on the corner, with 50 bucks in my pocket. A fella offered to give me a ride up to Memphis. He didn't have room for me on the seat – I had to hobo it in back, on top of his load of grain. We stopped in a couple of Delta towns – Lula, and Tunica, and Walls – before we came to Memphis. I told him to let me out at Union Station, and I walked from there to Beale Street.' These are all details that I gleaned from the documentary Judy lent me, but sitting across the table from Gatemouth the story comes to life.

'I knew some friends up there, and that first night in town I gigged with a four-piece band – trombone, saxophone, bass horn, and drums. We tore it up,' Gatemouth gleefully recalls. He put together a big band with Doug Jenkins, headlining the Amateur Shows at the Palace Theater. 'There weren't many nightclubs on Beale Street in the '30s. I know that sounds funny, but most of the clubs were around the corner. We had Pantene's Drug Store, the Zephyr Café, and Sticklin Cab. Then on the other side of the street was Eggleston Tailor, Bufferton's Tailor, and Marlin's Barber College. Right next to the Palace Theater, we had a place called the One Minute where we could eat a whole meal for ten cents. Pee Wee's Saloon was down at the other end of the street. I had a room on Beale Street for a dollar and a quarter a week, and I put myself into Booker T Washington High School, and played in the clubs at night.'

Back in those days, women singers ruled supreme on Beale Street. 'The jug bands and harp players played right out on the street,' Gatemouth says. 'They didn't feature them in the clubs – just the big orchestras back then. Folks would come downtown for the Midnight Ramble, all dressed up. Beale Street was the biggest known street in town.'

Blues shouters like Ma Rainey, Bessie Smith and Alberta Hunter controlled the scene – but Gatemouth quickly made his mark. 'I was billed as Arnold Dwight Moore back then', he recalls, 'when I got my first big break. The Elks Club was going to New York City with a 100-piece band, and they wanted me to sing the "Beale Street Blues" in front of the group. Back then, we didn't have no microphones, just a big megaphone – and they wanted me to sing with the band in a parade down in Harlem. Well, I sang the blues from nine o'clock in the morning till four o'clock that night. I almost lost my voice singin' and hollerin'!'

Soon after that, Gatemouth was performing at the 81 Club in Atlanta, Georgia with Ida Cox's Darktown Scandals. 'I was just 21 years old, singing "Stardust" to the crowd when this short, fat woman came barreling down the aisle. I opened my mouth – I had beautiful teeth back then – and she looked up and hollered, "Aw, sing it, you gatemouth son of a bitch." The drummer was laughing so hard he fell off his seat – it really tore up the show. I was so embarrassed – until the white man that owned the theater told me that he was gonna book me in a midnight show for 25 bucks.

'You don't know how much money that was back then,' Gatemouth laughs. 'I was already making nine dollars with room and board. Well, the next day, I was standing out on the corner when I saw a horse wearing a straw hat and a cowbell walk by. The horse had a sign on it – nothing on that sign but a great big mouth, and the words "Gatemouth. Midnight show." Well, you couldn't get through the streets to see me that Saturday night – it was that crowded. And I've been known as Gatemouth ever since!

'Now, turn off that tape recorder for a minute, and let me rest,' Gatemouth says. He stands and stretches, then offers to show us around his church. The Lintonia Chapel AME Church is a small building, yellow brick on the outside and homey brown panelling inside. Despite the prevalence of the AME religion in Mississippi, Gatemouth preaches to a small congregation that meets just twice a month. But the leisurely pace is fine with him: he can travel without worrying about his parish, preaching in Memphis and Chicago at whatever church – Methodist, Church of God in Christ, Baptist – will have him. He's in demand for weddings and funerals as well: he presided over burial services for Johnny Ace and Rufus Thomas, and even staged his own funeral in Birmingham, Alabama, in the 1950s.

Gatemouth opens a bottle of Coca-Cola and sits back down, ready to continue with the story. By now, I feel like we're old friends, and I smile companionably at him as he winds back up. I ask him about the Rhythm Club fire in Natchez, Mississippi. More than 250 people were killed when the club burned to the ground back in 1940, and Gatemouth remembers the event as if it happened last week.

'I was sitting on the bus with a little girl who liked my singing. All of a sudden, we heard some shouting, and looked out at the club. Two people got out, but everyone else – Walter Barnes [the bandleader] and everybody – burned up. It was a real tragedy – the party was for society folks, and they all died in the fire. There wasn't a way to get out – just one door, and nobody could find it in the commotion. The drummer and the bass player managed to knock a window open, and they were the only two to escape before the ceiling fell in. I was just lucky I wasn't inside,' he says, 'real lucky.'

I've been to Natchez, where a single plaque overlooking the Mississippi River commemorates the ghastly event. The Rhythm Club was actually located a few blocks away, on St Catherine Street, but tourists still pause to read the long list of party-goers who perished in the flames. Several blues musicians, including Leonard 'Baby Doo' Caston and Gene Gilmore, wrote memorial tributes to the victims of the Natchez Fire, but my own favourite is the sombre and spooky 'Natchez Burning' by Howlin' Wolf. 'Did you ever hear about the burning/That happened way down in Natchez Mississippi town,' Wolf growls menacingly. 'I stood back, was lookin', and the old building come tumble down.'

'You know, I have a pole from the Rhythm Club, a big ol' beam, in my living room at home,' Gatemouth says, bringing me back to the present moment. 'I got it when they were tearing the place down. You'll have to come out and see it.'

Gatemouth switches topics, jumping from his recording career for the National and King labels – 'I didn't make a penny royalty,' he says ruefully – to his days in New York at the Apollo Theater and the Cotton Club. He ran with all the major musicians of his day, and remembers every last one of them. 'My best buddy was Wynonie Harris,' he says,

'Wynonie and T-Bone Walker.' Then he tells us a story about auditioning for Nat King Cole's band, and playing with Louis Jordan, until, finally, I ask him about his conversion.

'Now, that's a story,' he says, his eyes twinkling. 'One Saturday night, I was performing in Chicago at the Club DeLisa. I had just walked out of a crap game in the basement – I'd won $700 – and I walked out on stage with just one thing on my mind. That was getting back into that game and getting rich! But I never made it back down there,' Gatemouth says mysteriously.

'Red Saunders's band was backing me up. They played my introduction, but nothing happened. I missed my cue, which had never happened before. The band started again, and I opened my mouth and started singing a gospel number that I remembered from when I was a little boy. "Shine On Me", it's called. Folks went crazy – they thought I was drunk, or that I'd lost my mind. Mike DeLisa came running from the back, hollerin' for them to put the curtains down. Well, I walked off that stage and right out the door. Never went back – a week later, I was attending classes at the Moody Bible Institute there in Chicago. It was the greatest thing that ever happened to me,' he confirms with a big smile. 'I've been preaching now for 53 years.

'No one has ever called me a great preacher, but people seem to enjoy me,' Gatemouth says. 'I'm the greatest religious entertainer in the world! You know, the only difference between religious songs and the blues are the lyrics. When I sang the blues, I sang about my baby. And now I sing about Christ.

'My first sermon was "He may be your man, but he comes to see me sometimes",' Gatemouth says with a grin. 'Well, that was the blues like Ma Rainey used to sing. And the one I really pack the houses with comes straight from the Bible. It goes, "I asked her for some, she wouldn't give me none, but she went and told everybody in town about it." That's the story of the woman at the well,' he guffaws.

And without further ado, Gatemouth begins the story of his own funeral: 'It was Easter Sunday, 1951, in Birmingham, Alabama,' he begins. 'I decided that I would come from death to life, so I had an undertaker made a wood casket for me. I climbed into the casket at four in the afternoon and stayed in there until midnight. I charged a $5 love offering to people who wanted to come to the wake and see me. More than a thousand people came by, and *Ebony* and *Jet Magazine* were there. Then, at midnight, I was resurrected.

'I reached into my pocket, pulled out a pair of dice and threw them into the casket,' he says. 'Next, I pulled out a beer can and a whiskey bottle – and threw 'em into the casket. A deck of playing cards – threw 'em in the casket. Then I hollered "Born Again!" and you never seen such shoutin' in your life. Everybody in that place went crazy!

'The next day, I went on the radio and told everybody I was going to the graveyard. I had my red Cadillac convertible loaded up with the flowers, the casket, the pallbearers, and everything. We had $38,000 in the casket, and I drove down Main Street and had the pallbearers carry that casket right into the bank.' Police Chief Bull Conner intervened, and gave Gatemouth 24 hours to get out of town. 'I left in 30 minutes flat,' Gatemouth laughs, 'as soon as I got my money out of the bank. I left Birmingham, and didn't go back until after Bull Conner was dead.'

When we've all composed ourselves, I ask Gatemouth to backtrack to his days on WDIA in Memphis. 'That was before my days in Birmingham,' he confirms. 'I had a gospel show that was on every afternoon at one o'clock. BB King – he was known back then as "the Peptikon Boy" – took over my show when I left. But every time I come to Memphis, they beg me to come on 'DIA. I always try to drop in and give my fans a little something.'

And now, it seems, he has some questions for me. Gatemouth wants to know when and where he'll be performing at the Music and Heritage Festival, and who will be backing him on stage. Then we follow his big black Cadillac back to the interstate, and head home in the twilight.

The next time I see Gatemouth, it's at the Center for Southern Folklore, where he's sitting on a stool in front of a captivated audience, a crackerjack band behind him. He's wearing an elegant pinstriped suit, a yellow silk shirt and a brimless gold cap. 'I was just a teenaged boy when I came to Beale Street,' he tells the crowd, 'and that was more than 70 years ago!' He pauses for a moment to let the significance sink in, then tells the band to 'hit it'. Judy Peiser nods at me from across the room, as Gatemouth swings into 'Darktown Strutter's Ball'.

'It's a very swell affair/All the "high-browns" will be there/I'll wear my high silk hat and frock tail coat/You wear your Paris gown and your new silk shawl/There ain't no doubt about it babe/We'll be the best dressed in the hall', Gatemouth sings, his head thrown back and mouth wide open. He stands up and clowns across the stage, movements he might've learned from Ida Cox back in the '30s. I close my eyes and let his voice take over, as the years roll back. And, for an incredible moment, Gatemouth, his band and everyone in that room are back on Beale Street, at the Palace Theater.

Then it's over, and Judy gets up on stage to introduce the next group. Gatemouth grabs a table near the door, where he sits signing autographs and selling cassette tapes for the rest of the day. He greets me like an old friend, then gently waves me aside when a newspaper reporter from Chicago sits down at the table. 'You better get this down, sonny, because I'm only telling it once,' I hear Gatemouth cajoling as I wander off. 'I was a boy soprano up in Topeka, Kansas…'

OL' MAN MOSE IS DEAD
Mike Evans

Another regular performer at the Center for Southern Folklore until his death in November 2002 was Mose Vinson, a veteran piano player who had been around the Memphis scene longer than almost anyone can remember. Born in 1917 in Holly Springs, Mississippi, in the early 1920s his family moved the 30 miles or so north to Memphis, where he learned to play piano and organ while still a child.

A meeting with the now-legendary Sunnyland Slim in the 1930s set him on the road to a musical career, though not one as successful as that of his mentor. He was a regular face on the Memphis club scene, playing with names such as BB King and Memphis Slim at venues like the Parlor Club in the 1940s, but he often had to augment his earnings from music with 'day jobs'. Indeed, it was as studio caretaker – doing janitorial and plumbing work – that he came into the orbit of Sun Records while they were still largely a blues-based outfit in the early '50s. He soon found himself recording a few sides for the label, in 1953, though none were issued at the time, only appearing in more recent years on retrospective Sun compilations.

The most acclaimed tracks he appeared on at Sun were as an accompanist, a year later, when he backed harmonica ace James Cotton on two classic sides of the same single, 'Cotton Crop Blues' and 'Hold Me In Your Arms', not long before Cotton moved to Chicago to begin his 11-year tenure with the Muddy Waters band. Also while at Sun, Vinson was to later recall, he would jam with the teenage Elvis Presley, the latter keen to check out the piano man's technique.

Although he was known to play outside the Memphis area from time to time (including notable folk and blues festivals in Chicago) in recent years, Mose Vinson was almost a permanent fixture on Beale Street when it became the home for the Center for Southern Folklore. 'He was synonymous with the Center,' Judy Peiser stated in Vinson's obituary in the *Memphis Commercial Appeal*. 'When we started doing public presentations from the late '70s, Mose was always there.' And the Center, as well as also featuring Mose on its annual Memphis Music and Heritage Festival, was responsible for his only solo album, *Piano Man*, released in 1997 and co-produced by Peiser, Jim Dickinson and Knox Phillips, son of Sun pioneer Sam Phillips.

He remained in residence at the Center when it moved to the mall-like Peabody Place, right until his death. His passing was widely mourned in Memphis, where he was remembered not just for his boogie-based barrel-house piano but also for his contribution as entertainer, and indeed teacher, to literally thousands of children and adults over the years. His funeral procession made its way down Beale to his interment at New Park Cemetery, and was followed by a musical tribute concert the following evening at the Center. Instead of floral tributes, the Center requested that contributions be made to the Mose Vinson Musicians'

Fund that it set up in his honour, to support and promote traditional Memphis musicians.

Mose Vinson's style, in keeping with fellow Memphian pianists Booker T Laury and Memphis Slim, was that of the prewar 'barrelhouse' pianists whose music bridged blues, boogie-woogie and jazz, a style that has all but disappeared in terms of live performers. He was the one of its last exponents, yet mostly unrecognised by the world at large. Jim Dickinson, keyboard player, producer and mainstay of the Memphis scene for many years, pinpointed this when he added to the tributes: 'All the Memphis piano men are undersung, but he may be the most, he was the guy who never got out of town.'

IN A TOWN THIS SIZE
Andria Lisle

Yesterday afternoon, I got a phone call from Charlie Musselwhite. 'I'm in Memphis for a week,' he told me, the words dripping off his tongue like slow-moving molasses. 'I'm hoping we can drive around and eat some soul food', he said, 'and listen to my new record.'

I'm at his sister's house on Mud Island a day later, knocking on the door. Charlie greets me with a friendly hug, then climbs into the passenger side of my VW Beetle. He's wearing a faded pair of black Levi's and shiny black cowboy boots, and a cool '50s-style bowling shirt. 'Man, I am hungry,' he drawls, raising his eyebrows as he rubs his tummy. 'Let's go eat, and then we'll head out to my old stomping grounds.'

We head down North Main Street to Alcenia's, just a few blocks away. BJ, the restaurant's owner, is an old friend of Charlie's, and she rushes over as soon as we walk in the door. 'I got your picture up, Charlie,' she says, nodding over her shoulder to an autographed photo next to the cash register. 'Now what will it be today? We just fried up a pan of catfish, and I got some pork chops coming up.'

Charlie grins – he is in hog heaven – and orders the pork chops and fried green tomatoes, while I settle for a crispy catfish filet. We're served iced tea in huge plastic tumblers, and once he is satisfied that lunch is on the way Charlie begins to talk.

'I was born smack dab in the middle of Mississippi, in Kosciusko, but I grew up in Memphis, Tennessee,' Charlie says. Raised in Memphis, he migrated to Chicago as a teenager in 1962, 'like thousands of others after those big factory jobs', then, five years later, he headed west to northern California.

Somewhere along the way – in Chicago, actually – he hooked up with Muddy Waters, Howlin' Wolf and Sonny Boy Williamson, dislocated Mississippians who'd also made the migration north. Charlie played harmonica, and he began sitting in on gigs with the bluesmen until, in his words, 'it just got better and better. I decided I should start paying attention – this is my way out of the factory.'

'I didn't have any kind of a plan,' Charlie insists. 'I didn't even entertain the thought of being a professional musician – it never crossed my mind. I just played the music because I loved it. But when I got to Chicago there was this whole blues scene going on, and when they found out I played they made me sit in. One thing led to another, and people were inviting me to play with them. I was just having fun – I was a teenager, I didn't have any responsibilities or anything.' Then, in 1967, he recorded an album, Vanguard's *Stand Back! Here Comes Charley* [sic] *Musselwhite's Southside Band*, that – gritty voice, brash harp and all – launched a career that has spanned more than three decades.

Yet Charlie maintains that his early days in Memphis influenced him the most – and he reinforces the sentiment on his latest album (his 26th), *One Night In America*. Here he's taken 12 seemingly disparate songs and used them to build a story – his story – of childhood in Memphis. 'All these tunes capture the feeling of the times I remember from the '40s and '50s,' Charlie says after lunch, when we get back into the car. As he loads the disc into my CD player, he adds the words, 'It was all I knew.'

While the album provides an aural snapshot, it helps to drive by his old house and really get a sense of the place. Charlie grew up on tiny Manhattan Avenue, a block off Summer Avenue in northeast Memphis. The run-down neighbourhood behind Leahy's Trailer Court – Baltic Street, Pacific Avenue, Gracewood Street – still reeks of blue collar life, crowded working-class bungalows surrounded by the seedy urban sprawl of Sweet's Truckers Lounge, second-hand furniture stores and acres of used-car lots. It's an area that – on the surface – hasn't changed much in the last 50 years, a neighbourhood that exerts a tight hold over its people. It's hard to imagine a teenager here with big dreams of any sort.

Yet this is a town where poor boys are known for making their fantasies a reality, and even in the neighbourhood behind Leahy's Trailer Court there were a few who made it: rockabillies like Johnny and Dorsey Burnette, who also resided on Manhattan Avenue, and Johnny Cash, who lived a block north on Tutwiler.

'Where I grew up', Charlie says, as we head east down Summer Avenue, past the thrift stores and boarded-up bars, 'music was everywhere – on the radio, at revival meetings, downtown on street corners, in houses and clubs. And just across Cypress Creek, there was a black neighborhood.' Despite the prevalent racial divisions of that time, the area held an inexplicable fascination.

Charlie turns up the volume on the car stereo, and we listen to an Americana-sounding track, his cover of Kieren Kane's 'A Town This Size'. Charlie's voice fills the car, and he moodily looks out of the window while we listen to the lyrics. 'In a town this size, there's no place to hide', goes the song; 'Everywhere you go you meet someone you know/You can't steal a kiss in a place like this/How the rumors do fly in a town this size'.

Finally, Charlie begins to speak. 'One of my first friends was a black boy named Clydell who also played the harmonica,' he says with a smile. But it was difficult for the two to get together, and Charlie relates a story that, half a century later, still burns him: 'One day I made the mistake of going into the grocery store where Clydell worked to talk with him. It never occurred to me that I was getting him into trouble or doing something wrong, but they called him in the back.

'The lady who owned the place marched up the aisle with her arms folded, and she really told me off. She said that it wasn't right for me to be friendly with black people, and that I've got my place and he's got his place. I was stunned – it was almost like being kicked in the stomach. I sure didn't mean to get him into trouble,' Charlie says softly. Suddenly his version of 'A Town This Size' takes on a whole new meaning.

'A couple of times he tried to get me into some black clubs,' Charlie remembers. 'Clydell would go in first and see if some music was happening, and when they'd see me come in they'd say, "Oh no, he's gonna get us in trouble," so yeah, there was some racism going on.'

We drive a few more blocks in silence, then Charlie continues. 'You know, the way I grew up was, "God made everybody, and if you mistreated anybody you were mistreating God, because we're all God's children." That's how I was raised. As a child, I remembered how the buses said, "Colored to the rear" – it was painted on the inside of the bus, just like that. There were separate water fountains and separate bathrooms, and I would ask my mother about stuff like that and she'd say, "Well, it's just the circumstances we live in."'

He still managed to learn some music from Clydell, and from Furry Lewis and jug-band impresario Will Shade, who lived at the east end of Beale Street. 'I'd ride the bus downtown, sit around someone's house drinking and playing music,' Charlie recalls. 'I'd get 78s from the Salvation Army and the used-furniture stores, and from Pop Tunes downtown. I was always curious, even before I got into playing music. Out of curiosity, I would buy anything that looked interesting – Greek music, all kinds of weird music from around the world. How it ended up in Memphis, I'll never know! But a lot of it had a bluesy sound to it – some of the same scales. I naturally gravitated toward blues. It just seemed to make so much sense to me. It was how I felt – when I heard that I understood it, I knew that feeling. 'The beauty of the blues', he explains, 'is how it can adapt itself to anything. Twelve bars and three chords is one of the most convenient ways to play, but that doesn't have to be the end of it.'

It's no surprise then, that Charlie samples blues, country, hillbilly, and rock 'n' roll on *One Night In America*, and effortlessly melds these styles, his own early musical education providing the common ground. He has help: guitarists Robben Ford, GE Smith and Marty Stuart, bassist T-Bone Wolk and drummer Per Hanson work together to supply the rootsy base, while Christine Ohlman and Kelly Willis provide sweet accompaniment to Charlie's rust-coated vocals and acoustic harp riffs.

Charlie's most famous childhood neighbour is represented here with a rousing rendition of 'Big River' – 'I used to see Cash driving by all the time in his Thunderbird,' Charlie remembers. 'Johnny seemed like he was one of us and was singing about the life we knew.' Ivory Joe Hunter is here, too – Charlie's shuffling version of the local R&B star's country-soul weeper 'Cold Grey Light Of Dawn' is superb. Jaunty lyrics aside, it's one of many dark and lonely moments on the album. The solitary mood continues with original numbers 'In Your Darkest Hour' and 'Ain't It Time?', songs that Charlie admits are about himself, or friends he knew. The gospel standard 'Rank Strangers To Me' also gets the lonesome touch – 'I grew up feeling like that,' Charlie laughs – while his take on Jimmy Reed's 'Ain't That Lovin' You Baby' provides a hard rockin' finish.

'I saw Jimmy Reed at the Cadillac Club,' Charlie recalls, before gently exclaiming, 'You know, Memphis has destroyed more history than most places in America ever had. They almost destroyed Beale Street, and would have if somebody hadn't thought about making money. They had not an ounce of compassion for the music or the people. That was a real wonderful neighborhood,' he says, then immediately corrects himself: 'It was actually pretty awful – poor and run-down – and I spent a lot of time down there and saw a lot of poverty. But instead of tearing it all down they could've fixed it. It didn't change the situation to tear it down,' he says, and he's right.

Oddly enough, it's a cover of a Los Lobos song that best sums up his childhood memories. We make a final lap down Manhattan Avenue, and turn up the car stereo: 'A quiet voice is singing something to me', Charlie croons in a gravelly voice, 'an age-old song about the home of the brave in this land here of the free'. Its driving beat compromised by a blast of downhearted lyrics, the song captures all the ups and downs of a blues-loving white boy growing up in the working-class neighbourhood behind Leahy's Trailer Court – 'one time, one night' in Charlie Musselwhite's Memphis.

BIG LUCKY MAN
Mike Evans

Another blues veteran, Levester 'Big Lucky' Carter died on 24 December 2002, aged 82. Carter was one of those many bluesmen who never experienced what one would call stardom; nevertheless he forged a reputation which rendered him much respected well beyond the South and his home base in Memphis.

Big Lucky was born in 1920 in the small Mississippi town of Weir, east of the blues heartland of the Mississippi Delta. Jessie Mae Hemphill and Ed 'Prince Gabe' Kirby, both established names in their own right, were blood relatives, but he was first attracted to the music via the great slide guitar players like Tampa Red and Blind Lemon Jefferson, and fashioned himself an instrument accordingly, putting four wire screen strings on a board and playing it (literally) with a bottleneck.

He didn't actually pursue a musical career until after serving in the army in World War II, where he had earned his 'Big Lucky' nickname for his gambling skills. It was after the war that he moved to Memphis, where he was invited by his cousin Prince Gabe to join his band, The Rhythmaires, who were playing at the Fiesta Room, on the corner of Orleans and Vance streets, at the time. He turned up with a guitar and what he later described as 'a little Mickey Mouse amp', but on Gabe's insistence he soon replaced these with a Gibson guitar and Fender amplifier. Now he was a professional – and playing just off Beale Street, no less.

While still playing with Prince Gabe, whose Rhythmaires were also sometimes billed as The Millionaires, he recorded for Sam Phillips at the Sun Studio in 1956, but the results made little impact. This was followed by sides for the Savoy label in Chicago, which in turn did no better in terms of sales.

Like many in the annals of Memphis music, his break came aided by local radio. It was in 1968, at which time he was doing a show on WDIA every Saturday afternoon with DJ AC Williams called (presumably after the old Louis Jordan number) *Saturday Night Fish Fry*. Williams arranged for Carter to get some studio time at Willie Mitchell's Hi Records, where he cut six sides under his own name for the Hi label, including two singles for the label's subsidiary MOC. The tracks, featuring the backing of Teenie Hodges and the Hi house rhythm section, have more than a touch of jazz about them, a fact that in some part explains Carter's late-in-life celebrity in Europe.

The tracks were released as part of a series called *Roots Of 21st Century Blues*, and whether this drew attention to Big Lucky on the other side of the Atlantic isn't clear. But there is a following for blues and jazz in Europe – particularly in France – that in proportion to the total population far exceeds that in its native United States.

Whatever, in 1998, when he was in his late 70s, he cut his first album, *Lucky 13*, for the British Blueside label, which went on to win a year-end readers' poll for best blues CD in the French magazine *Soul Bag*, and was honoured with the prestigious Big Bill Broonzy prize for best blues CD from the French Academy of Jazz. And despite the fact that *Lucky 13* was never released in America, it received home-grown accolades, including a critics' choice award in *Living Blues* magazine for Artist Most Deserving of Wider Recognition.

During his final years, Big Lucky kept playing around Memphis, and toured occasionally in Europe, under the management of University of Memphis musicologist David Evans. He also contributed to a Europe-only CD release produced by Evans entitled *The Spirit Lives On: Deep South Country Blues And Spirituals In The 1990s*. And, as well as being a regular performer at the Center for Southern Folklore and its Memphis Music and Heritage Festival, during his last years he was a frequent attraction at Wild Bill's, one of the most celebrated venues in the city.

WALKIN' THE DOG
Mike Evans

Marking the move from blues to early rock 'n' roll to soul, in its relatively modest way, Rufus Thomas's career – professionally involved with companies that included WDIA, Sun and Stax – was the evolution of Memphis music personified.

His family had moved from his birthplace of Cayce, Mississippi, to Memphis when he was a small boy, and in 1927, at the age of ten, he had started performing as a tap-dancer. By 1936 he had joined the prestigious 'Rabbit Foot Minstrel Show', a tent-show review for black audiences that had toured the segregated South since the late 1890s, and had just witnessed the departure of its most famous participant, the legendary Ma Rainey.

His role with the Minstrels was primarily as a comedian, and this 'entertainer' background was to stand him in good stead, for, although he made his singing début on record in the early 1940s with 'I'll Be A Good Boy', it was as host of the weekly Amateur Night on Beale Street talent show at the Palace Theater that he started to make a name for himself. All the up-and-coming artists would get up at the talent nights for $1 a time, including Rosco Gordon, Johnny Ace, Bobby Bland and BB King. Rufus did well on $5 as MC for the whole evening, and he stuck at it for 11 years.

The connection with BB King was cemented further when Thomas got a job as DJ on the all-important Memphis radio station WDIA, the first black-owned and black-targeted station in the USA. He had the one o'clock show, while BB hosted the better-placed three-in-the-afternoon *Sepia Swing Club*. When BB had to quit due to record success, making touring an increasing priority, Rufus took it over, where he stayed for many years. The blues and R&B content of WDIA's programming was crucial in the musical environment of Memphis back in the early 1950s, especially in the way it impacted on young whites listening to its all-black output – Sun Records' Sam Phillips and the adolescent Elvis Presley among them.

The Sun label was still almost 100 per cent blues and R&B in 1953 when Rufus Thomas cut his first big hit, an 'answer record' to Big Mama Thornton's 'Hound Dog' (later a huge smash for Presley) entitled 'Bear Cat'. Although the single made the Number Three spot in the national R&B charts, Rufus carried on gigging locally, DJing at WDIA and working his day job in a textile factory. Soon after, in 1954, Elvis began recording for Sun and the world changed for Sam Phillips, though not as much as it might have done in retrospect. Whatever, the label's main output quickly moved from R&B to white-dominated rockabilly-rock 'n' roll.

Rufus's fame might have spread no further than the immediate environs of Memphis were it not for the emergence in 1960 of the fledgling Satellite label (later changed to Stax), where he cut a side with his daughter Carla Thomas – ''Cause I Love You' – that became a regional hit.

Encouraged by this, Thomas became part of the label's pre-eminence in the rise of '60s soul music when he made the US Top Ten with 'Walking the Dog' in 1963, which was covered the following year by UK pretenders to the R&B throne, The Rolling Stones.

There followed a series of deliberately contrived novelty-dance records to emulate ''Dog', including 'Can Your Monkey Do The Dog?' in 1964, 'Do the Funky Chicken' in 1970, 'Do The Push And Pull' (1971) and 1972's 'Do The Funky Penguin'.

Anyone else would have been funked out by all this, but Rufus carried on, staying with Stax till the label folded in 1975, moving then to AVI. He continued broadcasting, recording and performing into middle – and then old – age, even making a rap record ('Rappin' Rufus'), singing at the 1996 Atlanta Olympics, and being dubbed 'The Official Ambassador of Memphis Music', along with his self-appointed title of 'the world's oldest teenager'.

A Memphis street was named after him, and he was honoured with a Pioneer Award by the R&B Foundation in 1992, but ill health dogged his final years and Rufus Thomas died of heart failure in a Memphis hospital in December 2001, at the age of 84.

SHOWTIME AT WILD BILL'S
By Andria Lisle

Folks can complain all they want about the dearth of good live music in this town – Monday through Wednesday, that is. But come Thursday, they'd better shut up, and head on over to Wild Bill's, the city's friendliest juke joint. Located just north of Rhodes College at the intersection of Vollentine Avenue and Avalon Street, Wild Bill's packs 'em in an astonishing four nights a week. At least twice a month, I navigate my way past the legion of Cadillacs and Lincoln Town Cars parked out front, and make my way towards the narrow glass-fronted door sandwiched in between three beauty shops and a meat market.

Most nights, the club is so crowded that I have to wait for William Story – Wild Bill himself – to clear a path for the door, which opens inwards onto the dance floor. I stand outside, a five-dollar bill in hand, getting my last few breaths of fresh air before diving into the steamy, smoke-drenched sweatbox of a club. Just 21m (70ft) deep, Wild Bill's nevertheless sees at least 100 patrons on any given night – 'Sometimes', Bill says with a laugh, 'I try to turn people away. I tell 'em I don't have any seats, but they don't care. They just want to come in and dance!'

The set-up is simple: three rows of tables that run the length of the room, with a bandstand just inside the front door, and a bar and jukebox in the back. The walls are painted a cheerful orange colour, which complements the paintings and photographs of Bill and his patrons that are pinned throughout the room. A ceiling fan keeps time above the band, while Bill watches over the scene from his stool, just inside the front door.

I've been coming here for ten years. Over that time, I've changed, but the club has stayed what it's always been – a homey neighbourhood juke joint. Students from Rhodes College come over, as do older black folk from the surrounding Klondike and Hyde Park areas. And, as Bill points out, 'We have people in from overseas every week.' It's hardly a surprise – Wild Bill's has been listed in everything from the *New York Times'* 'Sophisticated Traveler' section to Shangri-La's *Kreature Comforts' Lowlife Guide to Memphis*. As one of the only 'sure things' happening in Memphis, Bill's has become an international destination.

Most nights, The Hollywood All Stars provide the music at Wild Bill's. Led by bassist Melvin Lee, the loosely knit group has been a pivotal force on the local blues scene for the past two decades. Guitarists seem to come and go, but Lee – along with drummer Don Valentine – holds down the rhythm section with pride. The group plays a variety of music, running the gamut from hard-hitting gutbucket blues to unadulterated Memphis soul. From behind the drums, Don provides the steady, workmanlike vocals, serving up an Elvis medley and a Chuck Berry number with equal fervour.

Folks – black, white and every colour in between – pack the linoleum-covered dance floor from 10pm till 3am, pausing only for beer and bathroom breaks. Everyone else sits shoulder to shoulder at the long tables, good-naturedly ribbing each other's dates, and passing bottles of alcohol and buckets of ice up and down the room. I secure a seat against the south wall, and squeeze in between an older woman in a sequined dress, and a group of college kids in blue jeans. Fashion-wise, anything goes at Wild Bill's: I've seen men in wigs, girls in shorts and T-shirts; even, I think, a fellow in his pyjamas. On this particular night, tracksuits are, for some reason, prevalent on the dance floor. I count five of them on the sweating, blurry bodies out there before I give up and call to Buddy for a beer.

Buddy and his friend Mike are the two waiters at Wild Bill's, clean-cut, first-name-only men who cater to the neighbourhood crowd. They like the kids, too – especially those who pay $5 on a $3.25 beer and tell them to 'keep the change'. It's up to Buddy and Mike to keep the party rolling, and they do their best in the cramped room, moving at least six cases of beer a night. They do pretty good with set-ups, too, served to people who bring in their own bottles of booze. And Wild Bill's kitchen is open until 2am, selling cheeseburgers, hot wings and fish sandwiches to a hungry late-night crowd.

Within moments, Buddy is at my side – a miraculous feat, considering the backlog of people dancing in the aisle – with a cold quart-size bottle of Budweiser and two clean glasses. The woman next to me smiles, but demurs when I offer to top up her drink. 'It's my birthday', she tells me, 'and my friends are buying my beer tonight. Let them pay!' she say.

And then, before I know it, I'm on the dance floor, shakin' it with a man twice my age. He's an agile mover, and a much flashier dancer than I am, and before long I am panting from the effort. Don's singing Rufus Thomas's 'Walking The Dog', and my partner twirls me round and round. The couple next to us is doing a slow grind, while another woman drops her hands down to the ground and rubs her crotch all over her date. She shakes her hips exaggeratedly, a bluesy version of a dancer from a rap video, to loud hoots from the bandstand. At the door, Bill watches the scene before turning his attention to the group of people trying to get in. He stands up and pushes us all together, making room for the opening door. Six more people come in, dancing their way towards the bar. It's going to be a busy night…

As The Hollywood All Stars finish 'Walking The Dog', Don makes an announcement. 'We're gonna take a pause for the cause,' he says, as the band breaks into a brief shuffle. They struggle into their coats and head outside, to smoke cigarettes and bullshit with one another before it's time to go back on. A handful of folks follow the band out – aspiring young guitarists hoping for an invitation to sit in, wives and girlfriends, and even a few broke fellows hoping for enough spare change for another beer.

Inside, Wild Bill plugs in the jukebox, while Cedric, the house photographer, makes his rounds, snapping pictures of happy couples for a few dollars a piece. The beer continues to flow, and everyone is having a great time. After a few short minutes, Bill heads over to the bandstand and picks up one of Don's drumsticks. 'Showtime, showtime', he shouts over the din, banging away on one of Don's cymbals. He makes such a racket that Melvin Lee sticks his head back inside to assure him they're on their way.

And so it goes, for five or so hours four nights a week. Sometimes a horn player will come in the door, or a guitarist or guest vocalist, and the band will squeeze together even tighter on the bandstand to make room for the newcomer. Two red-hot saxophonists like to drop in late in the evening – presumably after their regular gigs – and by midnight they're punctuating the All Stars' riffs with sharp blasts of rhythm. Even later, moustachioed bartender Nathaniel Starks takes over the microphone for a soulful ballad or two, until, after a nod from Bill at the door, he reluctantly picks up his dishrag and heads back behind the bar.

After a few hours, it occurs to me that I've clocked in nearly 1,000 hours at Wild Bill's over the years, but I don't know much about the man at the door at all. I approach him at his post, and after a shouted conversation arrange a meeting for the next afternoon.

I am surprised to see nearly as many cars parked outside Wild Bill's on Sunday afternoon as there were the night before. Inside, I notice a dozen people enjoying a soul food lunch: fried chicken, greens, field peas and cornbread. Wild Bill is seated on a stool at the bar, drinking coffee. I realise that, in all those nights of drinking and dancing, I've never seen him truly relaxed before. He waves me over, and we begin to talk.

'Not too many people know my story,' Bill says with a wink. 'You're one of the first to ask.' I'm bursting with questions, but Bill is such a reticent speaker that I hesitate to break into his reverie. He sips his coffee and sighs, then sets it back onto the bar, wiped spotless after a busy night. 'I was born down in New Albany, Mississippi,' Bill tells me. 'When I was growing up down there, they had a little racetrack. I was just seven or eight years old, and I ran the rest of those kids down. That's why they call me Wild Bill,' he says with a sly smile. He's well into his 70s now, and it's nearly impossible to imagine this staid gentleman tearing around a dirt track with his bare feet.

'We moved to Marion, Arkansas, when I was nine,' Bill recalls. 'I left there in 1937, when I was just a teenager. The high water ran me away,' he says, referring to the devastating Mississippi River flood of that year, 'and I've been in Memphis ever since. I started driving a cab in 1948, and I haven't retired from that yet. I'm a co-owner of Citywide Cabs, and that keeps me pretty tied up.'

Bill Story has been running nightclubs since 1964. 'I've always loved music,' he claims. 'I never wanted to play – I just like to sit back and enjoy it. My first club was at 2110 Chelsea, not too far from here,' he recalls. 'It's been so long that I can hardly remember what it was called… The Pink Cat – that's it. Then I had a club called the L&H on Avery Street. When I left there, I came here – and that was ten years ago.'

For a man who's spent a lifetime inside nightclubs, Bill has little to say about the scene. 'We have as many white people coming in here as we do black. And they mix well – we don't have any trouble,' he tells me. I ask him about a few legendary juke joints on the Memphis scene – Club Manhattan and the Plantation Inn, but Bill shrugs in reply. 'I don't have time to go anywhere else in Memphis,' he says. 'I've never even been to the casino – I went to the dog track a few times when it first opened, but never went back.'

When asked about his favourite musicians, Bill demurs. 'Well, Melvin Lee has been playing with me since the 1960s, and I like his band,' Bill says. 'And Steve Nelson is one of my favorite players – he's such a showman. But he's busy driving a truck these days…' His voice trails off, and he looks into his coffee cup, eager to get back to business.

So I ask him about the Wild Bill's Social Club, a group that meets at the club on a regular basis. 'Well,' he says laconically, dragging out the word, 'there's ten of us in the group. They just went down to New Orleans to catch a ball game, but I didn't want to go – I didn't have *time* to go. I didn't want to go to the football game anyways – I was raised up in the country, and we didn't play ball down there,' he says with a snort. 'My wife, Lurlean, keeps getting after me to go somewhere else, but –' he looks happily at his surroundings ' – why leave?'

And with that, Wild Bill Story tips his hat, and excuses himself from his perch at the bar. Someone's at the front door asking about the band that night, and besides there's plenty of work to do. I thank him for the interview, and head home.

2 Soul City, USA

RACIAL COLLISIONS IN MEMPHIS
Andria Lisle

It's a rainy Saturday afternoon, and I'm cruising around downtown, looking for a parking space. As a local, I refuse to pay for parking, except in the most extreme circumstances. But the free lot I usually park in has been dug up for a new basketball arena that the city is building on Linden Avenue, just south of Beale Street. The construction crew is under a tight deadline and, even on the weekend, bulldozers and dump trucks roar up and down the block.

Until last week, the trucks – overloaded with dirt from the arena excavation – were headed to the north end of Mud Island, a sandbar situated just west of downtown Memphis, in the middle of the Mississippi River. Ken Hyneman, a local developer, had purchased the arena dirt to boost the floodplain on the 60 hectares (25 acres) he owns on Mud Island, and for weeks, the dump trucks came in at the rate of 70 truckloads an hour. The dirt piled up 11m (35ft) high until the island's banks could take no more: in the middle of the night, a sizeable chunk of Hyneman's land broke off and fell into the Memphis harbour.

For a while, at least, there will be no barges coming into Memphis, until the US Army Corps of Engineers are able to dredge the harbour back to its original depth of 3m (9ft). They've brought in a cutterhead called the Pontchartrain, billed to Hyneman at the cost of $30,000 a day. And at the north end of Mud Island, on the Auction Avenue Bridge, ice-cream vendors are doing big business where crowds have gathered to gawk at the spectacle. This is the biggest news in town, and coverage of the mudslide dominates local TV broadcasts as well as the daily paper.

I obligingly stand on the bridge for an hour, standing on my tiptoes to see the Pontchartrain do its work below. Pipes run from the red and white cutterhead to a spot in the river about a 400m ($\frac{1}{4}$ mile) away, well south of the I-40 Tennessee–Arkansas Bridge. Broken tree trunks and branches, which snapped under the weight of the mud, litter the harbour, and motors hum as the dirt is dredged from the murky depths. The air is thick with the stench of slippery muck. I don't want an ice-cream cone and, after hanging out for a few minutes, I don't even want the bottle of water I'd brought from my car. I've seen – and smelled – enough, and I eventually drive off, following the river south to Beale.

The Mud Island débâcle is somehow typical for Memphis, which is more of a large town than a small city, despite what the local government would have you think. We have a city mayor and a county mayor – one black, one white – and both seem to cancel each other out on major issues, although in a month Shelby County will inaugurate AC Wharton, our first black county mayor, who promises to shake up local politics even more.

From the Civil War to the Civil Rights Movement, in 100 years Memphis history is peppered with many such inconsistencies. It's a case of give and take in a town where it's wise to choose your battles carefully.

Just ask Jacqueline Smith, a protester who has lived outside the National Civil Rights Museum for nearly 15 years. Convinced that the museum – built, ironically, on the site of the Lorraine Motel, where Martin Luther King Jr was assassinated – is a tourist trap that distorts the legacy of the Civil Rights Movement, Smith is on a one-woman crusade urging visitors to boycott the facility. She spends up to 20 hours a day at her post, armed with press releases, a spray-painted bed sheet that serves as a protest flag, and a dozen good reasons why the National Civil Rights Museum is in the wrong.

A former employee of the Lorraine, Smith was evicted in 1988 when museum developers bought the fleabag motel, previously scheduled for demolition. Passers-by stop to sign her petition and hear her out, then – always – enter the courtyard of the museum and disappear inside. An estimated 125,000 people a year walk past Smith on their way to and from the museum, yet she continues to bide her time, determined to 'wait out' the enemy.

A few kilometres from the National Civil Rights Museum lies Forrest Park, where Civil War general and Ku Klux Klan founder Nathan Bedford Forrest is buried. A statue of Forrest astride his mighty charger King Phillip looks out incongruously over Manassas Street in a predominantly black part of town.

According to the Nathan Bedford Forrest Organization's website, the statue's dedication took place on 16 May 1905, with '30,000 southerners from seven states attending. Following the various speeches, Forrest's eight-year-old great-granddaughter, Kathleen Forrest Bradley, pulled the cord that unveiled the magnificent memorial as the band cranked up "Dixie".'

The moment celebrates the life of a man as complicated as the city he lived in: one of the South's first millionaires, the military mastermind was also a gentleman farmer and slave trader. Forrest gained fame for his prowess on the battlefield, but he was internationally reviled for an April 1864 skirmish at Fort Pillow, a Union outpost located on the Mississippi River bluffs some 80km (50 miles) north of Memphis. Confederate forces under Forrest's command executed a handful of the 250 black Union troops sequestered within the fort, allegedly because he was outraged by the sight of blacks bearing guns. Witnesses swore that the black troops surrendered, only to be massacred by Forrest's vengeful wrath.

Yet two years later, when free blacks set out to rebuild the First Baptist Church on Beale Street, which was burned by angry citizens during the war, Forrest was the only white Memphian to make a donation. What could have compelled this solicitousness towards his black brethren? I am tempted to ask the Klansmen who rally around Forrest's statue every few years, but my fear always gets the best of me, and when the white hoods line up on Manassas, I huddle on the couch in front of the TV set to laugh privately at their interviews on the evening news. Confronting the Klan in person is still risky business.

The racists who spout their diatribes on local TV aren't even from Memphis. They hail from Illinois, Indiana and Ohio, states well to the north of the Mason–Dixon line. They're drawn here by our city's terrible history – the wrong kind of history, as when Dr King was assassinated in April 1968. They're not aware that we have a black city mayor, Willie Herenton, who's been in office since 1991, or that more than half his 650,000 constituents are also black.

It's doubtful that they realise that such local musicians as Jim Dickinson credit the city's musical heritage to 'a racial collision in both directions' – the impact of two cultures occupying the same physical space. 'Memphis music', Dickinson sums up, 'is a direct result of that integration', with whites recording blacks, learning to play music from blacks, impersonating black musicians, and eventually performing alongside them. Dickinson himself was taught music by Alec, his family's yard-man – an exchange, he insists, that in the 1950s 'was not socially acceptable in any way, shape or form. It was not all right for teenage white boys to do that.'

Radio, however, could not be segregated, so the cultural revolution arrived, incongruously enough, over the airwaves. Pioneering the insurrection was Dewey Phillips, host of WHBQ's *Red Hot And Blue* radio show. Enthusiastic and unschooled, Phillips broke all the rules by programming, as music historian Colin Escott notes in *Good Rockin' Tonight*, his history of Memphis music, 'an eclectic mix of blues, hillbilly, and pop that would become an institution in Memphis'. Phillips's ability to pick hits, as well as his manic sense of humour and refusal to be pigeonholed, made tuning into his radio show a daily ritual for Memphis teenagers, white and black, setting the stage for sounds to come.

Less than 8km (5 miles) from the WHBQ studios, WDIA was making waves as the first all-black-programmed radio station in the country. Armed with local luminaries such as Rufus Thomas, Dwight 'Gatemouth' Moore, and Nat D Williams, 'DIA (as folks called it) was the voice of Memphis's black community.

But it's just behind Forrest Park, at 706 Union Avenue, where the seeds of integration really took root. Inspired by the success of WDIA and WHBQ, entrepreneur Sam Phillips opened the Memphis Recording Service 'with the intention of recording musicians from Memphis and the locality who I felt had something that people should be able to hear', he says. Recognising the power of the raw black sound, Phillips experimented with great historical (but not financial) success. Ike Turner, James Cotton, Rosco Gordon – even Rufus Thomas – recorded in the studio located just beyond the shadow of Forrest's statue.

In May 1951, Sam Phillips cut Ike Turner and The Kings Of Rhythm performing a manic number that went far beyond the traditional R&B sound. 'Rocket 88', which was ultimately credited to Jackie Brenston, the vocalist on the track, was licensed to Chess Records later that spring, and went straight to the top of the R&B charts. The song, an amalgamation of hard-driving blues and big-city boogie, was hailed worldwide as one of the first rock 'n' roll records, and – more importantly – as guitarist Calvin Newborn (who toured with Turner in the wake of his 'Rocket 88' success) recalls, 'It broke the ice for civil rights to begin.'

The ferocious sound behind 'Rocket 88' came by accident. On the drive up to Memphis from Clarksdale, Mississippi, a guitar amp fell from its precarious position on top of Ike Turner's car, breaking its speaker cone. 'We had no way of getting it fixed,' Phillips has recounted time and time again, 'so we started playing around with the damn thing. Stuffed a little paper in there, and it sounded good.' Rather than submerging the distortion, Phillips turned the amplifier up, and the result of his unorthodox approach caught the ear of a nation.

Phillips moved on to recording white musicians, but the sentiment, the spirit behind the music, was essentially unchanged. As Colin Escott emphasises in *Good Rockin' Tonight*, at 706 Union they 'did more than borrow the form of black music: they borrowed its fervor. Not a blatant copy – something new had been forged, and Sam Phillips was responsible.'

With other Sun artists, the story is the same. Poor rural white boys like Carl Perkins, Johnny Cash, Charlie Feathers and Jerry Lee Lewis all learned their instruments at the hands of neighbourhood black musicians. Local blacks, originators of the sound, hung around the back door looking for a way in.

Then came Stax. Brother and sister team Jim Stewart and Estelle Axton relocated their tiny studio from rural Tennessee to downtown Memphis in 1960, setting up shop in the unoccupied Capitol cinema on East McLemore Avenue. More unlikely purveyors of the Memphis Sound could not be imagined.

'I never thought of it till I got in it, and then I lived it, 24 hours a day,' remembers Axton, who was formerly a schoolteacher. 'When I wasn't working, I was dreaming about it.' Echoing Sam Phillips's sentiment, she says, 'We had an open-door policy. If you wanted to be heard, if you had something unique or different for us to listen to, well then, bring it in and we'd take the time to listen.' None of their plans were intentional – they just happened.

'I had scarcely seen a black person till I was grown,' recalls Stewart. 'I had no desire to start Stax Records; I had no dream of doing anything like that. I just wanted music, just anything to be involved with music.' Located in a black working-class community, Stax offered equal opportunities for blacks and whites. And once the door opened at Soulsville USA (as the studio was called), curious neighbourhood blacks began to stop in.

Carla Thomas. Isaac Hayes. David Porter. The Mad Lads. The Bar-Kays. The Astors. Booker T Jones… These names could serve as a roll-call for world-renowned black singers and musicians who grew up at Stax. Balancing the scales were white teens Steve Cropper and Donald 'Duck' Dunn, who, along with Jones and drummer Al Jackson Jr, formed The MG's – the rhythm section that became the core of the Stax sound.

Accordingly, one of the label's biggest hits came from Booker T And The MGs, who, after recording a blues instrumental, hastily cut 'Green Onions', a B-side for the single. 'The disc jockeys flipped it over and "Green Onions" was a million seller. That's just the way things happen sometimes,' Axton nonchalantly recalls.

Otis Redding appeared on the scene in 1962. 'Like almost everything else that happened at Stax, the arrival of Redding was both unforeseen and unplanned for,' writes author Peter Guralnick in *Sweet Soul Music*. 'He was only there in the first place because he'd driven his friend, Johnny Jenkins, up from Macon, Georgia.' But once recorded, Redding hit again and again with songs like 'Respect', 'Mr Pitiful' and 'Try A Little Tenderness'.

Culminating with his appearance at the Monterey Pop Festival in the summer of 1967, Redding, according to Guralnick, 'eventually opened up the world of southern soul to a large-scale white audience, making

Stax a byword in soul circles'. It all ended that December, when Redding's plane crashed into an icy lake *en route* from Cleveland, Ohio, to Madison, Wisconsin. His biggest seller, '(Sittin' On) The Dock Of The Bay', was released posthumously.

The Staple Singers, a prominent family group on the gospel circuit, were also hit-makers for the label. Led by patriarch Pops Staples, the group – Pervis, Cleotha, Mavis (and later Yvonne) – was drawn into the Civil Rights Movement by the words of Martin Luther King Jr. 'When we heard Dr King preach', Mavis ascertains, 'Pops said, "Now if he can preach this, we can sing it. This could be our way of helping." So we started singing protest songs!'

'Respect Yourself', their biggest Stax hit, evolved from the idea that black folks needed – and deserved – to be proud. 'Everybody is somebody' was an idiom Pops typically avowed. 'There's no big I and little you – God made us all.' On the Staples' version of the song, Mavis delivered the battle-cry in the second verse, her rumbling voice erupting at the phrase 'big ole man' on her way into the chorus. Pops's vibrato hooks, snug over the studio rhythm section, took the message home. Then Martin Luther King Jr – the man who made that notion a reality – was shot down at that motel on Mulberry Street, just a few blocks north of McLemore Avenue. Riots ensued, and it seemed that Soulsville – and all of Memphis – would never be the same again.

Though no one realised it at the time, Stax's days were also numbered. The 'Sound of Money', as the label once called itself, was financially destroyed after a bad distribution deal with CBS Records in 1972. Minor creditors forced Stax into bankruptcy in late 1975. That same year, drummer Al Jackson – Soulsville's heartbeat – was shot to death in his home. Just a few months later, Union Planters Bank shut Stax down in a foreclosure for default on a $10.5 million loan. Union Planters Bank sold the property to the Church of God in Christ (COGIC) for $10. The church effectively let the building rot.

While filming *Mystery Train*, director Jim Jarmusch captured the facility at its worst: McLemore Avenue deserted, the building covered in graffiti. This was Stax in the 1980s. By the time *Mystery Train* was released in 1989, COGIC had razed Stax with plans to build a soup kitchen. Other than an inconspicuous historical marker (courtesy of the state of Tennessee) encircled with weeds, there were few clues that the property was ground zero for soul fans.

Then on 20 April 2001, a crowd of 3,000 gathered at the former Stax site to witness the 'ground shakin' ground breakin'' for a planned $20 million Stax Museum of American Soul Music and Stax Academy and Performing Arts Center, both projected to open in 2003.

The day was overcast and windy, but jubilant musicians, fans and local politicians turned out to see fireworks explode as a backhoe symbolically dug into the earth. Isaac Hayes, Rufus Thomas, William Bell, Bar-Kays' bassist James Alexander, and The Mad Lads' John Gary Williams and William Brown were among the Stax luminaries present at what Curtis Johnson of The Astors described as 'a family reunion. Just about everybody who was anybody, and who worked with, or for, somebody at Stax, was here. It was all smiles, hugs, and love.'

Author Stanley Booth, who chronicled the rise and fall of Stax in *Rythm Oil*, attributes the new-found popularity of the Memphis Sound and subsequent Soulsville revival to an unlikely source: 'Evidence of its reality is the long, long time it took the politicians to claim it.'

Deanie Parker, who began her career at Stax as a clerk in the Satellite Record store – and is now president of Soulsville Inc, the non-profit organisation behind the museum project – takes a humbler view. 'I just want the neighborhood to sing again,' she says.

And as the Stax Museum of American Soul Music prepares to open its doors to the public, the dump trucks will resume their trek down Linden to Front Street and across the bridge to Mud Island. Oddly enough, I now realise, their route begins at Clayborn Temple, the meeting site for Dr King's final, disastrous march. It ends at Auction Avenue, close to the spot where Nathan Bedford Forrest bought and sold human beings like so many cattle.

It's possible that outside the National Civil Rights Museum, Jacqueline Smith can hear the trucks rumble from the arena site. I wonder if she smiles, thinking about Memphis's first NBA team and the money local taxpayers have spent courting the handful of young, black millionaire ball players.

Thanks to the influence of such Memphians as Mayor Herenton, AC Wharton, Deanie Parker, and even Sam Phillips and Jacqueline Smith, four years have passed since the Ku Klux Klan last darkened our door. It's a new day in Memphis, and as I pull into my parking spot the sun peeks out from behind the clouds. Maybe we'll become a city after all.

STAX RECORDS
Mike Evans

Sun Records and the still-standing studio at 706 Union Avenue have pride of place in the itinerary of any music fan visiting Memphis. While the Graceland mansion out on Highway 51 is a shrine to some, and a curiosity at least to even the most sceptical, Sun was where the music – and consequently history – was actually made. However, if we're talking historically, equal priority should be given to the name of Stax Records, whose musical legacy is there for us all to hear, but without the bricks-and-mortar physical presence of a tangible site that puts it on the tourist hit list.

When the original studio was allowed to change hands and subsequently (literally) disappear, what was left of the Stax phenomenon was the power of the recorded output itself, and the indelible mark it left on popular music –and the music business – throughout the 1960s and beyond.

Founder Jim Stewart (the 'St' in Stax), himself an aspiring fiddle player though professionally working in a bank, began recording local country artists in 1957, first of all using a relative's garage as an improvised studio. He even managed to release a single, a C&W number he wrote, with local DJ Fred Bylar singing, called 'Blue Roses'; he named the label Satellite ('Satellites were big at that time'). Aided financially by his sister Estelle Axton (the 'ax') – another bank employee – he purchased an Ampex recorder and relocated to the nearby town of Brunswick, Tennessee, 50km (30 miles) east of Memphis, where a permanent studio was set up in a friend's empty warehouse.

But, as Robert Gordon points out in *It Came From Memphis*, neither individual was planning to get involved in black music – the direction of the label (which was soon to be renamed Stax) came from Estelle's son Packy. As she recalled to Peter Guralnick in *Sweet Soul Music*, 'We had a little group. Steve Cropper was in that group. My son, Packy, was playing tenor sax. Charlie Freeman on guitar, Terry Johnson was the drummer, "Duck" Dunn – they all went to Messick High School, they were just a little rock group that called themselves The Royal Spades.'

Freeman, Johnson, guitarist Cropper and bass player Dunn were to become the backbone of the Stax house rhythm section, but before that The Royal Spades had a hit in their own right under their new name, The Mar-Keys. The Mar-Keys, with another sax player, Don Nix, trumpet man, Wayne Jackson, and pianist, Smoochie Smith, were a very early example of a white outfit playing black R&B, something that was commonplace by the middle '60s. And their one and only hit, the down-home 'Last Night' in 1961, was one of the pioneer crossover R&B hits that was hugely popular in both black and white markets – another music-business distinction which Memphis soul music, and Stax in particular, helped eradicate by the middle of the decade.

The rhythm section became The MGs (Memphis Group) who, with Booker T Jones on keyboards, had a series of Stax hits as Booker T And The MGs, starting with the international smash 'Green Onions' in 1962. The Mar-Keys' horn section, meantime, evolved into the Memphis Horns.

While still listed in the telephone book as Satellite, the fledgling label had moved back to Memphis in 1960 to occupy the former premises of the Capitol cinema on East McLemore Avenue, where it signed its first black act, Rufus Thomas. Thomas's first release with the company was a duet with his 17-year-old daughter Carla – ''Cause I Love You' – which became a big seller across the South. More importantly, it led to a distribution deal with the New York-based Atlantic Records.

Soon after the move back to Memphis, the name change put Stax on the map, along with Soulsville USA – glowing in bright-red plastic letters on the illuminated theatre marquee – which is what they dubbed the studio building itself.

Following Carla Thomas's solo follow-up, 'Gee Whiz (Look At His Eyes)' – which became the first national hit for Stax in 1961 – the label seemingly could do no wrong. Hit followed hit, with releases by Rufus

Thomas ('Walkin' The Dog', etc), Sam And Dave ('Soul Man', 'Hold On, I'm Coming'), Eddie 'Knock On Wood' Floyd, and Stax-produced hits for Atlantic that included one of the true anthems of southern soul – Wilson Pickett's 'In The Midnight Hour'.

There was even a Stax package show that toured Europe in 1967, stunning audiences everywhere with Booker T And The MGs, Carla Thomas, The Mar-Keys, Sam And Dave, Eddie Floyd, Arthur Conley and bill-topper Otis Redding. It was the same year that Otis reached his widest audience of all in the film documentary of the Monterey Pop Festival, and the year of his untimely death.

Despite increasing financial complications referred to earlier in this chapter, Stax continued to make its presence felt in the charts, nationally and internationally. Major hits by Johnnie Taylor, Booker T, Judy Clay and William Bell were eclipsed only by Isaac Hayes, who became a superstar name with the release of the soundtrack to the 1971 *Shaft* movie, which eventually won Grammies and an Oscar. Also on the cinema screens, *Wattstax* (1973) proved a concert-footage smash to rival *Monterey Pop* and *Woodstock*, with Stax luminaries Hayes, The Staple Singers, Rufus and Carla Thomas and Johnnie Taylor heading the bill.

Stax Records' place in American music history is assured, as one of the most popular soul labels ever – second only to Motown in sales, but equally important in its influence. In 15 years Stax had over 167 hits in the US Top 100 pop chart as well as 243 hits in the Top 100 R&B listings. Its history paralleling that of the Civil Rights Movement of the 1960s, Stax was one of the most integrated companies of any kind as well as being the fifth largest African-American-owned business in 1974. And the Memphis label outlasted most of its rivals, releasing almost 300 albums and over 800 singles between 1959 and 1975.

Stax's influence can be felt 30 years later in R&B, rock, pop, jazz, hip-hop and gospel. Stax songs have been covered by an amazing variety of artists including Aerosmith, The Rolling Stones, The Black Crowes, The Blues Brothers, Salt 'n' Pepa and En Vogue, as well as influencing R&B and rap stars such as R Kelly and D'Angelo.

For Memphis, Stax is critical historically as the most successful and international of any of the city's recording labels. According to

Soulsville USA: The Story Of Stax Records, in 1973 Memphis was the fourth largest recording centre in the world, and recording was the third largest commercial activity there. With over 200 employees, Stax was a major part of that activity: beginning with Rufus Thomas, it created the link between the roots of rock 'n' roll at Sun Records in the 1950s to the sweet soul music of the 1960s, through to the hard funk and disco of the 1970s. Stax provided a template of what an integrated company could be – from management all the way down to its bands, the label's open-door policy providing a creative opportunity and entrée into the music business for Memphians, black and white.

SOULSVILLE
Mike Evans

While Stax Records was certainly the most prolific soul record label from Memphis and the first name in quality soul music, Hi Records also thrived in the same area of town in the 1960s and early 1970s. Just down the street from the Stax studios, at 1320 South Lauderdale, Willie Mitchell's Royal Recording studio created numerous soul classics for the Hi label with Al Green, Ann Peebles, Otis Clay and OV Wright along with Mitchell's house band, The Hi Rhythm Section. The success of Stax and Hi encouraged other, smaller labels such as Goldwax Records, as well as creating a demand for other studios, including the famous American Recording. It was all this activity, not just the spectacular success of Stax Records, that made Memphis the Soul Music Capital of the World in the late 1960s.

This concentration of the music industry, plus the area's historical antecedents in the music's development, led to the area being dubbed – after the nomenclature adopted by the Stax studio building – Soulsville USA. Among many points of interest in the area are the birthplace of Aretha Franklin at 406 Lucy Avenue, as well as her father's (the Rev CL Franklin) church, the New Salem Missionary Church at 955 South Fourth Street. Memphis Minnie lived just past Aretha Franklin's birthplace (but many years earlier) at 1355 Adelaide, while David Porter and Maurice

White lived in the currently demolished LeMoyne Gardens, one of Memphis's toughest housing projects.

The legendary Johnny Ace, when he lived at home in Memphis, resided at 899 Ferry Court, right behind the Stax Studios. James Alexander of The Bar-Kays grew up at 898 Stafford, and many of the Stax musicians rehearsed at his house before going into the studio. The Blackwood Bros went to church at 1084 McLemore Avenue, at the First Assembly of God, where Elvis also worshipped, one block east of the Stax Studios. And, of course, one of the earliest and most prolific gospel composers, the Rev Herbert Brewster, preached the gospel at Trigg Avenue Baptist Church. Bluesman Memphis Slim's family lived across from Stax at 1130 College Avenue, while the 'Father of the Blues' WC Handy lived at 659 East Jennette. And that most revered of Memphis jazz families – that of Calvin and Phineas Newborn – grew up at 582 Alston, later moving to 588 Alston.

One block north of Stax, Elmwood Cemetery's imposing property is one of the city's greatest hidden charms. While the great 1930s bandleader Jimmie Lunceford and gospel legend Lucie Campbell are the most famous musicians to be buried in Elmwood, viewing the amazing – though often kitsch – artwork of the tombstones is worth an afternoon's visit to this historic location.

The most exciting recent development as far as the area is concerned is that a non-profit organisation named after the district, Soulsville, has been set up to put into motion a long-awaited project, the Stax Museum of American Soul Music, located on the original site of the Stax studio at 926 East McLemore. Adjacent to the museum will be the Stax Music Academy, which will develop and teach the future musicians of Memphis music, with the focus on inner city youth.

The Stax Museum of American Soul Music, due to open in spring 2003, will include displays of many of the elements that made Stax Records a uniquely integrated recording studio, label and business during a decidedly non-integrated period of time in the United States. The museum will demonstrate that Stax Records became one of the most influential record labels of all time and the fifth largest minority-owned business in the US in 1974. Stax Records's strength relied on its policy, which allowed anyone with any talent to come through the doors and contribute creatively. The 'open-door policy' of Stax Records was its trademark from day one and created long-lasting music careers for many people who would otherwise have had no opportunity in the music industry. Stax had an integrated group of employees at a time – especially in the South, when such integration was uncommon. Women had key roles in running the company many years before the Equal Rights Amendment was enacted.

Visitors to the museum will tour through the re-creation of the main studio (Studio A) with its sloping floors (originally the studio was a cinema) and 'Voice of God' movie speakers. The museum will show how the Stax artists and writers created songs, brought them straight into the studio, and recorded them. Key players in the Stax, Hi and Goldwax Records stories will tell their stories through documentary films and interviews. Soul fans will learn how soul music grew through the roots of gospel music, and memorabilia such as contracts, costumes, instruments, posters and awards will be displayed. Artefacts from the Stax and Hi record labels as well as other soul record labels will be presented. The Satellite Record store will be rebuilt in its original location, once again selling the Memphis Sound. The self-proclaimed aim of the Museum is to 'immerse the visitor in the funky sounds of sweet soul music', showing how the Stax sound has influenced music 30 years later.

HI TIMES WITH WILLIE MITCHELL
Mike Evans

Among the movers and shakers who have forged the musical legacy of Memphis, few rank higher than Willie Mitchell, first of all as the crucial A&R (Artists and Repertoire) man responsible for the artistic development at Hi Records, then as proprietor of the equally influential Royal Recording Studios.

Well before Mitchell got involved, Hi Records was founded in 1957 in the wake of the huge success of Sun Records, with an investment of $3.50 by Ray Harris. With two partners, Bill Cantrell and Quinton Claunch, who worked on production for Sun and Meteor Records in the mid-1950s, they approached Joe Cuoghi (who was later to be President of Hi) at Popular Tunes record store, which included a jukebox service. Joe had better financing and industry contacts than the others.

The first success came in late 1959, with a hit by the Bill Black Combo, 'Smokie-Part 2', Bill having been bass player on the original Elvis sessions at Sun and also part of his subsequent touring band. Harris and Black had developed a unique bottom-heavy beat sound which became the Hi instrumental trademark in the early '60s, with hits by Black and his guitarist Reggie Young, 'yaketty sax' player Ace Cannon and trumpeter Willie Mitchell. The label became known as the 'House of Instrumentals', in fact, some observing that 'Hi' could have been short for 'Hit instrumentals'. And, as part of this success, Mitchell had his share of instrumental hits, starting with 'The Crawl' in 1961, followed by 'Sunrise Serenade', '20–75' through to his biggest instrumental smash, 'Soul Serenade', in 1968. But it was as house arranger rather than performer that Willie Mitchell made his mark on the sound at Hi.

Mitchell was born in Ashland, Mississippi, in 1928, moving with his family around 1930 to Memphis. He played trumpet with his high-school band, and even played on BB King's first sides while still a teenager, then formed his own 17-piece band until he went into the Army in 1950. Just previous to his Army service, he'd studied arrangements and scoring with pianist Onzie Horne, a former employee of Duke Ellington who would become MD at King Records, then later for Isaac Hayes.

Returning to Memphis in the mid-1950s, Mitchell formed a new 18-piece outfit, working residencies including Danny's Club in West Memphis, then the Manhattan Club and the Plantation Inn. The band's line-up included all the best Memphis jazz talent of the period, including Phineas Newborn Jr, Charles Lloyd, Booker Little, George Coleman – all destined to be big names in their own right – plus the rhythm section that would become one half of the original Booker T And The MGs, bass player Lewis Sternberg and drummer Al Jackson. As Peter Guralnick points out in *Sweet Soul Music*, 'To young whites like Steve Cropper and "Duck" Dunn, Jim Dickinson and Packy Axton, who made the PI (Plantation Inn) their second home, bands like Willie's were the pinnacle of cool and provided a level of musicianship and formal elegance to which they could scarcely aspire. To Memphis's fledgling "music industry" these bands, with their natural reservoir of reading musicians, were a resource to be tapped.'

In 1960 he got his first real involvement with a record company, the Home of the Blues label, where he performed the various roles of house musician, recording artist and producer, in the last capacity working with the popular Memphis vocal group The 5 Royales and the R&B stylist Roy Brown. It was then that he started to develop his horn arrangements, which anticipated the Hi and Stax sound. Then, after a chance meeting with engineer and label founder Ray Harris, Mitchell was invited to make some records (as performer) at Hi. As well as his modestly selling singles, however, he was soon to became house arranger, and his backing group The Hi Rhythm Section.

With this loose amalgam of hypertalented musicians, Willie Mitchell went on to define a new black music style, though (as at Stax) both black and white musicians played on many sessions. He used an old eight-track recorder pieced together from two Ampex four-track machines, which operated on 'tube' (valve) technology as opposed to 'solid state', the 'tube' work being essential to the Mitchell sound. The drums were tuned and then miked in such a way that they became the centrepiece of the backing tracks.

The Rhythm Section consisted of Al Jackson or Howard Grimes on drums, Bobby Emmons on organ, guitarist Reggie Young and Tommy Cogbill on bass. The regular horn players were Andrew Love, Ben Cawley, Charles Charmers, James Mitchell, Gene Miller and Wayne Jackson. With a line-up change that introduced the Hodges brothers (Teenie Hodges on guitar, Leroy on bass and Charlie on organ), between 1964 and 1969 the combo had no fewer than eight R&B hits under Willie Mitchell's name, including '20–75', 'Bad Eye', 'Mercy', 'Soul Serenade', 'Prayer Meetin'', '30–60–90' and 'Uphard'.

Hi, however, was still largely regarded as the home of the instrumental (and the occasional novelty) hit. What Willie realised they needed was some vocal hits to restore the balance. He started in this direction with some sides by OV Wright, which resulted in a hit in 'Eight Men, Four Women' in 1967, followed by some LP tracks with Memphis R&B star

Bobby Bland. But the real breakthrough in the vocal stakes for Hi, with Mitchell at the helm, was with 21-year-old Ann Peebles.

Born on 27 April 1947 in St Louis, Missouri, Peebles began singing gospel in the choir directed by her father when she was only 9 years old. The only female to date to have cut solo albums for Hi, she saw her 1969 début single on the label, 'Walk Away', become a minor hit, and the fourth, 'Part Time Love' a major one the following year. But her biggest success was to come with the magnificent 'I Can't Stand The Rain' in 1973, which many consider to be the defining example of the Hi Records sound, and which John Lennon cited as one of his all-time favourites.

Willie Mitchell's major foray into vocal production reached its peak, however, and for ever changed the fortunes of Hi Records – and his own – when he literally discovered Al Green working in a club in Midland, Texas, in 1968. It meant a new direction for soul music as he and Green, in the words of Peter Guralnick, 'came up with an old idea phased in a new way, the last eccentric refinement of Sam Cooke's lyrical gospel-edged style as filtered through the fractured vocal approach of Otis Redding and the peculiarly fragmented vision of Al Green himself'.

After 1969's shaky start, 1971 saw the first of a string of charting singles beginning with 'Tired Of Being Alone' and 'Let's Stay Together' and culminating in 1974's 'Sha-La-La'. A couple of lesser hits later, Green, beset by personal problems, split from Mitchell, made some self-produced solo albums, then went back to the Church (where he had started as a singer) and famously set up his Full Gospel Tabernacle Church in Memphis (this is dealt with in detail later).

Other Mitchell-led vocal projects at Hi included work by Otis Clay and Syl Johnson, but none came anywhere near the commercial crossover success achieved with Al Green or Ann Peebles. The mid-1970s disco boom militated against the kind of soul represented by Hi (and Stax, for that matter), and in 1979 the company was sold to Cream Records.

Willie Mitchell carried on as proprietor of the Royal Recording Studios, the same premises where he cut all the Al Green hits, and remains there to this day at 1329 South Lauderdale. The technical stuff has been upgraded, much else stays as before, and Willie Mitchell is still very much part of the fabric – not just of the studio, but of Memphis itself.

SOUL QUEEN
Mike Evans

Carla Thomas, the daughter of Rufus Thomas, was one of the core artists that represented the essence of Memphis soul, and the Stax sound in particular. Born in Memphis in 1942, Carla first performed with the Teen Town Singers while still under ten years old. She was persuaded to cut ''Cause I Love You', a duet with her father, which was released on Satellite (later Stax) in 1960. The line-up itself guaranteed attention – as well as her brother Marvel on organ, the single featured Robert Talley on piano, Steve Cropper on guitar and a then-unknown Booker T Jones on baritone sax. The record was important if only because its success in airplay and the sales across the South led directly to the fledgling label getting a distribution deal with the mighty Atlantic Records in New York.

Her next record, and first solo effort, was made in late 1960, and again she proved herself to be an asset to the label: 'Gee Whiz (Look At His Eyes)' provided their first national hit when it made the *Billboard* Top Ten.

Her next sides were the subject of a Satellite/Stax distribution wrangle with Atlantic (who insisted they had signed to all of Satellite product, rather than just Rufus/Carla duets), with the result that her releases ended up on Atlantic although she was still signed to Satellite. Whatever, some strong material followed, including an 'answer' record to Sam Cooke's 'Bring It On Home To Me' titled 'I'll Bring It On Home To You' in 1962, 1963's 'What A Fool I've Been' and 'Let Me Be Good To You' in 1965.

Her name back under the Stax logo, the sensational 'B-A-B-Y', written by Isaac Hayes and David Porter, reached the American R&B Top 3 and pop Top 20 in 1966, followed by a series of duets with Otis Redding that saw her heralded as the 'Queen of Soul'. A version of Lowell Fulson's 'Tramp' introduced the partnership in 1967, with 'Knock On Wood' appearing later in the year, both making the US Top 30. 'Lovey Dovey' was the final collaboration with Otis before his death in the plane crash that also killed four members of his backing group, The Bar-Kays.

Although further singles in the duet formula with William Bell and Johnnie Taylor were unable to capture the magic she had achieved with

Otis, Carla remained with Stax until its bankruptcy in 1975. Through the following years of the '80s and '90s she made no records, although she did tour occasionally with the Stax revival shows, appearing, along with her father, at the Porretta Terme Soul Festival in 1991. She still lives in Memphis, and lately has been making live appearances more regularly, one of which recently led to a brand-new live recording.

The occasion was a 2002 birthday party that Hollywood actor Morgan Freeman was throwing for his wife, Myrna. He asked producer David Less to assemble the best musicians and arrangements to be found in the Mid-South, fronted by Carla Thomas. The result was an album released on the Memphis International label, *Live In Memphis*, with the cream of Memphis players including Spooner Oldham on piano, Stax alumni Ronnie Williams on organ, Bobby Manuel on guitar and current Booker T And The MGs drummer Steve Potts, plus songwriting veteran Dan Penn on backing vocals.

The horn section of Jim Spake (sax) and Scott Thompson (trumpet) played true to the original arrangements of Carla's catalogue of blockbuster hits, bringing additional enthusiasm, drive and funk to the mix. With the added vocals of Mad Lads' lead William Brown and Reba Russell – a Memphis vocal legend in her own right – Carla revisited her greatest hits in a celebration of the classic Memphis soul sound.

THE MEMPHIS HORNS
Mike Evans

When Andrew Love and Wayne Jackson started playing together as part of the Stax house band in the early 1960s, little could they have imagined that, more than 40 years later, they would be known as a saxophone and trumpet duo the world over.

Wayne got his start in West Memphis, strumming guitar and singing current pop songs – he especially remembers the old Vaughn Monroe number 'Ghost Riders In The Sky' – in childhood talent shows. Andrew, on the other hand, began his career playing sacred music and gospel hymns like 'Amazing Grace' in Memphis's Mount Nebo Baptist Church, where his father, Roy Love, was the pastor. Wayne took up the trumpet and trombone, developing the trumpet in particular, and the two's paths converged once they both started playing on the Mid-South gigging scene, sitting in with bands and so on, and picking up the odd session date.

Wayne Jackson joined The Royal Spades (who famously changed their name to The Mar-Keys when they were signed up by the fledgling Stax record company) soon after they had a hit on their hands with 'Last Night' in the most celebrated of Stax line-ups that included Steve Cropper and 'Duck' Dunn, Don Nix and Charlie Freeman.

Andrew Love, meanwhile, was getting regular session work at Hi Records, where future MG's drummer Al Jackson suggested he try his luck with Stax. He was soon in the house band, along with Jackson (no relation to Al), and the two gelled immediately, both musically and personality-wise. Together they created the distinctive horn sound that very quickly became a Stax trademark across the world, with hits from the likes of Otis Redding, Sam And Dave, Carla and Rufus Thomas and the rest. Andrew recalls when he first played with Wayne: 'I loved how our tones blended and so did Wayne. We have a unique sound. We've been together ever since.'

As part of the Stax–Volt revue, they toured Europe in 1967. They were there providing the backing when Otis Redding – with his spine-tingling version of 'I've Been Loving You Too Long' – stole the show from The Who, Jimi Hendrix, Janis Joplin and other superstars of the mid-1960s at the Monterey Pop Festival that same year (immortalised on film by Don Pennebaker).

In 1969 they took the crucial step of incorporating officially as The Memphis Horns, a name that had already begun to stick with them informally on the music scene. They were now a freelance unit, open for session work for any artists who wanted an injection of Memphis soul on their records. From there on, the work just never stopped coming in, with names from across the spectrum booking their services. They are still amazed by it all: 'For about ten years, we were making number one records daily,' says Wayne. 'It would be King Curtis one day, Tony Joe White the next day, Dionne Warwick the next and then Elvis.'

They are still operating as a unit, with a track record that reads like a scroll though a history of recent popular music, with the likes of Aretha

Franklin, Wilson Pickett, Albert King, BB King, Jimmy Buffett, Peter Gabriel, Steve Winwood, U2, Al Green, Willie Nelson, Lenny Kravitz and Sting just the tip of the iceberg.

Billing them as 'The Most Recorded Horn Section in American Popular Music', their website quotes Robert Gordon, who describes them working in the studio as 'like getting a glimpse of angels speaking'. We can make less than satisfying attempts to analyse their success or define their sound, but, as Gordon concludes, 'Nothing explains The Memphis Horns better than their quarter century of music.'

3 If Beale Street Could Talk

TALKIN' BEALE STREET BLUES
Mike Evans

For anyone visiting Memphis with an interest in the city's music heritage, Beale Street – at least the section which runs from Riverside Drive against the Mississippi in the west to the intersection with Danny Thomas Boulevard in the east – is a prime point of call, a must-see, regardless of the sequential impact of urban decay, redevelopment and then the tourist trade. Of course, one only has to look at the monochrome photographs of the bustling thoroughfare when it really *was* the hub of Memphian music life to realise that what exists today is at best a shallow imitation, at worst an irrelevant aboration, of its former self. Having said that, a stroll down Beale can still be an entertaining diversion – like so many examples in the worldwide 'heritage' industry, a result of, rather than celebration of, a place's actual history. And, in the case of Beale, it's quite a history.

From the early 1800s, as Memphis became a magnet for immigrants from all corners of the globe, homes, shops, churches, theatres and the rest sprung up along Beale Street, which by the 1840s had become part of an affluent enclave of the city. The grand Hunt-Phelan home, which still stands today near the east end of Beale, is testament to this.

In the aftermath of the Civil War, many emancipated black slaves settled in the area, which was devastated in the 1870s by a series of cholera and yellow fever epidemics, as a result of which over half of the population had died or had fled Memphis – in just one month, over

5,000 people died and a further 25,000 left the city. Significantly, the African Americans, who had a much greater immunity to yellow fever, assisted the sick, tended to the dead and helped to rebuild the city after the disease had passed.

The epidemics left the city devastated economically, and the black community who had remained in the Beale Street area became directly involved in its renaissance. By the early 20th century it had become a bustling district again, Beale Street itself full of shops, churches…and nightlife. It was the latter that made it a mecca for young musicians, and by the 1920s the area had acquired an anything-goes atmosphere and 'wide-open' reputation, with the booming nightclubs, theatres, restaurants, stores, pawn shops and, of course, hot music accompanied by the inevitable gambling, drinking, prostitution, murder and even voodoo alongside. There on Beale and the adjacent streets, all manner of musical entertainment was available, from the big vaudeville shows and talent nights at the Palace Theater and the Daisy, to the jug bands and lone musicians playing the street corners.

The Great Depression of the 1930s took its toll, as it did everywhere else, followed by World War II that likewise affected every aspect of life. But Beale was still a lively hot spot after the war, in the late 1940s, as jazzman Herman Green recalled in an interview on his own website with Jerry W Atwood: 'It was 1945. I was about 14 or 15 years old. That was a whole different Beale Street. Where Handy Park is, was a big wide open space and it was the market. People would come from all over and bring fresh vegetables and fruit and anything else you can imagine, and sell all day Saturday in the market. There would be pick-up trucks loaded with watermelons and dogs running around and a real crowd all over the street. It was where everybody came to see and be seen. I guess I played in every place that there was. Sometimes we would get a dollar for playing in a bar and sometimes we could get on a stage show, but a lot of times we just set up on the street and put an empty can (chip bucket) in front of us and played, and people would put pennies and nickels and dimes in the chip bucket and we would make a little money.'

Many of the actual clubs weren't on Beale itself, but in the surrounding streets, but even so Beale Street was the de facto musical hub of Memphis, with saloons and bars being where musicians playing the clubs gathered socially; places like the legendary Pee Wee's Saloon, where WC Handy and his band made their first HQ in Memphis in 1909, and where the 'Father of the Blues' was reputed to have written the first-ever 'official' blues song, 'Memphis Blues' (originally as 'Mr Crump' with reference to the then-city mayor). Pee Wee's, which survived into the early 1990s, was at 315 Beale, which now houses, unrecognisably, a branch of the Hard Rock Café chain.

Similarly in the '40s and '50s, another musicians' gathering place was Mitchell's Hotel, located at 207 Beale Street. Andrew 'Sunbeam' Mitchell and his wife Earnestine (who went on to run Earnestine and Hazel's Lounge on South Main Street) ran a hotel and upstairs club, helping struggling musicians with a bed when they were homeless or a bowl of chilli when they were hungry and a place to jam after the other clubs had closed. He was something of a modest philanthropist, even buying young musicians instruments to get them started. And during the Civil Rights struggle he made the hotel available for meetings and rallies.

Over the years, Sunbeam ran many clubs in the Beale Street area, including the Club Handy, the Domino Lounge, the Flamingo Room and the Hippodrome. He managed BB King in his young days and, when Little Richard was struggling for work in the early '50s, Sunbeam gave him a job wiping down the tables so he could be near the music.

Talking to Ross Gohlke for *Bluespeak* in February 1998, the late Big Lucky Carter remembered Sunbeam's in the '40s and '50s: 'The greatest musicians you had was upstairs at Sunbeam Mitchell's. All of the musicians would come through up here. He had lodging for them, he had food – his specialty was chilli. It was hard to find a hotel then. Musicians would come through here, they'd stop by Sunbeam's upstairs and play for their supper. That was the baptizing place for musicians. If you come out of there, if they said you was a musician, you was a musician.' Sunbeam Mitchell died in 1989.

The largest entertainment establishments on Beale were the two theatres, the Palace and the Daisy (which later became the site of the Beale Street Blues Museum), the Palace being famous for its Amateur Night on Beale, which was hosted by schoolteacher/journalist Nat Williams and then blues singer Rufus Thomas, as Herman Green describes: 'We were the band for the Palace Theater. The Palace has been torn down, but it was right next to where the New Daisy is now. Those were the days, in about 1948 and 1949, when we had Amateur Night on Beale and the Midnight Ramble. It would be difficult to try to describe all that went on and all the different music people and musicians that came to town to play the Palace.

'On any given night you might see T-Bone Walker, Big Joe Turner, and many others that are legends now and gone from us. Rufus had a partner we called "Bones" and they would warm up the audience with an act called "Rufus and Bones". They were kind of a black Dean Martin and Jerry Lewis, with Rufus doing the straight lines and "Bones" doing all kinds of crazy things. I doubt if you could name any famous black music person that we did not play with during those days. Ike Turner, Bobby "Blue" Bland, Muddy Waters, Howlin' Wolf, Johnny Ace, Little Junior Parker, Albert King and just about everybody else would come to Beale Street, including many of the Delta bluesmen that were unknown then. Later, after I left, Elvis Presley used to come by, when he was just getting started.'

But, with population shifts and changes in leisure habits, the glory days of Beale were coming to an end, and by the 1960s, when much of the street was derelict, there was even talk of 'urban renewal' – bulldozing down the once bustling neighbourhood. Some of the old buildings were in fact lost, but (in 1966) Beale Street was placed on the National Register of Historic Places, and by the early 1980s a programme of renovation was taking place. Community and government investment in the Beale Street area encouraged new businesses such as clubs, theatre renovations, shops and restaurants to return to the area, but – almost inevitably – much of the heart and soul of the place as it *had* been had long disappeared with the juke joints and saloons.

Taking a walk eastwards up Beale these days, the first big establishment – perhaps significantly – is a classic case of a tourist-aimed development replacing a genuine historical site. It's Elvis Presley's Memphis on the corner of Second Street, an eating and entertainment facility that presents mainstream-friendly rock 'n' roll acts and such, the décor and menu oriented to promoting the 'King'. Ironically, the site was previously occupied by Lansky's clothes store, where Elvis – and the bluesmen of Beale Street whose sartorial style he emulated – famously bought his 'Memphis flash' clothes in the 1950s.

The same side of the street brings us to the Blues City Café, famous for its BBQ ribs and steaks sold by the pound (plus live bands), while across the road is another place with a famous name in neon – BB King's Club. Although highly tourist-oriented, you do get the genuine article here when BB appears a couple of times a year, and most of the live acts like Ruby Wilson and soul singer Larry Springfield are worth a listen – if you can avoid the distraction of noisy parties (most of whom, you suspect, have never been in a blues club before) 'letting their hair down'.

Other places like Kings Palace Café and the more flamboyant Rum Boogie Café perform a similar balancing act of presenting solid, professional (albeit predictable) blues and soul bands to audiences of the curious rather than the committed, though the tiny Blues Hall annexe of the Rum Boogie, featuring mainly acoustic artists and seating for about 50, has a more 'authentic' ambience.

Further up Beale, it's even more of a shadow of its former self. Where Memphis jazz singer Joyce Cobb had her enterprising club until recently, there's now a trendy cocktail lounge, although the dynamic 17-piece Memphis Jazz Orchestra that played Mondays there can still be found at Alfred's on the corner of 3rd Street.

The non-musical enterprises on Beale are, naturally, dominated by shops catering just for the tourist trade. The Memphis Music record store a couple of doors up from BB's at 149, though carrying the obligatory souvenir ephemera, does at least have a decent selection of blues, jazz and rock 'n' roll discs, plus a mail-order facility, and the resident 'bluesologist' Dr Malcolm Anthony was extremely helpful when I last visited a couple of years ago.

A little further up from Memphis Music, there stands A Schwab's Dry Goods Store, which despite the urban planners' attempts to knock it down, remains the one true testament to a bygone era – it is still standing since 1876 and virtually unchanged since the middle of the last century, when Beale Street certainly had (to paraphrase Mr Handy) something to talk about.

FOCUSING ON BEALE
Andria Lisle

A discreet bronze plaque at 333 Beale Street declares the structure at the southeast end of the entertainment district the Ernest C Withers Building, but its exterior yields little clue as to the treasures within. It's not until you enter an unmarked entrance between 'Eel Etc' and a tattoo parlour that you see – at the end of a corridor – two tan doors marked 'Withers' Photography Studio.'

Although he's been at this location for less than a decade, Ernest C Withers has been a commercial photographer in Memphis since the end of World War II. Working on Beale, Withers took portraits of the performers – and the audiences – at the Flamingo Room, Club Paradise, the Hippodrome and other clubs, documenting what he calls 'a separate America'. Augmenting his policeman salary (he was one of the first blacks to join the city's force in 1948), Withers made '$50, $60 a night – maybe $100, being seen, making pictures' for $1.50 a piece.

Withers turned in his badge to work full-time as a photographer in 1950. It was just in time, for he caught the Memphis blues scene, the rise of R&B and the rumblings of rock 'n' roll with his camera. He also documented the Civil Rights Movement – from Emmett Till's murder trial, to the integration of the Little Rock school system, to the final days of Martin Luther King Jr. The two subjects often crossed over: thanks to revolutionaries like DJ Dewey Phillips, Sun Records' Sam Phillips, and Jim Stewart and Estelle Axton at Stax, the Memphis music scene was integrated long before the rest of the world, and Withers has the pictures to prove it.

Many of his pictures – BB King and band lined up in front of their tour bus, Howlin' Wolf performing at a grocery store, Elvis Presley backstage at a WDIA Goodwill Revue – have become an indelible part of the American music psyche. Yet for every published photograph, Withers has thousands more, never before seen, and just as fascinating. The file cabinets in his office are overflowing with untold histories in black and white, and I often stop by to ask him about Stax Records, or Sam Cooke, or the scene at the Hotel Men's Improvement Club. Other times, I drop in to find out what's happening in Memphis today – at 80 years young, Ernest C Withers is still going strong.

One rainy Wednesday afternoon, I duck into Ernest's office to catch up on things. A phone is ringing as I walk down the hall, and Ernest waves me to a spot on the couch as he answers the call. 'Withers here,' he says, sounding like a newsman straight out of the '40s – which, of course, he is. He reaches for a Bic pen – his shirt pocket is full of them – and scrawls down a bit of information. After a few moments, he hangs up, removes his brimless kente-cloth cap, and scratches his head. 'Come here, girl,' Ernest finally says. 'You can help me with this. We need to help file an obituary.' Before I even know the name of the deceased, I am dialling numbers and sending faxes, helping Ernest get the word out. Within the hour, a preacher, solemnly dressed in a grey suit, stops in to pick up an archived photograph. Ernest makes a few solicitous enquiries about the impending funeral service, jotting down the date on his calendar.

Soon after, a young man comes in with a letter regarding an upcoming awards ceremony at an area school. Ernest will be presented with a plaque, and he's got to put together a presentation detailing the last days of Dr King. Then two middle-aged sisters arrive, hard at work on a family tree. Ernest has a manila envelope ready for them, containing a portrait of their grandmother on her wedding day. The women are ecstatic, and Ernest relays what memories he has of that long-ago afternoon. He gestures around the office at the stacks of photos that cover his desk and file cabinets, and promises to find more pictures of their grandmother when he has the time.

Whenever I stop in, I do what I can to help Ernest organise his work. It's a futile attempt, however – he still photographs 15 to 20 events a week, and having to sort the negatives and photographs that come from the developer every day is a losing battle. I straighten up the prints in his office according to size and subject, and mail out a few bills and requested pictures. Then I leave the rest to his daughter-in-law, who is much better at keeping his things straight than I am. Luckily, the Panopticon Gallery in Boston has most of Ernest's negatives in storage.

'C'mon, girl – let's grab us some lunch,' Ernest says, breaking my reverie. He's already in his raincoat, and I hurry to the door to catch up with him. We dash through the rain puddles to his car, parked on the Beale Street cobblestones outside. I don't have to ask where he's taking me – we always go to the Gayhawk, a fabled black café on Danny Thomas Boulevard, on the south end of downtown. Ernest has been a regular diner at the Gayhawk since it opened some 50 years ago, and he relishes the conversation as much as he does the plate-lunch special.

Lunch at the Gayhawk is a long-established ritual – Ernest bows to the waitress on duty, then introduces me as 'his white daughter', a position I am honoured to hold. Then we grab our trays, and make our way through the cafeteria-style line. Without fail, Ernest points to a sign that declares that customers *must not* waste their food – 'You will be charged for any food remaining on your plate', chides the handwritten notice. Ernest guffaws and pats his stomach. 'We won't have that problem,' he says with a wink. A veritable who's who of Memphis's black community drops by our table to pay their respects. Local politics, from the latest Michael Hooks scandal to the Ford dynasty's current victory, are the order of the day, and by the time we finish our bowls of peach cobbler we are as well informed as Mayor Herenton himself.

Sated, we return to the studio. I have a copy of Ernest's latest book with me, and I want to ask him about some of the photographs. The book, *The Memphis Blues Again*, contains copious notes from editor Daniel Wolff, but I want a firsthand account of several of the portraits inside. Ernest sits down at his desk with a glass of water, and looks at the book's cover photograph of Lionel Hampton.

'This picture was made at an affair at the Hippodrome on Beale Street,' Ernest says. 'Memphis was on what was known in those days as the chitlin' circuit – a separate circuit. When people go to blues shows now, there's a combination of all people. But back in those days it was ninety-nine and forty-four hundredths percent African-American people – it wasn't a mixed crowd.'

Ernest's mind is as sharp as a steel trap, and his words paint a picture of a Beale Street long forgotten. 'The Hippodrome was at the east end of Beale, between the Hunt-Phelan home and the Martin Luther King Labor Center,' he tells me. 'It was originally a skating rink – when that declined, they turned it into a one-night-stand facility. At other places, black people had to go up through the back to see the big acts – the acts were African American, so why did the African-American people have to sit up in the gallery? So the Hippodrome was opened for blacks only. It held five or six thousand – and it was always a packed house. They booked Roy Brown, Lionel Hampton, Erskine Hawkins, Fats Waller... A lot of musicians played there!'

Then Ernest leans in to scrutinise the photograph. 'I captured the emotions of the people looking on at Hampton while he beat the drum. He was exciting to watch,' Ernest exclaims. 'Drumming affects the psyche of people – it was just a psychic moment.' I turn the pages until we're staring at a picture of Elvis Presley and Rufus Thomas at a WDIA Goodwill Revue, in December 1956. Rufus, clad in buckskins and an Indian headdress, has both arms extended toward the camera while Elvis, wearing a pinstriped coat, clowns behind him.

Ernest smiles, remembering the moment. 'Elvis visited backstage that year, and he was just charismatic enough to go out on the stage with Rufus. To see the image now, everybody knows Elvis. But this was an unusual moment, because there were no interracial shows in that day and time. People reacted to him, but they didn't react to the "legendary-ness" of Elvis – he was just a young white kid that came to the show and went out and did the twist with Rufus.'

I turn the page again, and we gaze at a dreamy portrait of Carla Thomas, Rufus's daughter. 'This was before Carla cut "Gee Whiz" and became a star – at this time, she was just a young girl from The Teen Town Singers and the *Big Star Show*. When Carla was a young girl, I used to make pictures at the *Big Star Show*, which was broadcast on WDIA every Saturday. Afterwards, I'd ride Carla and the rest of The Teen Town Singers downtown, where they could catch a bus or a streetcar home. Carla was a pretty girl – just as beautiful as she could be,' Ernest recalls.

I flip through the book until I find a photograph of Ray Charles playing the saxophone. 'Oh,' Ernest says, taking the book from me, 'this was from an appearance at the City Auditorium – a blacks-only show. Nothing at that time was integrated,' he says. 'Memphis was a separate town. White people used to come on Beale Street to the Palace Theater on a special night for white attendance at the Midnight Ramble. At a given time, the black theater switched to whites only. They didn't put signs up – it was just understood – "no black people". And the same thing would happen for black people at the City Auditorium.'

Ernest points out saxophonist Hank Crawford, seated behind Ray Charles. 'Hank was a Memphis boy, but by this point he'd already left Memphis and joined Ray Charles's band,' Ernest tells me. 'Hank was a graduate of Manassas [High School], where WT McDaniels was the band instructor. McDaniels' band The Rhythm Bombers used to compete with Professor Lucky Sharpe's band out of Douglass High. Professor McDaniels never got much credit in the annals of history, but he trained Evelyn Young, Frank Strozier, George Coleman and Hank Crawford – the seeds of yesterday that developed into the musicians of today.'

The Memphis Blues Again ably reproduces Ernest's pictures, but it takes the photographer himself to weave the narrative, explaining the significance someone like Professor McDaniels had on Johnny Ace and Tuff Green, who in turn influenced Ike Turner and Elvis Presley. Ernest is a very democratic photographer, who considers all of his subjects valid – whether photographing blues guitarist BB King or gospel soloist Queen C Anderson, he caught their 'spotlight' moment, capturing it for all time.

This is what I've been looking for – the details of a long-lost Memphis from someone who's lived the life. I turn the page again, and ask Ernest about another photograph. We continue, uninterrupted, for the better part of an hour. Then, at a quarter past two, Ernest rouses himself, reaching for his camera bag. 'C'mon, girl,' he says, 'I've got a church concert to photograph.' He makes a quick phone call, then heads out the door, where the future of Memphis music awaits.

'IF YOU CAN'T FIND IT AT SCHWAB'S...'
Mike Evans

Like in all great cities of character, there are places in Memphis which truly take you back in time, and no more so than a visit to the unique A Schwab's Dry Goods Store at 163 Beale. Across its creaky wooden floors you can explore aisle after aisle of bizarrely diverse merchandise, from outsize ladies' underwear to dog muzzles, hot barbecue sauce to love potions, snow-globe souvenirs to do-it-yourself voodoo manuals. Schwab's was founded in 1876 as a family business and has remained so ever since. It is proud of its motto – 'If you can't find it at Schwab's, you're better off without it.'

Like most things in Memphis, particularly on Beale Street, the store's history has its links with the blues: it was one of the country's first ever businesses (if not *the* first) to sponsor a blues radio show. Entitled *Bluestown*, the programme was broadcast to an African-American target audience by local station WHBQ, from 1943 to 1947. Schwab's sold blues records – not something one would normally find in a general store of that kind – at three for $1 back then, and lent them to the station, whose own library was somewhat limited. (WHBQ's place in the history books was assured, however, when in 1949 it became the venue for the pioneering DJ Dewey Phillips, who, almost single-handed, launched R&B, rockabilly and early rock 'n' roll to a genuinely mixed-race audience in the South.)

Schwab's, like much else of Memphis culture, survives despite the city rather than because of it. Talking to Robert Gordon in *It Came From Memphis,* the proprietor Abraham Schwab recalled how he had dug in his feet, refusing to move, when the shop was threatened with demolition as part of President Nixon's urban renewal programme in the 1970s. As he wryly commented at the time, paraphrasing an often-made observation, 'Memphis has torn down more history than most cities even have.'

4 Jazz In Memphis

CALVIN'S BOOGIE
Andria Lisle

One afternoon, I head over to Calvin Newborn's apartment on Camilla
Street. He lives on the ground floor of a high-rise located near the
University of Tennessee Medical Center, just a few blocks east of Beale
Street. I park my car at one end of the parking lot and, by the time I ring
the buzzer in the lobby, Calvin's there to let me in.

Calvin, the last surviving member of Memphis's first family of
jazz, turned 70 this year, but his smile and step are much livelier than
I thought possible in a man that age. He greets me with a hug, and
my gaze travels from his bright eyes to his strong, compact hands.
His skin has a warm, reddish hue, and his entire body glows with a
mixture of divine intelligence and unbridled energy.

Calvin's talk is full of his recent trip to New Orleans, where he
performed alongside Big Jay McNeely and Rev Dwight 'Gatemouth'
Moore. Afterwards, Calvin played his own set, leading a small combo
through a riveting version of 'Calvin's Boogie', his signature number
first recorded back in 1950. The crowd of music fans at the three-
day Ponderosa Stomp went wild when Calvin débuted
autobiographical lyrics for the song. While he says his singing 'could've
been better', it's obvious that he was pleased with their response.

It's been a big year for Calvin – he got a degree from Southwest
Community College in May, and has a job lecturing at the Stax Music
Academy for the summer. He's bursting with plans for the future,

including an autobiographical play and documentary film, but first I ask him to tell me about the old days of Memphis music, when the lines between blues and jazz were perpetually blurred.

I know the bare bones of the Newborn family background: Patriarch Phineas (Finas) Newborn Sr married Rosie Lee Murphy in rural West Tennessee in the 1920s. They moved to Memphis just in time for the Depression; soon after, Rose was sent to her folks' farm in Whiteville to give birth to Phineas Jr in late 1931. Back in Memphis, Finas worked days as a cook's helper and spent his nights playing the drums in local bands. His talents were prodigious, and he soon went to work with Jimmie Lunceford's Chickasaw Syncopators, performing at the Palace Theater's Midnight Ramble on Beale Street. 'It was just Junior, and Mother and Father,' Calvin tells me. 'They settled in Orange Mound, right before I was born.'

Orange Mound, the first all-black urban community in the South, is still an active neighbourhood today. It straddles an area just south of the Norfolk-Southern railway yard, between the University of Memphis and Midtown. These days, the original patina of the neighbourhood is dusty and faded, but driving past the Newborns' old house on Marechalnell Street, I can easily imagine what Orange Mound must've looked like in all its glory. Even today, Melrose High School and the legendary Brown Derby nightclub still stand, while the Southern Heritage Classic and the community's annual Christmas Parade are two must-see events, replete with spangled high-steppers, marching bands and even a black Santa Claus.

Calvin's smooth, sonorous voice draws me back into the conversation. 'When we lived in Orange Mound, my brother and I walked to Beale Street to see the Midnight Ramble. We had heard my dad going on and on about the Palace Theater, so one Saturday we played in the park until dusk, then followed the railroad tracks all the way down to Beale.' Calvin and Junior ate hot dogs and went to the evening movie at the Palace, hiding in their seats until the Midnight Ramble began.

'Back then,' Calvin explains, 'Beale Street was black like Harlem. It was so different – almost impossible to describe. *Everything* was black. I felt more comfortable than I have ever since, probably because I'm black,' he says, pinching his skin with a chuckle.

Finas's sons literally grew up with musical instruments in their hands. Before they were out of elementary school, the two took first prize at the Palace Theater's Amateur Night show, where Calvin brought down the house singing 'Your Mama's On The Bottom, Papa's On Top, Sister's In The Kitchen Hollerin', When They Gon' Stop'. 'I hadn't reached my teens yet,' Calvin says with a smile, 'but was already hooked line and sinker on show business! I didn't see anything that I didn't like – it made me feel grown up to be around all that cursing. It was like a circus – it really appealed to me.'

'Phineas and I both started out on piano,' Calvin tells me. 'But after two years, I quit taking lessons because he monopolized the keys. He was a child prodigy – all Junior cared about was playing the piano.' So a family friend on the Beale Street scene offered to help Calvin pick out a guitar. It was BB King, who'd recently arrived in Memphis from Indianola, Mississippi. 'BB helped me pick out a big guitar to learn on. He already knew how to play, although he couldn't count – he played 9-bar blues and 13-bar blues,' Calvin laughs, picking up a battered acoustic guitar to demonstrate.

'I could already read music, so I decided I was gonna take classical guitar lessons. I went to the only classical teacher in town, a white man. He slammed the door in my face, saying, "Boy, if I teach you it'll run the rest of my students off." I got rejected a lot,' Calvin says with a shrug. 'All these resentments built up inside, and I started acting out.' While he's talking, Calvin deftly tunes the guitar he's holding, then runs through a series of Segovia-inspired riffs.

When Junior was 17 and Calvin was 15, they joined their father's Finas Newborn Orchestra at the Plantation Inn in West Memphis, Arkansas. 'I despised the white world back then,' Calvin tells me. 'We played at the Plantation Inn for four years, while I was enrolled at Booker T Washington High School. I didn't know it, but white people motivated me to play jazz – that's right. Some white fella would come up to me high as a kite and drawl, "Boy, could you play 'Sweet Potatoes In Sandy Land'?" and we would make up a song right on the spot! We got tips like crazy,' Calvin says. 'I kept a pocketful of money and wore a suit to school every day. I even stopped and got my shoes shined every morning – I was as clean as the Board of Health! But at the same time, we were drowning our feelings, just swallowing our resentments. They were just festering inside of us.'

The summer of Calvin's ninth-grade year, he went on the chitlin' circuit with Roy Milton's band. 'That's where I got my honorary degree in R&B, battling Red Prysock,' Calvin explains. 'That was also the last time I saw Big Jay McNeely, when I played with him that summer. That's why it meant something to me to play with him in New Orleans – it's 53 years later, and Big Jay is still screamin',' Calvin chuckles, his laugh filling his small apartment.

In 1950, Finas's band moved back across the river to Clifford Miller's Flamingo Room in downtown Memphis. 'I was the featured attraction of the show, playing "Calvin's Boogie" while dancing with the guitar behind my head, between my legs, sliding on my knees, and playing in the air,' Calvin recalls. Ernest Withers' photographs attest to Calvin's unique acrobatic skill. 'My hang time was like Michael Jordan's, but I was dunkin' the guitar!' Calvin boasts. 'I was known as Flying Calvin, the king of after-hours blues on Beale Street.'

'Phineas was an introvert,' Calvin explains. 'The only thing he cared about was the piano. I, on the other hand, was an extrovert. I called it a spiritual fight between us – he was so good, and I was always trying to get the attention, which is why I became such a showman.'

A young Elvis Presley befriended the Newborns, and openly studied Calvin's moves on the guitar. 'At the Flamingo Room one night, Daddy told me to let Elvis play my guitar,' Calvin tells me. 'He wrecked the house (and my guitar) tearing off strings, while doing my moves, and singing, frantically.'

'Elvis was the first colorblind person I knew,' Calvin laughs. 'He was a frequent visitor at our music shop on Beale and at home. He sent us Christmas cards and gave my brother an expensive gold watch. The last time my mother saw Elvis was at our cousin Rev Brewster's Trigg Avenue Baptist Church. After listening to Queen Anderson sing "Peace In The Valley", Elvis told her he was gonna make a record; he called her "Mama

Rose". And she told him, "Cast your bread on the water, and many times it will return, Elvis; and I say it will have butter and jelly on it." The first record Elvis recorded was "That's All Right, Mama" – it might've been a tribute to Mama Rose,' muses Calvin.

In 1955, Calvin followed Junior to New York, where The Phineas Newborn Jr Quartet opened for Count Basie's band 12 weeks that year. 'Basie catapulted us from Beale Street to Broadway,' Calvin says affectionately. But trouble was on the horizon, for in 1951, Calvin had married Wanda Jones, the lead vocalist and trombonist in Finas's orchestra. 'Wanda was a really talented girl,' Calvin remembers. 'She could sing like Billie Holiday. But she had a real bad drug habit, and it eventually killed her.' In New York, Calvin developed a heroin and cocaine addiction of his own.

Then, in 1965, Finas was playing with The Hall Miller Animal Circus Band, headlining an act that featured the elephants dancing to his drumbeats. He had a bad heart, and doctors had warned him that if he didn't give up the drums death was imminent. Unable to quit, Finas sat in with Junior's group at a Los Angeles nightclub. 'He walked off the stage', Calvin tells me, 'and dropped dead.'

While Calvin was focusing on his own problems, his older brother's world came crashing down around him. Already diagnosed as mentally ill, Phineas was living in a halfway house in Memphis when he was attacked and badly beaten in January 1974. His cheekbone was fractured, and both arms severely injured. At the Veteran's Hospital, Phineas was largely uncooperative, and he was unable – or unwilling – to give any information about his attacker. When Calvin returned to Memphis to help take care of Phineas, he discovered an entirely different Beale Street. He saw 'tourists gazing at a map and looking puzzled outside the Visitor's Information Center', and 'a station wagon stopping at WC Handy's house', where its driver took a snapshot, then sped off. Musicians like Calvin Newborn were no longer so welcome in the rebuilt entertainment district. Nevertheless, he picked up gigs wherever he could.

Phineas recorded one more album for Atlantic, 1974's *Solo Piano*, and he made a triumphant return to the stage before dying of cancer in the summer of 1989. A few days after Phineas's death, Calvin checked himself into the Memphis Mental Health Institute. While inside, he took 'a fearless and total inventory' of himself, and began treatment for his drug problem.

After his release, Calvin wrote and published his brother's biography, a book called *As Quiet As It's Kept: The Genius Of Phineas Newborn, Jr*. He has been clean and sober for more than a decade, and now has a degree in Substance Abuse Counseling. Calvin calls it the Newborn Redemption. 'God gave me this life, and I wouldn't have lived it any other way,' he says, his eyes glowing with excitement. 'My conversion came about through my music – the original piece that I'd recorded as "A Piece Of The Pie" has become "A Peace-Making Pie". And listen to this – I'm gonna play this one at the Gibson Lounge next weekend.'

Calvin picks up his favourite guitar, a beautiful hollow-bodied Ibanez, and starts to play a familiar tune. He clears his throat, and begins to sing 'Lush Life' in a smooth tenor: 'I used to visit all the very gay places/Those come-what-may places/Where one relaxes on the axis of the wheel of life/To get the feel of life from jazz and cocktails', and as he mouths the words my mind wanders through all the stories I've heard this afternoon. Somehow, Calvin has taken the old Nat King Cole standard and turned it upside down, plucking the guitar strings with a hard-won defiance. 'So,' he sings, 'I'll live a lush life in some small dive/And there I'll be/While I rot with the rest of those/Whose lives are lonely too'. The lyrics are heart-wrenching, but they clearly illustrate a path that Calvin could've taken, yet chose to avoid. He ends the song with a glistening arpeggio, then immediately launches into a jubilant version of 'Calvin's Boogie'. He's played these notes for nearly 60 years, but today they sound like a brand-new composition.

His voice, too, is clear and pure: 'Move right into the groove/Because you can't lose with Calvin's boogie/Shake your body down/And 'round and 'round to Calvin's boogie'. Calvin's eyes gleam with excitement as his slender red fingers move up and down the frets, bending the notes with ease. 'There's no better way to lose the blues than Calvin's boogie,' he sings triumphantly; 'There's no mountain high/That you can't climb with Calvin's boogie'. The words ring with a joyful optimism, clearly a mantra that has gotten him through thick and thin.

HERMAN GREEN DOING HIS THING
Mike Evans

Tenor sax player Herman Green has been a mainstay of the Memphis jazz scene for ever. Currently the head of Jazz Studies at the Lemoyne-Owen College in Memphis, Green has performed with such jazz legends as John Coltrane, Miles Davis and Clark Terry, and was in Lionel Hampton's Band for eight years. But (perhaps a more natural stance for a Memphis musician than most others) his history has straddled not just jazz but the blues, rock and soul that made the city famous. And he avoids categorisation – he doesn't even try to separate his jazz playing from his blues playing, as for him it's one and the same thing.

As early as 1953 Herman was playing the clubs on Beale Street when his friend, the then-unknown Rufus Thomas, asked him to join him for a session at Sun Records. It was the session that produced Thomas's first big hit, 'Bear Cat'.

Likewise, even earlier, when the equally unknown Riley 'Blue Boy' King first played professionally, it was Herman he asked to put a band together. Riley, of course, soon became known as BB. In an interview with Jerry W Atwood for his own website, Herman recalled how BB, was booked onto the pioneering all-black radio station WDIA and needed a band just to play 15 minutes of music plus a jingle for a miracle 'cure-all' called Peptikon that was sponsoring the show: 'Riley asked me to help him get the band together. We played everyday, live, for 15 minutes and helped sell Peptikon. Riley sang the jingle. But it worked out good, because we had a band together, so if a job came up we just took the Peptikon Band and played.'

His affinity to jazz as much as blues dated right back to his first regular gig, which was with The Al Jackson Band (Al Jackson being the father of The MG's' drummer Al Jackson) at the Palace Theater, which stood on the site of the present New Daisy at the top end of Beale Street. It was the late 1940s, and it was a big band in the swing style of the day. Of course, being on Beale meant that a lot of the time they were backing R&B artists like Joe Turner and T-Bone Walker, so from the start the demarcation between musical styles was healthily blurred.

Then a totally different residency came about around 1953, with a small outfit including Willie Mitchell and Phineas Newborn Jr, at a nightclub in West Memphis called the Plantation Inn. Here the all-black band, including a variety of vocalists, wowed an all-white audience who had never heard anything like it before, an audience that included (from time to time) the young Elvis Presley.

Green's real involvement in jazz came about via his being drafted into the Army at the time of the Korean War, however. After his tour of duty in Korea, in 1955 the 23-year-old found himself in a bar near the airport in San Francisco after the military plane taking him home to Memphis had an unplanned delay. He was fascinated by the trio playing there, who were playing the kind of jazz-blues he was familiar with, but with a whole new edge that was new to him.

He decided there and then to stay over a while and see what was happening on the 'Frisco club scene workwise, and soon fell in with the local players, who were in fact the vanguard of what was then the latest thing, 'West Coast' jazz. Herman was soon playing in the house band at the Blackhawk, a now-legendary venue in the jazz history books, and between 1955 and 1957 he played with the very best, including Miles Davis, Dave Brubeck, Cannonball Adderley and such.

In 1958 he became leader of the house band in a 'Frisco club called Box City, a late-night after-hours venue (it didn't even open until 1am) catering for musicians who'd already played their evening engagements, and wanted to relax and (usually) jam. In Box City, and subsequently clubs including the Say When and the Jazz Workshop, Herman's band would play host to the biggest names passing through town.

It was while he was playing around the San Francisco clubs, making something of a name for himself, that Herman came to the attention of the great Lionel Hampton, the vibes-playing bandleader who was by that time a genuine jazz legend. Hampton offered him a job, which he stuck with on and off for the next eight years, during which time he settled in New York for about three years.

It was a time of much experimentation in jazz, and while in New York Green met, and became good friends with, the tenor sax giant and great experimentalist John Coltrane. Herman later recalled, 'Everybody wanted to experiment, everybody wanted to try something new, but there was no one that had that innovation of music like John. Even today when I do a sax break and I get way out in outer space, I still turn to the others in the band and say, "Hey, I'm doing my John Coltrane thing."'

After the Hampton job, Herman decided it was time to return to Memphis, where he has been part of the musical fabric ever since. As well as session work at Sun, Stax and almost every other major studio over the years, he has taught music to hundreds of students, in 2002 being cited as the Best Woodwind Teacher and Music Teacher of the Year by the Memphis chapter of the Music Academy. He and Calvin Newborn were both invited to play at the Winter Olympics in Salt Lake City, and Herman continues to appear around Memphis, of course, in regular residencies at various bars and cafés, including the Soul Café, and the Zanzibar jazz lounge and eatery, both recent additions to night-life on South Main Street.

His recent album (*Hernando Street Blues*) with The Memphis Blues and Jazz Quartet was critically acclaimed. The Quartet, which Herman put together for the album, features some of the cream of the Memphis music fraternity, comprising: BB Cunningham Jr, bass player for Jerry Lee Lewis and former lead singer for the smash hit group, The Hombres; Tony Thomas, who was voted the best keyboard player in Memphis by his fellow recording artists; Terry Saffold, who plays drums for The Platters when they are on tour; and Nokie Taylor, a trumpet player for Isaac Hayes and who has appeared on over 60 Stax recordings in his time. Guest artists on the LP, as well as numerous top local musicians, included Austin, Texas guitar star Jimmie Vaughan, who was reciprocating Herman's guest appearance on his own Grammy-winning (as Best Traditional Blues Album of the Year) *Do You Get The Blues?*

Herman Green's concept for the album is a tour of his Memphis, San Francisco and New York musical roots: from 'Up Highway Forty-Nine', the Blues Highway travelled by the early blues players to get to Clarksdale; to the nightclubs of 1950s Beale in 'Memphis After Midnight'; to the title track, which evokes the night Elvis Presley invented rock 'n' roll; to 'Stone Cold Experiment', on which Herman is still adding to the legacy of Memphis jazz and remembering his days with John Coltrane.

'I CAME AND I STAYED' – JOYCE COBB'S MEMPHIS
Mike Evans

Not a native of the city, but an established and highly respected resident, Joyce Cobb is a fine jazz singer and composer, university teacher, radio broadcaster and recipient of numerous awards, whose name was given greater prominence during the 1990s when she was the only female proprietor on Beale Street to have her own club carrying her own name.

Born in Okmulgee, Oklahoma, in 1946, her early life involved a few changes of address due to her academic instructor parents moving around a lot, before settling in Nashville, where she first sang as a child in the choir at her grandmother's church. When college called, she attended Central State University in Wilberforce, Ohio, majoring in Social Welfare, and it was in nearby Dayton that she got her first gig, via a guitarist friend who lived in the same condominium. They rehearsed for six months in the basement of the building, and managed to get a job with the Ramada Inn circuit, making more money per week than she would ever hope to make in social work.

Back in Nashville, Cobb began to make a name for herself performing at Opryland, and consequently getting work on local radio and TV. But her first real break looked like it had come when, in the mid-1970s, she was signed to Stax Records of Memphis, albeit as a country singer.

'I was going to be the next Charlene Pride,' Cobb explained to Bill Ellis in the Memphis *Commercial Appeal* in 2002. 'At that time, Jim Stewart was interested in a subsidiary label that handled country music. He heard my demo from Nashville. He thought my voice sounded right, and I was black and he thought that would have been a good move. I think OB McClinton and I were the two signed to that deal.' Unfortunately, the signing came just as Stax was going under. 'Almost made it – it's all about timing…'

Things took a more positive turn in 1979, when she made a single for the Shoe record production company. Cobb was playing dates at the Holiday Inn in Memphis when she was approached by Shoe's Wayne Crook, who suggested she stay in town and write some material for a possible recording deal. This she did, and one of the results was an R&B

number called 'Dig The Gold', which Shoe placed with the Cream label. The single sold well, especially on the West Coast, and reached Number 42 in the *Billboard* chart.

Things were on the up, and the next step was an album. *Good To Me*, released by the major label RCA, was Joyce Cobb's début LP, and that too was to feature in the *Billboard* best-sellers, peaking at Number 11. Settling in Memphis, she had another single out in the early '90s for Willie Mitchell's Waylo Records, 'Another Lonely Night', which did well in the UK and led to some European tours, including one with Otis Clay. Other star names who helped widen her exposure when she appeared with them included Taj Mahal, Muddy Waters, The Temptations, Ashford And Simpson and Al Jarreau.

Then, in April 1992, she opened Joyce Cobb's club, right there on Beale Street. Although her repertoire was broad, taking in pop, rock, even a little country or disco, here she was able to indulge her first love, jazz, and oversee appearances by the best of local jazz talent as well. Even when she was not officially on the bill, if she was not working elsewhere Joyce was usually to be found in the club, and more often than not would end up 'sitting in' with whoever was playing that night.

Having sung with The Memphis Symphony Orchestra many times, Cobb has been voted Best Female Singer on four different occasions by the Memphis chapter of the National Association of Recording Artists and Songwriters (NARAS). NARAS has also given Cobb the Premier Vocalist Award in 1986, 1988 and 1996. The *Memphis Flyer Magazine* voted her and her band the best in Memphis and the Beale Street Merchants association voted Cobb the Best Female Entertainer in 1995.

Since the early '90s, Cobb has been a contributing volunteer presenter on the WEVL community radio station in Memphis, on which she has hosted shows covering Memphis music old and new, her own 'pot-pourri' of vocal music, a programme covering classic swing and bebop, and a reggae show. She also holds down an academic post, teaching voice in the Commercial Jazz department at the University of Memphis.

She's gone back into the recording studio from time to time, most recently with the Dixieland-style ensemble The Beale Street Jazz Band, with whom she cut two albums at the end of the '90s. And, if all that wasn't enough, Joyce Cobb still never stops gigging around the Memphis area and elsewhere, usually with her regular outfit, Cool Heat.

And she's always venturing into pastures new. In her review show *Delta Blues Women*, first performed in 2001 backed by a six-piece band, Joyce Cobb weaves the stories and songs of Ma Rainey (the 'Mother of the blues'), Bessie Smith (the 'Empress of the Blues') and those of other classic singers, like Lucille Bogan, Sara Martin, Mamie Smith and Victoria Spivey, into a fascinating journey through the Mississippi Delta, celebrating the blues as the cornerstone of American popular music.

In 2002, Cobb was the recipient of the 18th Annual Women of Achievement Award, which recognises the contributions of women in the life of Memphis. In her acceptance speech, she acknowledged the importance her adopted city had played in her career: 'Memphis has embraced me to the point of making it very comfortable to live and pay bills and do what I like to do, which is music. It hasn't been very difficult from clubs to festivals to travel to symphonies to big band and Beale Street. I came and I stayed.'

IRWIN SHEFT, JAZZ EVANGELIST
Mike Evans

Celebrated as the home of blues, soul and rock 'n' roll, Memphis has nevertheless a strong jazz tradition. The vast majority of the clubs that flourished in and around Beale Street in its heyday from the '20s through the '50s featured jazz more than blues, and even R&B was only coming in, in the late '40s and early '50s, as the scene there was starting to subside.

This list of great jazz names to come out of Memphis is considerable, going back to the great pre-World War II bandleader Jimmie Lunceford, who is buried in Elmwood Cemetery and taught in a high school in the city for years. The list is particularly strong on piano players, including Lil Hardin (who played in Louis Armstrong's Hot Seven and later became Lil Armstrong), Donald Brown and, of course, the great Phineas Newborn; and there are trumpet players (Booker Little, Marvin Stamm) and sax players, from Hank Crawford and George Coleman to Charles Lloyd and Sonny Criss, and guitarist Calvin Newborn.

Most of these musicians had to leave town to make it, in the early days up to Chicago, later New York and, from the '50s onwards, often to the West Coast. But there was always a thriving live scene and plenty of work for the musicians who stayed behind. That fact comes out in the examples of seminal players like Willie Mitchell, who, while making their name as R&B, soul or pop musicians, often came from a jazz background, and formed the backbone of the arranging and session-playing fraternity at the important record companies and studios like Stax, Hi, American, Ardent and so on. The 18-piece big band that Willie Mitchell formed on his return to Memphis in the mid-'50s is testament to that, featuring in its ranks the best of the Memphis players of the day including Phineas Newborn Jr, Charles Lloyd, Booker Little, George Coleman and drummer Al Jackson – some line-up!

It's this fact of musical history that is central to the *raison d'être* of the Jazz Foundation of Memphis, set up by jazz promoter and enthusiast Irwin Sheft. Through the World Class Jazz Series established in 1985, the JFM has promoted on a non-profit basis concerts by top names that have included Phineas Newborn, Milt Jackson, Joshua Redman and Diana Krall. Why does a city need a specific organisation to support jazz, especially one as musical as Memphis? Sheft answers thus: 'Why subsidise the symphony, the opera, the ballet? Jazz, as we have said, is America's classical music; it is recognised around the world as the fine arts music of this country. As such, it deserves a prominent place in the hierarchy of the arts that compose the cultural ambiance of great cities.

'But there is another equally cogent reason for supporting serious jazz. Jazz is an integral part of that preeminently marketable and very varied Memphis music spectrum, The Memphis Sound. In fact, more jazz musicians from Memphis – at least ten – are at this moment internationally acclaimed than any other kind. One, George Coleman, is considered one of the five greatest living saxophonists; another, the late Phineas Newborn, perhaps the greatest pianist of all time. You don't have to go to New York to hear the best. The World Class Jazz Series is here.'

But to continue to fulfil its mission of bringing true jazz greats to Memphis, as well as presenting local artists and producing educational seminars for listeners, it must, like similar programmes in other cities, have funding. Which is why Sheft, with evangelical fervour, keeps up a relentless lobby of individuals and corporations who might want to support jazz.

In his unrelenting propaganda war for jazz and community funding of jazz, Sheft draws the parallel with cities that have subsidised jazz programmes: 'Lincoln Center – the home of the Metropolitan Opera, the New York Philharmonic and New Your City Ballet – now has year-round jazz programming. The Smithsonian in Washington has expanded its jazz program with a resident orchestra. The United States Congress recently declared jazz a "rare and valuable national American treasure to which we should devote our attention, support and resources..." Atlanta has a world-class jazz series. So do Charlotte, Hartford, San Francisco and most other major cities.'

He points out that these other places have had major jazz programmes funded by government or corporations, whereas since 1985 the World Class Jazz Series has staged over 80 concerts by the world's premier musicians including Sonny Rollins, Dave Brubeck, Wynton Marsalis, Diane Schuur and Milt Jackson, relying exclusively on ticket sales. 'That does not work in other cities, and does not work anywhere for the symphony, the opera, the ballet, theatre, et cetera. Or for our series, as I have learned the hard way – by losing money.' So donations to the JFM would be used to make good some of these loss-making – but, as Sheft and many others see it – essential ventures.

Whatever, jazz in Memphis will always survive, as jazz has survived elsewhere as long as musicians are around to play it. But Irwin Sheft is quite right in concluding that, for an artform to resist sterility, it has to have an audience, not just one that buys the records but one that has a chance to go out and hear the real thing live.

5 Sun Stroke

SAM PHILLIPS AND UNION AVENUE ROCK 'N' ROLL
Mike Evans

The first time I visited the Sun Studios building, I was staying at the downtown end of Union Avenue, at the Radisson Hotel, just a block away from the more prestigious Peabody. It was the summer of 1992 and heatwave time, but like mad dogs and Englishmen are supposed to I decided to walk it, a midday Sun rendezvous so to speak. Most of Union east of the Greyhound Bus Terminal that stands next door to the Radisson seemed to consist of that archetypal American space guzzler, the used-car lot, so the 1.5km (1 mile) or so trudge to number 706 was hot, dusty and visually uninspiring, to say the least. Equally unprepossessing was the building itself, a red-brick affair with Venetian blinds shading the windows, and the familiar bright-yellow Sun Records logo the only concession to its status as a must-visit for music fans worldwide.

And it's not just the much-recounted story of how Elvis got his first break there – indeed made his first earth-shaking commercial sides there – that draws the crowds. The building, from its days as the mundanely named Memphis Recording Service, was the venue for the very genesis of rock 'n' roll.

Sam Phillips was born in 1923 in Florence, Alabama, a part of the world that, during the years of the Depression in which he grew up, was as steeped in racial bigotry and discrimination as any part of the segregated South could be. Phillips studied engineering and the basics of broadcasting at college, following through with radio announcer jobs first at stations in Muscle Shoals, Alabama, Nashville and finally Memphis, where he was what would now be known as a sound engineer for live dance band programmes from the grand Skyway Ballroom of the Peabody Hotel.

But Sam had other enthusiasms. As well as the swing bands, he had always been captivated by the sounds of black America, from back in his childhood when he was aware of Negro church music, then via his uncle-in-law, who had launched an afternoon radio show (*Atomic Boogie Hour*) in Bessemer, Alabama – beaming black R&B to a predominantly white audience – after leaving the Muscle Shoals station where he had hired his young nephew. And in Memphis he soon became aware of a similarly radical broadcasting venture on the part of pioneering DJ Dewey Phillips (no relation) with his five-nights-a-week *Red Hot And Blue* show on Radio WHBQ beaming from the Gayoso Hotel just up the street from the Peabody.

Inspired by his wild namesake, who started revolutionising the Memphis airwaves as early as 1949 with a potent mix of gospel, blues, R&B, boogie and straight pop, and ended every commercial break with the message, 'I don't care where you go or how you go, just tell 'em Phillips sent you', Sam managed to raise $1,000 to convert an empty auto shop at 706 Union into a recording studio. The Memphis Recording Service opened on 2 January 1950 with the selling line 'We Record Anything – Anytime – Anywhere' offering recording and transcription facilities for local radio stations, advertisers and private individuals.

It was the latter facility that famously attracted the 18-year-old Elvis when he walked in to make an acetate as a gift to his mother, but that was a couple of years after Sam also declared his aim to record black artists in the South who might otherwise have not had the opportunity. That mission was the foundation stone for the Sun record label, which initially Sam test-bedded with a single release he launched in collaboration with Dewey on a one-off label called The Phillips, featuring a local multi-instrumentalist Louis Joe Hill. They pressed just 300 copies of the single, the only one to appear on the short-lived label.

Sam went on to record various blues and R&B artists like BB King and Howlin' Wolf for other labels before starting his own. In fact, it was one such leasing exercise in May 1951 that saw the recording of what many consider the first real rock 'n' roll record, 'Rocket 88' by Ike Turner's Kings Of Rhythm, which went out on the Chicago-based Chess label under the name of its lead vocalist Jackie Brenston, and made the top of the national R&B charts.

The leasing arrangements were mainly with RPM Records in Los Angeles and Chess, but after a legal wrangle between the two companies over Rosco Gordon's 'Booted' Sam decided it was time he formed his own label as the natural outlet for the burgeoning amount of talent passing through the studio. With funding from a fellow local broadcaster Jim Bulleit and Sam's brother Judd, the Sun Record Company was launched in March 1952, and for its first two years – before it historically signed Elvis Presley in mid-1954 – put out hillbilly, gospel and, predominantly, southern blues. And crucially, despite the brevity of their formal partnership as label entrepreneurs, Sam and Dewey Phillips forged a close association that meant that the Sun product had instant exposure on the local airwaves.

The advent of Elvis, of course, changed everything, not just in the wider world out there but at Sun Records itself. His style (forged in just ten sides released on Sun), as well as laying the basis for the rock 'n' roll revolution in popular music generally, was also the template for a specific genre that came out of the fusion of country music and R&B-inspired rock – rockabilly. In the words of writer Peter Guralnick, 'It was called rockabilly, because it was not the clankety rock of Bill Haley and his Comets nor the hillbilly sound of Roy Acuff and Ernest Tubb but a fusion of the two.' Carl Perkins, one of its great practitioners and Sun protégé, called it 'blues with a country beat', and after Elvis's contract passed to RCA for the princely sum of $40,000, Perkins – along with Jerry Lee Lewis, Roy Orbison, the young Johnny Cash, Billy Lee Riley, Ray Smith and others – came to define the post-Elvis 'Sun sound' that was to dominate the label's output.

And, while rockabilly certainly wasn't exclusive to Memphis – Buddy Holly, Gene Vincent, Ricky Nelson, Eddie Cochran and many more all demonstrated its influence – this southern white-boy R&B was best represented at Sun, and arguably was exemplified at its purest (and most sexy) in Elvis's 'Baby Let's Play House', recorded at 706 Union Avenue in March 1955.

By 1958 Phillips decided that the conditions at Union Avenue were too cramped for the new multi-track recording equipment he needed to install, so new premises were found at 639 Madison Avenue. As a consequence, although seasoned veterans (including ex-Elvis Sun guitarist Scotty Moore, who was studio manager) concluded the new place had none of the atmosphere of its predecessor, the old Sun Studio stood empty at 706 Union for a quarter of a century.

Eventually Moore and other members of the 'Class Of '55' persuaded Sam Phillips to return the original studio to its former glory. It has remained a working studio ever since, a fact proudly stressed to visitors to the restored site.

The tiny studio (or approximation thereof) – where so many now-historic audio artefacts were laid down, often with a one-take ease that belied their quality, at other times in painstaking overnight sessions until they got it right – is now the focus of a one-room 'tour'. The addition of a café and gift shop to the premises confirms its status on the Memphis heritage trail, but that doesn't undermine the definite frisson created by the simple knowledge that within those walls reverberated echo-enhanced sounds that literally changed the world.

NO MORE DOGGIN'
Andria Lisle

May was going to be a busy month. I had a trip planned to Arkansas, another to Mississippi, and wanted to take my time driving through the Delta before the weather got too warm. My car was packed, and I was ready to hit the road; however, I consulted my calendar before leaving town. I wanted to make sure I was home in time to see R&B legend Rosco Gordon, who was due to arrive at the end of the month.

The dapper 68-year-old pianist was on his way to his home town of Memphis to perform at the WC Handy Awards, the annual music event presented by the Blues Foundation. We had plans to rendezvous at the Orpheum Theater, a grand old building at the west end of Beale Street, shortly before the awards ceremony. I loved hanging out with Rosco, and nothing, I assured him, would cause me to miss our date.

We'd met in the summer of 2001, when Rosco came to Memphis to headline the Center for Southern Folklore's Music and Heritage Festival. He was easygoing and quick-witted, as comfortable hanging out with Rolling Stones bassist Bill Wyman (a big fan) at an impromptu practice session as he was performing for thousands on an outdoor stage. As a festival volunteer, it was my duty to drive Rosco around town for the week, accompanying him on his daily adventures. By the time he left Memphis, we were old friends.

The Big S Grill, on Dunnavant Street just south of McLemore Avenue, was our favourite lunch spot – Rosco particularly dug the small ply-walled room backlit in red and green. Named for owner Sam Price, the Big S ranks as one of the coolest neighbourhood joints imaginable. Its humble exterior – a white wood building with fortress-styled windows and a foreboding black door – belies the friendly atmosphere and good food inside. Everyday without fail, Sam would punch in the numbers for 'No More Doggin'' on the jukebox as we walked in the door, while chef JC Hardaway would come out of his tiny kitchen to take our lunch order.

I favoured the grilled cheeseburger, and Rosco would order a chopped shoulder sandwich, extra hot. We always shared a plate of French fries, hand-cut by JC, whose culinary expertise has been hailed worldwide in books, newspapers and even a documentary film. I'd order a quart of beer with my lunch, but Rosco, a diabetic, was content with a diet soda and ice. After our meal, he'd scoot over to a stool next to the bar – the Big S really is a cosy joint – and drop his change into a fruit machine. Bathed in the warm red light, he'd sit for hours, nodding to the regular patrons as he occasionally amassed (and often lost) small fortunes on the blinking screen.

'It's a waste of time for me to gamble, because I never win,' Rosco would laugh as he'd come back to the table for a bite. 'But I love it – and you've got to have some kind of vice, right?' Rosco loved to talk about the legendary poker games that would last for days, and note wistfully the day that he 'almost' won the New York State Lottery. 'I can come *this close*,' he'd tell me, with a gleam in his eye, measuring the space with his fingers, 'but I never win!' And then he'd ask Big

Sam for change for a $20 bill, tapping the counter impatiently until he was back on his stool at the video poker machine.

Back downtown, we'd drive past the National Civil Rights Museum, built on the site of the Lorraine Motel, where Martin Luther King Jr was assassinated in 1968. More than a few of Rosco's children were conceived at the Lorraine, he'd tell me, before asking – with a wink – if I felt like stopping in. Other days we'd park on the cobblestones in front of Ernest Withers' photography studio on Beale Street, and pore over old pictures in his front office. Along with the Civil Rights Movement, Ernest captured the heyday of the Memphis blues scene, and he also photographed Rosco's wedding and many Gordon family gatherings.

In the afternoons, Rosco and I would cruise the tree-lined boulevards of South Memphis while he'd reminisce about the old days, before he played with the famed Beale Streeters, a local group that included such talents as Johnny Ace, BB King and Bobby 'Blue' Bland.

'Bobby started out as my chauffeur,' Rosco told me as we headed down South Parkway one sunny afternoon. 'Then one night he was driving me to a gig over in Arkansas, and he started singing. "Hey, baby," I told him. "We've got this thing all wrong – you're the one who should sing, and I should be your chauffeur." I said, "Tonight, man, you're gonna be doing the singing." So I put him on stage and headed over to the dice table. Bobby sang all night, and I shot dice all night. After that, I wrote "Love You 'Til The Day I Die" for Bobby and I to perform together. But the song just died on the charts – it was on the flip side of "Booted", and nobody ever turned that record over,' Rosco lamented. 'And "Booted" was a huge hit, but I only got $800 for it.'

According to Rosco, the youngest of eight children, his sister was the real musician in the family – he would just play around on the piano keys when she wasn't practising her scales. 'I would play that old piano every day,' he told me. 'It became a thing with me – it got to where I had to play. But I wasn't *studying* music – I was just horsin' around.'

Nevertheless, Rosco's talent took him to the old Palace Theater on Beale, where he won an amateur contest when he was just 16 years old.

('It was a Wednesday night', Rosco remembered, 'and Rufus Thomas was the MC.') From there he went to WDIA radio, where he hosted his own 15-minute show under the watchful eye of DJ Nat D Williams, who, in the daylight hours, was Rosco's history teacher at Booker T Washington High School. From WDIA, Rosco went on to The Beale Streeters and Sam Phillips's Memphis Recording Service.

'Sam was one of the greatest producers I ever worked with,' Rosco said. 'He knew what he was looking for, and he didn't care how long it took to get what he wanted. When we cut "The Chicken", we went in at 9pm and stayed in the studio until four in the morning! But we got most songs in four or five takes. If we hit wrong notes, we'd leave 'em in if they were something we were really *feeling*,' he would laugh.

At the Union Avenue recording studio, Rosco cut a handful of songs featuring his signature loping piano beat, including 'Booted', which, licensed to Chicago's Chess Records, topped the R&B charts in 1952. His next release, 'No More Doggin'' (released on the RPM label), took his rhythmic approach a step further: Rosco accented the off-beat on the number, creating the shuffle sound ('Rosco's rhythm') that became the foundation of Jamaican ska music. He was not yet 18 years old.

In 1956, Rosco hit again with the novelty number, 'The Chicken', written for his pet – and stage partner – Butch, a fluffy white Bantam rooster. 'I had a suit made for Butch that was just like mine,' Rosco told me. 'When I'd snap his bow-tie, he'd take five steps forward and five steps back and shake his head. Everyone thought he followed my moves, but the truth was that I took his lead!' While Rosco rocked on stage, Butch made the rounds on the floor with a tip cup around his neck. 'He was the moneymaker,' Rosco laughed. 'I bought our first Cadillac, but Butch paid for the second!' The duo were immortalised in the 1957 film *Rock Baby, Rock It*, and also in one of Ernest's classic photographs from the same era.

But Butch died after about a year, and Rosco never found another bird to replace him. Soon after this, Rosco quit the business too: he left Sun after a flap with Sam Phillips over the publishing rights for 'The Chicken', which Rosco had sold to the Houston-based Duke Record label.

'After that, Sam lost interest in me,' Rosco recalled in a *Living Blues Magazine* interview in September 1980 that I uncovered after his visit. 'He thought I betrayed him, which I'm sure I did now. He never did any more business with me. He gave me the proper manly respect, but as far as recording me again, no way. I even drove down to Memphis to see him. The only thing he said was, "I see you're still wearing those $200 shoes." But he didn't want to record me anymore. I said "I got some stuff," but he said, "Well…"'

'Sam got hit twice by [Duke owner] Don Robey. But I didn't know any better. Money was money to me. They'd give me two or three hundred dollars for a record session, and that was it,' Rosco remembered in the interview.

Frustrated after he was denied royalties on 'Just A Little Bit', his biggest (and oft-covered) hit, Rosco focused on raising a family in Queens, New York. 'I never got any artist's rights on it when it came out on Vee-Jay [in 1959],' Rosco told Hank Davis of *Living Blues Magazine*. 'I just got paid for the session, got $250 up front. Later, when it was really selling, I went to the label. I told them I could really use some money. Calvin Carter called out to his secretary to give me a check for $25. I had tears in my eyes, told him to keep the money…' The record, he learned, eventually sold more than four million copies worldwide.

Rosco stayed out of the limelight for two decades, focusing instead on his own Bab-Rock label. He released his own singles on the tiny imprint, as well as duets with his wife, Barbara Kerr, and their 6-year-old son, Marcus. Subsidising his musical career with a less glamorous job pressing trousers in a dry-cleaners, Rosco did not return to the stage until after Barbara's death in the 1980s.

Then Rosco's comeback album, *Memphis Tennessee*, released on the Stony Plain label in 2000, garnered him a Handy nomination. Fuelled by this recent success, Rosco was riding high. He wowed the audience when he took the stage at this year's Handy Awards, appearing alongside fellow Memphis Recording Service alumni Ike Turner, BB King and Little Milton for a scorching version of BB's 'Three O' Clock Blues'.

As part of the festivities, I accompanied Rosco to a dinner honouring Sam Phillips. We were whisked up the elevator to the Skyway in the

Peabody Hotel, and wined and dined along with the rest of the international blues scene. I howled at Rosco's dismay when his unwitting waitress served him a platter of baked chicken – in deference to Butch, he told her, he never touched the stuff. She returned with a skimpy serving of potatoes and gravy, which he begrudgingly moved around the plate.

In typical fashion, Rosco hammed it up from our table in the corner, anxious to return to his hotel room to watch the last innings of a baseball game. He had money on it, I later learned – Sam Phillips be damned! As soon as we were able to get out of there, we headed across the street to the Hampton Inn, where Rosco had a room for the week.

Rosco's team – the San Francisco Giants – won that night, and we celebrated Barry Bonds' home runs over cold Coca-Colas from the hotel room fridge. After the game, Rosco turned down the volume on the TV set so he could tell me about his family. He had several sons, he told me, and a handful of beautiful grandchildren. 'I gave up performing music for 20 years,' Rosco said. 'I continued to write and record, but I labored for my family. I quit running up and down the highway as a promise to God, until my sons were raised.

'I am so proud of them,' Rosco told me. 'They're my men! But once they were grown, God let me get back on the road. Music is my life, you know, and God wants me to be happy.' He sat, basking in the glow of the moment, then got up to walk me down to the hotel lobby.

Later that week, Rosco performed for a packed house at a midtown bar. A TV crew was filming the event, and things ran behind schedule. When it came time for him to play, Rosco was nowhere to be found. I eventually located him in the back of the club, shooting pool with a pretty girl. He grumbled a bit when I interrupted him, pulling him to the stage before his game was finished, but winked as he settled down at the piano. 'Let's get high,' he sang, and the crowd roared. Rosco shuffled and stomped, and we all had a real good time.

The next day, Rosco left Memphis for Nashville, where he cut several tracks for a new album, then returned home to Queens. I was busy and didn't get a chance to call immediately and thank him for such a wonderful week. Of course, I regretted it later, but at the time I just couldn't slow down.

None of us foresee death when it comes knocking, but even so Rosco's passing on 11 July seemed particularly unexpected. Somehow Ernest heard the rumour by Friday morning, and he immediately called me to confirm it. It was a full day before we got the complete story: apparently one of Rosco's beloved sons discovered his daddy's body in his New York apartment, hours after he'd taken his final breath.

Doctors said that it was a heart attack, but I'm just glad he went fast. I'm glad, too, that Rosco's last trip to Memphis was a triumphant one. 'The feeling that I get when I see an audience having fun is incredible,' Rosco told me after his final performance, obviously moved by the crowd's reaction. 'Nothing could ever compare!' Somewhere up above us, I know that he and Butch are entertaining the angels, dancin' and doggin' around.

'STEP IN MY ROCKET AND DON'T BE LATE'
Mike Evans

Objectively speaking, it's as pointless a task to try to nominate one single disc as the first rock 'n' roll record as it is to try to identify the first jazz record, the first punk record or whatever. But, like the man said about the Oscars, someone's got to win it. And 'it' in the case of the premier rock platter is – by common consent – 'Rocket 88' by Jackie Brenston And His Delta Cats.

There have been other contenders to the title, of course (indeed someone produced a book on the subject a few years ago), ranging from Fats Domino's 'The Fat Man', released in 1950, to Bill Haley's 'Rock The Joint' (though, in 1953, already a cover of a 1949 R&B track). But it's 'Rocket 88' that has become accepted as *the* one: it's certainly a remarkable record in its own right, and arguably as important a product of the early-days Memphis Recording Service (pre-Sun) studios as the first Elvis sides a couple of years later. In many ways the genesis of the record is a microcosm of the birth of rock 'n' roll, with 20-year-old Sam Phillips its midwife.

Jackie Brenston was born in 1930 in Clarksdale, Mississippi, and after three years in the Army returned to his home town in 1947, at

WC Handy brought the city to prominence with his sultry 'Memphis Blues'. Today, his statue looks somewhat forlorn as it looks out over Beale Street from behind the confines of the Budweiser Pavilion

Paul and Elvis MacLeod at Graceland Too, their shrine to the King of rock 'n' roll

Memphis musician and producer Jim Dickinson at Sun Studio

Nancy Kossman, proprietor of Delia's Stackhouse in downtown Clarksdale, Mississippi

L-r: Guitar legend Hubert Sumlin and Henrietta and Charlie Musselwhite. Like Hubert, Charlie made the long journey from Mississippi to Chicago to play the blues

The King's presence is felt everywhere at Graceland Too, even on the stairway to 'Elvis Heaven'

706 Union Avenue, home of Sam Phillips's Memphis Recording Service and Sun Studio

Bentonia guitarist Jimmy 'Duck' Holmes playing the blues

Photographer Ernest Withers with Ike Turner in Clarksdale, Mississippi. Ernest has been photographing Ike since the 1950s

The Smithsonian donated their exhibit for the city's Rock 'n' Soul Museum, currently housed in the Gibson Guitar Factory just south of Beale Street

Rev AD 'Gatemouth' Moore singing the 'Darktown Strutter's Ball', just as he's done for the last 50 years

Guitarist Calvin Newborn in a reflective mood, with his prized instrument. Calvin is the last living member of Memphis's first family of jazz

The front door of the
Big S Lounge, Memphis's
best barbecue joint

Rosco Gordon
hamming it up at
the pool table, moments
before going on stage
in Memphis. This
concert was one of his
last performances

Mark Twain joked that a pyramid on the Mississippi River would mean the end
of Western civilisation. He would surely disapprove of this sports arena, built in
the late 1980s and already out of date

BB King's Blues Club,
named for its owner,
who made his name as
the Peptikon Boy on
local radio station WDIA,
first came to Beale Street as
a poor teenager from
Indianola, Mississippi

Othar Turner, the
last living master
of the cane fife.
Well into his 90s,
Othar shows no sign
of slowing down

Othar Turner
choosing a piece of
cane to make a fife.
A primitive wind
instrument, the fife
has only two sounds:
high and low

Graceland, Elvis Aron Presley's last Memphis home, in all its glory

Elvis sightings are a common occurrence in August, when thousands of fans converge on Memphis for Death Week

North Mississippi Allstars Luther and Cody Dickinson shakin' 'em all down on stage, Fred McDowell-style

Outside the Blue Front Café in Bentonia, Mississippi. This Delta juke joint is one of the oldest in the state

Paul and Elvis MacLeod had a tailor make each of them a replica of Elvis Presley's infamous gold lamé suit, worn on the album cover *50,000,000 Elvis Fans Can't Be Wrong*

The Lorraine Motel, where Dr Martin Luther King was assassinated on 4 April 1968. Despite the protests of people like Jacqueline Smith, the motel has been turned into the National Civil Rights Museum

Roger Stolle, owner of Cat Head, a new business in downtown Clarksdale. Roger and his wife Jennifer recently relocated to the Delta, pulled by their love of folk art and blues music

A crowded Beale Street. The late Rufus Thomas once said, 'If you could be black on Beale Street for one Saturday night, you'd never be white again'

Beale Street after the party is over

which point he began playing saxophone. Although a new face on the local music scene, he soon fell in with a larger-than-life character who at 18 was already a local DJ on station WROX, a pianist and noted sharp dresser and – most importantly – had a band. His name was Isaiah 'Ike' Turner, it was 1950 and he was ready to rock.

Turner's band was called The Kings Of Rhythm, they'd got together at high school, and were all crazy about rhythm and blues and jump-band records. 'We called ourselves The Kings of Rhythm because we'd take stuff off jukeboxes,' Turner recalled in *Mojo* magazine in 2002. Just as the band seemed to be gelling nicely, the lead singer Johnny O'Neal upped and left for the bright lights of Cincinnati, where he'd secured a deal with the King label. Ike, though he sang himself, was a vocalist short, and Brenston got the job, doubling on sax.

Next to enter the picture was BB King, still billed professionally as 'Blue Boy'. He'd already met Ike, but when he heard The Kings Of Rhythm for the first time he suggested they should be making records, and promised to put them in touch with Sam Phillips in Memphis, with whom he'd recently done some recording himself. Sam's ambitions with his Memphis Recording Service were just taking shape, and he was keen to get worthwhile new talent, into the studio – particularly unheard-of blues and R&B artists – so in March 1951 Ike Turner got the call that was to change their lives. They made for Memphis in Turner's Chrysler, toying with ideas for a new song on the way.

From the days of the classic singers like Ma Rainey and Bessie Smith, sexual analogy and innuendo has been a regular feature of blues lyrics, while nothing in postwar American culture had acquired more sexual connotations than the automobile. Like flashy clothes, sleek cars became a status symbol (especially for those who couldn't afford them), whose very design and advertising emphasised the sexual parallels in their ever-more streamlined design, smooth surfaces and power-driven performance. In 1951, the fastest saloon on the road was reckoned to be the eight-cylinder Oldsmobile 88; magazine ads for the car even featured a man and woman astride a space rocket, one for the 1952 model announcing, 'Johnny and Lucille, Oldsmobile's singing sweethearts, invite you to ride the "Rocket".'

So by the time they got to Memphis, after an eventful journey that involved a flat tyre and a run-in with the local highway patrol – plus the famous incident of the guitar amp falling off the roof – they had a song almost finished for their record début, 'Rocket 88'.

Sam Phillips has told the story over and over again of how the distorted guitar sound was achieved by default when he stuffed the damaged speaker with paper, but there was much more to the record than that. There was a frantic dynamic to it – with its booting saxes and Brenston's exhilarating vocal, it was like nothing Sam had heard before. During the session they went on to record a Brenston-voiced flip side, 'Come Back Where You Belong', plus two Ike Turner vocals.

The credit on the singles has been a bone of contention with Ike Turner ever since, though his view seems to have mellowed over the years. The two sides on which he sang lead were billed as Ike Turner And His Kings Of Rhythm, while the Brenston single was credited to Jackie Brenston And His Delta Cats – a far funkier name, in retrospect. Phillips, who was yet to set up his own label, leased the two 78 singles to Chess in Chicago in the April, with the result that by the end of that month 'Rocket 88' had entered the national R&B charts, hitting the Number One spot in the June.

But the success of 'Rocket 88' had far greater effects than could be measured in mere record sales. First of all, it confirmed for Sam Phillips the value of the local airplay kick-start it had received from DJ Dewey Phillips, leading to an informal collaboration which was to reap further benefits in the future. Second, it convinced Sam that those benefits would be best realised on his own label, which manifested itself as Sun the following year. Last, it heralded a new, wilder take on R&B, which would soon be labelled 'rock 'n' roll'.

In the wake of 'Rocket 88', Ike – despite his anger at the label credit he didn't receive – eventually went on to bigger and more long-term success after parting company with Brenston. Jackie, meanwhile, didn't even make it to a follow-up hit, 'My Real Gone Rocket' being a resounding flop later in 1951. And, although he was to rejoin The Kings Of Rhythm, staying with them until the early '60s, it was as baritone sax player, Ike allowing him to sing the occasional song on live dates, but never, *never*, 'Rocket 88'.

RED HOT ROCKABILLY
Mike Evans

Along with names like Warren Smith, Malcolm Yelvington, Sonny Burgess and Ray Smith, Billy Lee Riley was part of a whole stable of performers who came to represent the rockabilly sound pioneered at Sun. While not in the same league in terms of record sales as their label mates Jerry Lee Lewis, Carl Perkins, Roy Orbison or Johnny Cash, they nevertheless were the core of the labels' association with rockabilly, which had come to dominate its output after Elvis's success and subsequent move to RCA.

Born in 1933 in Pocahontas in the foothills of the Ozark Mountains in northeast Arkansas, when he was three his family moved to Osceola, another small Arkansas town on the banks of the Mississippi River. It was cotton country, and his father, a house painter by trade, would join his older sister picking cotton to make ends meet. For a year or so, when things were really bad, the Riley family even had to live in a tent.

But what he did pick up on from an early age was something money couldn't – the music around, particularly blues and country music. He learned to play harmonica while still a child, and he and his friends would go over to the black part of town to listen to the music whenever they got the chance, just kids sitting in the doorways of bars and juke joints, picking up on the sounds.

It was the classic recipe for rock 'n' roll, as he explained to Robert Gordon years later in an interview for the *Blue Collar Blues* sleeve-notes: 'I was raised up mainly around the old gutbucket blues. Those days, we couldn't listen to blues on radio, no one played it. I used to hang around and listen to all the black guys playing blues. When I got into playing music, I got into country. I did pretty good imitations of Hank Williams, Lefty Frizzell, Hank Snow. And in 1955, I got into the rock 'n' roll thing and started doing that. They're all actually part of each other, but when you combine it, you come out with all these different ideas.'

After a nine-month stay in Tupelo, Mississippi, through 1948 – where, coincidentally, the young Elvis Presley resided until November of that year – Riley joined the Army. It was the time of the Korean War, though he was never posted abroad. He was honourably discharged from the service in 1953, returning to Jonesboro, Arkansas, where his parents were living by that time.

The first thing he did coming out of the Army was to put together a hillbilly band, which soon found itself playing high-school dances and local clubs, as well as appearing on three radio shows each week. Then, after getting married in 1954, he moved to Memphis the following year to open a restaurant with his brother-in-law; it was a move that would prove crucial in his yet-to-be-launched musical career.

By the time he had settled in Memphis, Billy Lee had broadened his musical skills over the years to include guitar, bass and drums, as well as harmonica and vocals, in his accomplishments, though when he met up with guitarist Jack Clement (after the latter had hitchhiked a lift from him) it was just as vocalist that Clement invited Riley to join The Dixie Ramblers, a dyed-in-the-wool country outfit that also included bass player Ronald 'Slim' Wallace.

But it was another venture involving Wallace and Clement that was to involve Billy Lee Riley more fundamentally. The two showed him a recording studio they were building in Slim's garage on Fernwood Street. It was to be called Fernwood Studios, the idea being that they would also launch a label of the same name, and to Riley's delight they asked him if he would be their début artist.

In March 1956 they made their first recording, a bluesy number called 'Trouble Bound' and a more straightforward country song, 'Think Before You Go'. Jack Clement then took the tapes to Sam Phillips at Sun to have an acetate master made, and when Sam heard 'Trouble Bound' they immediately did a deal to release it as a Sun single, just as long as they cut a similar rockabilly-style song for the flip side.

Riley dutifully wrote a suitable B-side, 'Rock With Me Baby', which he and Clement recorded in a local radio station. The result went over to Sun, Sam giving Billy Lee a recording contract and Jack Clement a production deal. So the involvement with Fernwood never happened, but Clement and Riley became part of the fabric of Sun Records over the next few years.

The line-up on 'Rock With Me Baby' (which also included bass player JW Bruner) featured guitarist Roland Janes and drummer JM

Van Eaton, who with Riley formed the core of the Sun sound, serving as the house rhythm section. They subsequently recorded together as The Little Green Men, a name taken from Riley's next release, 'Flyin' Saucers Rock And Roll'. It was the era of the 'flying saucer' scares that had hit all the news media in America, as well as spawning a whole new craze in comic books and sci-fi movies, so the record had a topical gimmick as well as being at the cutting edge of the contemporary rockabilly sound that was now the Sun trademark.

It was during his early days at Sun that he came across a young guy sitting at the piano, playing like he'd never heard it played before. The pianist, it turned out, was Jerry Lee Lewis. Riley invited him to play gigs with his band, but Sam Phillips wasn't happy about the Louisiana kid playing on Riley's records. He did, however, appear on both 'Flyin' Saucers Rock And Roll' and 'Pearly Lee', the B-side to Riley's third single, 'Red Hot', while making a name for himself with his own Sun début, 'Crazy Arms'.

Billy Lee and his Little Green Men were now part of the Sun establishment, and as such toured with the Sun package show, which included Johnny Cash, Roy Orbison, Carl Perkins, Warren Smith and, later on, Jerry Lee Lewis. Riley left Sun briefly in 1958 for a one-record deal with Brunswick Records, after a disagreement with Sam Phillips over marketing his material, but he returned and recorded three more releases – 'Baby Please Don't Go'/'Wouldn't You Know', 'No Name Girl'/'Down By The Riverside' and 'One More Time'/'Got The Water Boilin' Baby', before leaving in 1960. During his time at Sun, he or part of the band were on recordings with Johnny Cash, Roy Orbison, Charlie Rich, Bill Justis plus most of the label's lesser-known names.

During the '70s and '80s, Billy Lee Riley found a whole new audience in Europe, as had many of the blues players that were his contemporaries, and here he would tour with a rockabilly package show and take part in rockabilly festivals in England, France, Germany, all over – where, in fact, rockabilly was enjoying a new cult status.

Then, in 1994, he got together for the first time in 30 years with his old partners, Roland Janes and JM Van Eaton, for a new album, *Blue Collar Blues*, which kicked off with a rewritten version of 'Flyin' Saucers

Rock And Roll'. On the sleeve-notes he's quoted as saying, referring to a vocal range that everyone from Sam Phillips onward found amazing, 'Funny thing about the way I sing, each one of those voices I consider my natural voice. When I'm singing blues, I'm not telling myself to do it this certain way. If I'm singing a country thing, it comes out country. Same with rockabilly and rock 'n' roll. It's a natural thing. That's what I am.'

6 Baby, Let's Play House

THE HOUSE THAT ELVIS BUILT
Andria Lisle

This August marked the 25th year since Elvis Aron Presley left the building for good. On 16 August 1977, the astonishing life of Elvis officially concluded, his unconscious body discovered in an upstairs Graceland bathroom at 2:30pm. Doctors in trauma room 1 at Memphis's Baptist Hospital, though they tried, were unable to put the spirit back into the body. Personal physician Dr George Nichopoulos pronounced the King of Rock 'n' Roll dead, saying, 'It's all over – he's gone.' Elvis was a mere 42 years old.

A quarter of a century later, Elvis still reigns supreme. To quote media expert Gilbert Rodman, author of *Elvis After Elvis*, 'His body may have failed him, but today his spirit, his image, and his myths do more than live on: they flourish, they thrive, they multiply. For a dead man, Elvis Presley is awfully noisy.'

And nowhere is Elvis noisier than in his adopted home town. He came to Memphis from Tupelo, Mississippi, in 1948, an overprotected 13-year-old with parents Vernon and Gladys Presley. Less than a decade later, thanks to Elvis's career, the Presley family moved from government-assisted public housing to the Graceland mansion. At the height of his success, the Presleys could have lived anywhere, but they preferred the familiar environs of west Tennessee.

If Memphis is the epicentre of Elvis Presley's legacy, then the Graceland mansion is ground zero. Built in 1939 on 200 hectares (500 acres) in suburban Whitehaven, the estate received its name from the original owner, Dr Thomas Moore, in honour of his wife's great-aunt Grace. Elvis paid more than a $100,000 for the 18-room limestone house and accompanying 5.5 hectares (13.5 acres) in 1957. He immediately redecorated, installing a 4.6m (15ft) couch in the living room, a soda fountain in the basement and a 2.5m (8ft) square bed in his own room. Outside accoutrements included the now-legendary front gates with the musical notes, a swimming pool and a chicken coop to house Gladys's pet poultry.

Livestock ran amok – on occasion, there were donkeys running around the backyard and peacocks roaming the front lawn. After hearing that geese were good for keeping the grass down, Elvis drove a Cadillac across the Mississippi state line and returned with a back seat full of birds. Uncle Vestor often manned the front gates at Graceland and even encouraged lovesick fans to write messages to the King on the fence that surrounded the estate. Even now, Elvis fans from around the world add their graffiti to the limestone wall, which is sandblasted clean every few years.

When Elvis died, he was buried at nearby Forest Hill Cemetery. At least 50,000 mourners lined Elvis Presley Boulevard for his final journey, and more than 2,200 floral arrangements decorated the Presley mausoleum for his funeral. After a brief spell at Forest Hill, his body was disinterred and brought home to the backyard. Elvis, Gladys and Vernon now rest side by side in Graceland's Meditation Garden, which fans can visit for free in the early morning hours. Lisa Marie Presley, Elvis's daughter and sole heir, owns the estate, which is in turn run by Elvis Presley Enterprises. Officially opened in 1982, Elvis's final home attracted more than half a million visitors in its first year of business.

Today, those 500,000 people seem small potatoes. According to Todd Morgan, EPE's public relations director, 'Any nine days in the summer we're gonna see 30,000 people or more.' While they have yet to tally the final count, EPE expects that more than 75,000 fans will have visited Memphis for 2002's 25th anniversary of Elvis's death, which is called International Tribute Week by Graceland employees, but locally referred to as Death Week. Do the maths – at $25 a head for Graceland's Platinum Tour, that's a heck of a lot of sequinned belts! 'Of course,' Morgan is quick to point out, 'not all of them toured Graceland – some came only for the candlelight vigil.'

The vigil – a 16 August tradition – is a favourite Death Week event for hardcore Elvis fans and curiosity seekers alike. The street in front of Graceland is closed down as the fans walk single file up the hill past the mansion to the Meditation Garden to pay tribute to the fallen King. Slow-burning candles are *de rigueur*, and many more clutch flowers, teddy bears, love notes and other personal items to deposit at the ready-made shrine.

It's quite a scene – five years ago, there were so many fans that it was eight o'clock the next morning before the last person made it through. 'We didn't know what to expect this year,' Morgan says, while the evening news showed a wild, weeping throng making their way to the King's tomb through a pouring rainstorm. It was an emotional three-ring circus starring beehived grandmas and jumpsuited old men amid people on foot and in wheelchairs, on crutches and walkers and, occasionally, collapsed on the kerb, too devastated for their pilgrimage to continue.

Surveying the scene, I realise that Elvis fans come in all ages, shapes and sizes. 'We don't have hard demographics,' Morgan insists. 'It's very broad-based – a real range.' Surprisingly, a lot of fans are 35 and younger, which means that they were very young – some not even born yet – when Elvis died. 'It's always been this way,' Morgan maintains. 'We get letters from 5-year-olds and teenagers. We always know when it's term-paper time: we get swamped with letters from kids doing their papers on Elvis.'

But how do young people – inundated with N*SYNC and Britney Spears on MTV and elsewhere – find out about Elvis? 'It happens on its own,' Morgan says. 'For us the proactive part, the challenge, is to simply get his work in front of audiences, making sure they see and hear him. Elvis does the rest. He's such a powerful person when it comes to that. Elvis is everywhere. He just permeates the culture,' Morgan says with a grin. 'Try to sit home one evening and flip through channels and not hear his name. He's everywhere. There's always news coverage about Elvis, there's always some book about Elvis, there's always something…'

In Holly Springs, Mississippi, 50km (30 miles) southeast of Graceland, there's a man who has taped every TV programme that has mentioned Elvis since the King's death. He also has more than 55,000 newspaper clippings that he says substantiate 'the King's unparalleled influence on international pop culture at large and in the universe'. Meet Paul MacLeod, the world's (and, according to him, the galaxy's) biggest Elvis fan.

Paul's fascination with the King began in 1954, when he purchased Elvis's first single, 'That's All Right, Mama'/'Blue Moon Of Kentucky,' cut at Memphis's Sun recording studio that same year. The sound of that 78 turned Paul into a zealot, collecting anything and everything he could find with an Elvis connection.

In 1974, the short, swarthy man – who does bear a slight resemblance to his idol, right down to the gold lamé suit hanging in his closet – named his only child Elvis Aron Presley MacLeod. Serita, his wife, eventually had enough: 'It's me or Elvis,' she said. Paul chose his first love – Elvis – with barely a regret. Two decades later, his collection blossomed into a tourist attraction in its own right.

Graceland Too, as Paul's abode is called, has since been visited by hundreds of thousands of fans, including (at last count) 3,000 Elvis impersonators. The decaying ante-bellum mansion is home to a mind-boggling collection of Elvis memorabilia, including Elvis quilts, telephones, recordings, scrapbooks, videos, carpet, and even a Stairway to Elvis Heaven.

Paul has dedicated his life to tracking down every mention of Elvis Presley in the media and recording any information – minutiae included – about him. Six TVs and VCRs capture every glimpse of Elvis that can be tuned in over local cable. Whether it's an Elvis movie, an Elvis impersonator, an Elvis picture or song in the background, or even an Elvis joke, it makes no difference. The moment is recorded, logged into a journal and then filed away for later reference.

Tours – which cost just $5 – leave visitors reeling. Students from the nearby University of Mississippi often stop by for a lesson in kitsch, while my own visits, often under the cover of night, leave my head pounding for days. For a few months afterward, I imagine Paul faithfully adding another line to his logbook every time I chance upon an Elvis mention in the local paper or on the ten o'clock news. Elvis has truly become his life's undertaking.

Back in Memphis, EPE acknowledge Paul MacLeod's effort, but make no attempt to endorse it. 'Any sincere expression of love and respect for Elvis is great,' Todd Morgan drolly remarks. 'People express their interest in Elvis in all kinds of ways, and some of the ways they choose to do it are quite fascinating. Now, there are things people do that involve our trademarks, and that can be a problem.'

But in the mid-1980s, when EPE took charge of the Presley estate, the trademark situation was out of control. 'Long before he was laid in the grave,' Elvis biographer Peter Guralnick sagely notes in *Careless Love: The Unmaking Of Elvis Presley*, 'the legend of Elvis's success had been retailed over and over again.' A ragtag collection of souvenir shops across the street from the Graceland mansion sold everything from vials of Elvis's sweat to 'Love Me Tender' shampoo and 'Blue Suede Shoes' bedroom slippers (with a rubber Elvis doll head affixed to each toe).

EPE eventually bought out the stores' leases and put an end to what their website calls 'an unsightly blemish of tacky souvenir shops'. Today, the high-end stores that replaced the so-called eyesore sell officially licensed paraphernalia only, carefully folded Elvis denim shirts vying for tourist dollars alongside genuine 14-carat gold TCB lightning-bolt necklaces and hip-shaking Elvis clocks.

It's no secret that EPE takes its merchandising very seriously. While he demurs on citing numbers, Morgan divulges that 'our per-caps on merchandise are always very strong and beat out a lot of other attractions around the country. So many people who visit tell us that they have to take something back for their friends,' he says proudly. 'People who come to Graceland always have a shopping list!'

The official International Tribute Week celebration for 2002 – the 25th – promised to be special. 'It's the biggest Elvis Week we've ever had,' Morgan says. 'Because of a lot of things going on, particularly a promotion with RCA and AOL, Elvis is really out there – even more than usual. Elvis Week is huge!'

The first-time 'Elvis Happening' parade on Beale Street was attended by 10,000 flag-waving fans. The event, which kicked off Elvis Week, featured Army tanks, vintage sports cars, 40 Harley-Davidson motorcycles, the NASCAR Elvis car, a *Jailhouse Rock* float and 51 tonne (50 ton) howitzer guns against an unmistakably patriotic backdrop. Parade marshals included Sun Records founder Sam Phillips and Elvis guitarist Scotty Moore, who were flanked with 28 hound dogs throughout the event. Dance parties, charity fundraisers, impersonator contests, and even a pool party at Elvis's pre-Graceland residence on Audubon Drive in East Memphis filled the nine-day calendar, which culminated on 16 August – Death Day.

More than 20,000 fans spent the early evening hours of the 16th at Memphis's Pyramid arena, a looming tomb-like structure on the Mississippi River. 'At 8pm,' Elvis's official website proclaimed, 'the real Elvis Presley stars via video in this concert event with his real, original bandmates live on stage.' Live footage of Elvis shared the stage with a who's who of Presley band members via special effects and 21st-century technology, Morgan explains. 'Elvis himself starred in the show – he sang lead.' James Burton, Ronnie Tutt and the rest of the early '70s TCB Band appeared on stage, as did Elvis's back-up singers, The Sweet Inspirations, the Jordanaires and members of The Imperials and JD Sumner And The Stamps. Elvis's first drummer, DJ Fontana, also performed, and Priscilla and Lisa Marie Presley – who married actor Nicolas Cage just the week before – were on hand for the sold-out concert.

But you didn't have to spend big bucks at the Pyramid – Elvis's spirit lingers on in other Memphis locations as well. Wanting to avoid the crowds, I put in a copy of his *Memphis Record*, recorded at American Studio in 1969, and cruised around town in the rain. Punching up 'Long Black Limousine', I drive by Lauderdale Courts, the housing project that was the Presleys' first home in Memphis. Their apartment was at 185 Winchester Avenue, number 328. In the laundry room below the Presleys' apartment, 18-year-old rockabilly and occasional Golden Gloves boxer Jessie Lee Denson gave Elvis his first guitar lessons.

After months of practice, Elvis and his friends began to throw dances in the basement beneath the main office at Lauderdale Courts. They'd serve Cokes and popcorn and play records – admission ran to 25 cents a couple. Still shy, Elvis would never dance. Despite his fear, he started singing and playing the guitar for his friends. Ballads from the likes of Kay Starr, Perry Como, Hank Williams and Eddy Arnold were all part of his repertoire. Elvis would hide in the corner of the dark basement, shielding his face from his friends – but he was scarcely invisible.

Today, the North Memphis neighbourhood is considered to be a bad part of town and, aside from a few street people wandering around, the once-bustling Lauderdale Courts stand empty. They were slated to be demolished a few years ago, until preservationists stepped in with a plan for extensive renovation. From my car, I look up towards the Presleys' darkened window as Elvis's voice fills the air: 'When you left you know you told me that some day/You'd be returning in a fancy car for all the town to see/Now everyone is watching you and you finally had your dream/You're riding in a long black limousine.' A chorus of female singers chime in to drive the song home as I sit and contemplate the King's fate.

Next, I drop by Elvis's school, Humes High, at 659 Manassas Street. While everyone else wore jeans to class, Elvis favoured dress pants and a sports coat – as if he were a movie star, classmates remembered. In October 1952, Elvis performed in the annual Humes Minstrel Show. The 17-year-old guitarist played to a packed house midway through the evening. A senior, Elvis became an overnight sensation at Humes. 'It was amazing how popular I became after that,' Elvis noted. 'Then I graduated.'

Now a middle school in a low-income black neighbourhood, Humes High nevertheless retains some sense of its former glory. In a recent visit to Memphis, Bob Dylan stopped by, just so he could stand on its auditorium stage and reflect on the momentous performance that took place 50 years earlier. Today, the worn wooden platform seems way too small to contain Elvis's talent, yet it manages to hold its own in local Presley mythology.

So does Sun Studio. It's been almost half a century since Elvis unleashed the power of rock 'n' roll with Scotty Moore and Bill Black in the nondescript building at 706 Union Avenue. In those days, Sam Phillips's Recording Service and Sun label were hardly a tourist attraction. Even locals scarcely glanced at the small storefront on the west side of town and, had anyone noticed the activity going on inside – bluesmen like Howlin' Wolf and Ike Turner coming and going, wannabe singers recording acetates for $3.98 plus tax, and hillbilly groups like Scotty and Bill's Starlite Wranglers trying to catch Phillips's ear – they would've shaken their heads and walked on, hardly aware that within those four walls a revolution was under way.

When Sam put Elvis (who, in the beginning, was one of those $3.98

customers) together with Scotty and Bill, nothing gelled until the group took a break. Elvis was fooling around on his guitar when the blues song 'That's All Right, Mama' popped into his head. 'All of a sudden,' Scotty told Peter Guralnick, 'Elvis just started jumping around and acting the fool, and then Bill picked up his bass, and I started playing with them.' Sam stuck his head out of the control room to ask the trio what they were doing. 'Back up,' he said. 'Try to find a place to start, and do it again.' And the rest, as they say, is history.

As I drive east past Sun Studio, headed home, I think back to the Elvis conference I attended earlier in the week. The day-long academic seminar, entitled *Is Elvis "History"?*, was held at the University of Memphis, with authors Greil Marcus and Michael Bertrand on hand for a scholastic debate. Peter Guralnick addressed Elvis's influence on the Civil Rights Movement, while Memphis Mafia hangers-on Bill Morris and Jerry Schilling fended off some truly inane questions from the sold-out crowd in attendance.

It was after lunch when the mood lightened. Sam Phillips, a rumoured no-show, took control of the microphone for what he called some 'down-home preachment'. At 79 years old ('that's 12 years and three days older than Elvis,' he says), Sam is a real raconteur, famous for flinging his arms and rolling his eyes in grand old southern Baptist style. Dressed in a khaki suit and starched white shirt, which accentuated his dark, wavy hair and untrimmed beard, he carried himself with an almost religious force.

'You would not have Elvis Presley and his fantastic influence were it not for hardship,' he told folks in the front row. 'If Elvis could've done it, he wouldn't have charged his audience a dime to get into his shows!' Sam went on to discuss the commonality of people – the desire to love and the desire to be loved. He paced and pounded his fist for emphasis, and the entire scene was nothing short of biblical.

'We're all a part of this,' Sam said, and the room snapped to attention. With a few more words, he took us back to that summer of 1954. 'When I started in the recording business, I worked my ass off thinking day and night, wondering who gave a damn. I liked all that gutbucket stuff – the deep Mississippi hollers and hymns. Then Elvis came into the studio. I was looking for the common denominator – and he was it. I couldn't classify him as black, or country, or pop, and that fascinated me. I wanted to see just how far he could go, so I messed around until he finally hit on something. We had to find that path that would turn into a broader road. That was my job – to work with people and find the natural instinct in them that they didn't know they had.'

Sam worked us into a frenzy, then reached deep for a line of corroborative scripture. He came up with this: 'There's some doors in life that we need to open for each other, and that is the axle on which this wheel turns.'

'Fear not,' Sam concluded, raising a fist to the heavens. 'The spirit of Elvis Presley will never go away. It will find an intuitive way of getting into people's hearts and getting their honest response.' He sat down as we gave him a round of thunderous applause, unanimously swept away by his unwavering faith.

GRACELAND, GRACELAND
Mike Evans

'The Mississippi Delta was shining like a National guitar...' The lyrics of Paul Simon rang in my head as I made my first visit to Graceland over a decade ago, initially not entering through the fabled wrought-iron gates but up the short driveway leading to the red-brick offices of Elvis Presley Enterprises (in a building that had previously been a church), just next door to the 'mansion', as the folks there call it. Even the short taxi ride from downtown Memphis was accompanied by the buzz of anticipation as Highway 51 became Elvis Presley Boulevard, a civic honour bestowed on that otherwise unremarkable stretch of road back in 1972. It's a road that leads, nevertheless, deep into blues country, through Jackson, Mississippi, and eventually to New Orleans on the Gulf of Mexico.

I was there to supervise, as editor, the planning of a photo shoot for a book celebrating the house itself and the treasures therein. It was to be a room-by-room account of what the fans get to see when they visit this shrine of shrines, and some (though not all) parts of the property they don't see. Todd Morgan, EPE's Director of Communications (and self-styled house 'Elvisologist') was to be a personal guide and general coordinator for myself, the book's designer and Gil Michael, the Memphis-based photographer who was to handle the actual shoot. Accordingly, unlike the tourists being bused from the reception centre on the other side of the road, we were escorted by foot through the gates with a nod and a wave of acknowledgement from the security guard on duty.

Like when meeting someone famous, whatever 'objective' mind-set you are determined to adopt and however blasé you are anxious to appear, the familiarity bestowed by fame can still have a strangely distorting effect. So it was as the winding path through the trees gradually revealed the house that we've all seen a thousand times in photographs, the Neoclassical façade with its white pillars in stark contrast to the 20th-century modern brickwork that constitutes its actual structure. Was it smaller than I imagined, or just further away than it seemed, up there beyond the gently rolling lawns?

Although that first visit was during 'opening time', with families and individuals filing through the various rooms literally by the busload – mostly ordinary working-class folk, mostly American, mostly white – we were privileged during the next two weeks, by the nature of our mission, to see the real detail of Elvis's habitat privately, during the hours of darkness.

We were able to examine close up the mock antique furniture in the Dining Room, the '60s sunburst clock in the Living Room (shoes off on the white carpet), the wall full of television screens in the TV Room, the ripped baize where someone miscued in the Pool Room, the exotic beasts carved into the furniture of the Jungle Room that Elvis had purchased in a one-off 30-minute shopping spree in a local store.

When it rains in Memphis, it can really rain, especially with the warm monsoon-like downpours that come in summer and will soak clothes through to the skin in an instant. It was during one such storm, about ten o'clock at night, while we were working in the eerily lit Jungle Room, that we were surprised by the sudden entrance from a side-door of an old black lady, her ebony face shining in the half-light, wrinkled like a walnut. 'Guess I'll take the dog a walk, before it starts to rain,' she announced, leading a fluffy white canine out into the night, oblivious of the weather. It transpired she was the nurse to Elvis's Aunt Delta, who still resided in the house at that time (Delta died in 1993), the dog being Delta's little Pomeranian, Edmond II.

The next time I was to work at Graceland was in 1995 for a book, *The King On The Road*, which told the story of Elvis as a live performer through the hundreds of posters, reviews, tour schedules, set-lists, backstage passes and other touring ephemera amassed in the vast archive that EPE have been assembling through the last decade, much of it from the personal collection of Elvis's manager, Colonel Tom Parker.

The Colonel had literally glued all the cuttings in huge leather-bound scrapbooks over the years. Every morning for a couple of weeks the author Robert Gordon (Memphian writer and now good friend) and myself would don the obligatory white gloves before prising open these mammoth tomes in order to find what gum-stained pieces of history might lie within.

I found myself in the archive once again in 2001 to research a 600-picture celebration of the life of the King to coincide with the 25th anniversary of his death in August 2002. Now holding nearly 50,000 photographs as well as the other memorabilia, the recently digitalised archive – like the Graceland operation itself – is more streamlined and user-friendly, though nothing much changes up in the house on the hill. The purpose-built 'exhibit' spaces displaying trophies, costumes and such have been modified to accommodate more material since 1992, but the rooms where Elvis lived and breathed are still as they have been, as if frozen in time, since he finally left the building.

The visitors across the road still wait in line for their tour tickets, visit the automobile museum and souvenir shops, marvel at the golden washbasins aboard the *Lisa Marie* private jet (which always seems weirdly stranded, incongruous at the edge of the busy highway), before boarding their bus for the final station of their pilgrimage. It's easy to be suspicious of so conspicuous a money machine, and indeed mock the sincerity of the faithful, but to ignore it – like an agnostic avoiding the Vatican when in Rome – is to miss an essential piece of the jigsaw that makes up the full picture of Memphis, Tennessee.

7 Singing Sanctified

AL GREEN'S WONDERFUL WORLD
Andria Lisle

Waking up in time for church on Sunday morning can be a Herculean task in Memphis. Saturday nights run late – all local bars are open until at least three o'clock in the morning, while several clubs on Beale Street serve beer until dawn. Hell-fire and brimstone are hardly the perfect prescription for a night spent drinking and dancing. In fact, if you ask the musicians in the late-night joints, most will tell you that they were forced to make a choice between Saturday night and Sunday morning a long time ago – there are few who can straddle the barrier between the sacred and the secular without flak from either world.

But some local heroes have managed to make the crossover, including Clarksdale native Sam Cooke, Johnnie Taylor of The Soul Stirrers and Delta guitarist Pops Staples. And, more recently, Arkansan Albert Greene, who has made the journey in reverse, trading in a music superstar's success for a more humble role, pastoring a South Memphis church.

Greene (he would not drop that 'e' until his solo career took off) got his start singing in a family gospel group, playing revivals and country services in the dirt-poor Delta communities south of Memphis. Then, in the 1950s, the Green family traded in their hard-scrabble rural life for an equally tenuous home in the city. They relocated to Grand Rapids, Michigan, where young Al formed The Soul Mates, a group heavily influenced by the Motown sound. After cutting the surprise smash 'Back Up Train' in 1967, Green hit the road alone, booking a series of dates that corresponded with the crisscross route of a Greyhound bus.

A chance meeting with Memphis producer Willie Mitchell at a Texas nightclub one year later led to one of the greatest pop music collaborations of the 1970s – under Poppa Willie's tutelage, Al scored big with 'Tired Of Being Alone' at the start of the decade, and racked up hit after hit over a seven-year run. Green put aside his religious upbringing to sing about the passion between men and women – yet, as his trademark falsetto soared over the lyrics, his soul sank under the weight of his secular success.

In Green's autobiography *Take Me To The River,* he tells of receiving the Holy Spirit in a Disneyland hotel room as early as 1973: 'I couldn't have been asleep more than an hour or two when I was suddenly awakened by the sound of shouting,' he writes. 'I sat bolt upright in bed, frightened that some crazy fan had broken into the room. The shouting continued, and as I listened, I realized that the voice wasn't threatening so much as excited and happy, as if someone had just walked into a surprise party with all his oldest and dearest friends in attendance. There was something oddly familiar about the voice, as well. Where had I heard it before?'

'It was then that I realized that the voice was my own! And while the words that I shouted were of no earthly tongue, I immediately recognized what they meant. I was praising God, rejoicing in the great and glorious gift of salvation through His son, Jesus Christ, and lifting my voice to heaven with the language of angels.'

From that moment on, Green vowed to commit himself to God, although more earthly matters continued to get in his way, culminating with a 1974 incident when a female friend poured a pot of boiling grits on his bare back, then killed herself in his bathroom. While he was recovering from his third-degree burns – an arduous eight-month process – Green devoted his spare time to Bible study, immersing himself in the healing power of God's word. He learned that 'no man can serve two masters' and that, if he tries, 'he will end up hating the one and loving the other'. As Al saw it, he had to choose between God and Willie Mitchell, and without any hesitation he parted company with the hit-making producer.

One spring afternoon in 1977, shortly after cutting *Belle* (his first album since splitting with Mitchell), Green was driving through South Memphis when God told him to turn down Elvis Presley Boulevard. The north–south street runs from midtown to the Mississippi state line, through the heart of Whitehaven, the once rural area that has become a popular suburban enclave. Dozens of strip shopping centres, the Southland Mall, and Presley's mansion line the busy six-lane corridor, which in June 1971 was renamed Elvis Presley Boulevard. Street signs proclaiming the name change were put up six months later, but after legions of fans stole the metal signs as fast as they were erected the city quit reinstalling them. A testament to their popularity, official Elvis Presley Boulevard street signs are available in the Graceland gift shops, and to this day, the north–south road remains unmarked.

'As I passed by the gates of Graceland, I couldn't help but wonder whether the Lord wanted me to stop off for a tour,' Green has often quipped. But he turned down Hale Road, drove through a four-way stop, and slowed down in front of a small, run-down church on the south side of the street. This, he realised, was what God intended for him, so Green bought the Full Gospel Tabernacle ('pews, pulpit, hymnals, and all') and set about earning his degree as a fully ordained minister.

Unless you've grown up in the Pentecostal tradition, a service at the Full Gospel Tabernacle is an eye-opening, jaw-dropping, spine-tingling experience. Things begin around 11 o'clock in the morning and wind down about three hours later but, rest assured, the time passes quickly. Rev Green's congregation is a small but loyal one, with about 100 parishioners in attendance on a regular basis. Clad in their Sunday best, they're easy to spot – just look for the sequinned gowns and feathered hats in the front pews. Tourists and non-practising Christians tend to skulk in the back, more eager for a glimpse of the famous reverend than a dose of old-time religion.

Green preaches as he sings, employing theatrics, emotion and an overflowing passion for his subject, educating his regular flock while enlightening the curiosity seekers with grace and dignity. On this Sunday morning, I sit in a pew in the middle of the room, listening to a woman read from the church bulletin. She informs us that Brother Sylvester is doing better after his heart surgery, asks us to pray for Sister Louise and her daughter, who were injured in a car wreck, then reminds us of the Wednesday-night Bible-study class, held in the church offices. Finally, Rev Green stands at the front of the church, flanked by one stout pastor and three watchful deacons, ready to deliver a sermon about worshipping false idols. The choir sways behind him, as he begins to read from the Old Testament.

'Ol' King Nebuchadnezzar set up a golden image for his people to worship. He called them all together, and then he ordered them to prostrate themselves in front of it,' Green says, as we reach for our Bibles, searching for the corresponding verses in the third book of Daniel.

'"Accordingly, no sooner than all the peoples hear the sound of horn, pipe, zither, triangle, dulcimer, music, and singing of all kind, than all the peoples and nations of every language prostrated themselves and worshipped the golden image which King Nebuchadnezzar had set up,"' Green reads as we follow along. When he pauses, a few women in the front row shout out an amen.

'But Shadrach, Meshach, and Abednego wouldn't obey,' Green tells us. 'Ol' King Nebuchadnezzar was outraged, and he ordered them thrown into a fiery furnace. The furnace was heated up seven times its usual heat, and the three men were thrown into the blaze. Yet the King saw four men in the furnace – Shadrach, Meshach, and Abednego, and a fourth who looked like a god. The fire had no power to harm the bodies of these men: the hair of their heads had not been singed, their trousers were untouched, and no smell of fire lingered around them.'

Rev Green is jubilant, and he lifts his robes to show off his own silk trouser cuffs and shiny black shoes as he dances around, mimicking the action of the three Jews who refused to bow down to a false god. 'You know, folks, I used to worship a golden image,' he tells us. 'I would hear that horn, and prostrate myself right on down.' The four-piece band, set up at the right side of the altar, sits at attention as the organist plays a pumping riff. 'Keep it down, y'all,' Rev Green instructs, but the choir behind him is ready to erupt.

'I used to sing that stuff, songs like "Love And Happiness",' Green says, teasing us with a few lines of the Number One hit. 'Let me tell you', he sings, 'about the power of love/Make you do right/Love will make you do wrong/Make you want to dance/Love and happiness…' The rest of the band joins in on the second bar, but as quickly as Green begins the tune it's over, and he switches gears to a gospel number. 'Clap your hands for Jesus,' he cries, and the entire congregation is on its feet. The Holy Spirit is on the move, and a dozen church ushers – ladies clad in white dresses, armed with blankets to cover overzealous worshippers – are on high alert.

'I used to sing "Call Me", but now the Lord sings those words to me,' Green says, nodding to a pair of tourists on the back row. 'It's all in the way you feel,' he croons, 'if love is real, come to me,' and his words are like an epiphany. The Holy Spirit is now in the house, entering every body that will receive Him, causing a riot of amens to ripple through the room. The congregation claps in time, and for the next 30 minutes we all belong to the Lord.

When the service is over, I realise that I am starving, and I head outside to my car. But I'm waylaid by a few friendly parishioners, who want to offer a hug and a handshake before they depart – and then, suddenly, I'm standing with Rev Green himself. He and his wife are greeting the newcomers, and Green offers kindly advice to his fans, and then, reluctantly, agrees to sign autographs. 'Y'all came to see me, but you're leaving with the Gospel of the Lord,' he says, before gently extricating himself from the throng and heading to the gleaming silver Rolls-Royce parked just outside the front door.

Ten minutes later, I'm ordering a plate of fried chicken, collard greens and cornbread stuffing at Stein's Family Restaurant. This soul-food joint is located just 3km (2 miles) away from the Full Gospel Tabernacle – and a few blocks south of Willie Mitchell's Royal Studio – but I barely make it in the door before the kitchen is closed. The small storefront café is packed with churchgoers, and Sunday is always a sell-out – some weeks, the restaurant owners call it a day at 3pm, having served up their allotment of chitterlings, mashed potatoes and meatloaf in just a few short hours.

I sit with a family of five: Mama and Daddy and a serious young man in a suit flanked by two cheery sisters in matching dresses and hair ribbons. The girls polish off a slice of lemon pie amid promises to finish their homework before dinner, and I have to smile at their earnestness. After one last sip of iced tea, I make my way to the counter to pay my ticket – $5 for a heaping plate of food. Even though I'm the only white person in the place, I feel at home. We are all filled with the Holy Spirit, I realise, as I look around the restaurant. We are all blessed…

On Tuesday afternoon, I return to the Full Gospel Tabernacle for a conversation with Rev Green. I am a little intimidated about my one-to-one with the sex-symbol-turned-preacher, and take care dressing that morning, anxious to look my best. Green's assistant, Lolita, greets me at the front door of the church, then leads me down a hallway to the reverend's inner sanctum. The office is brightly decorated, with Bible verses and inspirational messages covering the panelled walls, and stacks of literature piled on Green's desk and work table.

Green crosses the room to shake my hand, and I feel a warm energy when our fingers touch. His personality dominates the room, and by the time I sit down I am breathless. He's wearing a comfortable sweatshirt and a pair of faded blue jeans, and comes across disarmingly casual, getting the conversation started by talking about his many books.

'I have the inspiration of a student – I like to study,' he tells me. 'I need to know so many things! There's so much stuff to inspire a person that has to feel like – this is something that I have to do. I have to do it, I have to do it, *I have to do it*. It's like praising God. I learned to praise Him – He showed me how, and I've never forgotten it.'

And, like that, we're off and running. 'Wanting to play music was a draw, a magnetism,' Green says, his bright eyes meeting mine. 'I started in seventh grade singing in the glee club, and I did it until the 12th grade. I got straight 'A's in there, except for one time. So I was drawn to music.

'I didn't know that I wanted to be a musician when I was a boy in Arkansas. I remember that I kept stealing my brother's guitar. My older brother kept telling me, "Don't tune the guitar, don't twist the knobs on it." But I kept stealing it every day – I'd go in the basement to play it. He'd come home from work and he'd hit the guitar – "Blang, dong, dong" – it was out of tune. He'd say, "Albert, have you been messin' with my guitar?" I'd say, "No, I haven't touched it." Man, he'd take me around the corner – "Ka-boom!" "Albert, I told you, you leave that guitar alone!"'

When Green laughs, his eyes crinkle and his entire body shakes. It's an infectious moment, and I have to join in. By the time he resumes the story, I am completely at ease.

'That was on Sycamore Street in Grand Rapids, Michigan,' Green recalls. 'There was something about that musical instrument that I just *had* to play it. I just couldn't help myself. Sometimes I'd walk up and just touch it, and then I'd keep going. I was just whacked out, I guess, in the brain! I just needed to feel it, needed to touch it...'

Green's biblical hero is Moses. He identifies with the idea of the divine birthright and the concept of giving up celebrity to cast your lot with the sick and needy. 'I can relate to that,' he wrote in his autobiography. 'I know what it's like to leave behind the glitter and glamor of the world to seek out a poor and plain existence. I too have walked through the wilderness to find my place at the base of the mountain of God.

'God delivered me from the Egypt of my own vanity and pride, and delivered me to the humblest of circumstances, a place where I could discover the spiritual rewards of sacrifice and service. Like Moses watching over Jethro's flock, so too I was brought to a lowly station to minister to the needs of the poor of spirit.'

But in his office, when I ask about his heroes, he wants to know what I think of Louis Armstrong. I'm confused by this turn in the conversation, but Green smiles as he tells me about Satchmo. 'You know,' he says, 'I knew Mr Armstrong's music, but it didn't appeal to me until I came across a concert on TV one night and got to see how he really put everything into his music.

'He had this basket,' Green recalls, 'and he kept tossing his white handkerchiefs in the basket. He'd use one up and throw it down, and he'd have a pile more. It was *so* good.' He leans back in his chair, eyes closed, savouring the memory.

'At the end of the program, he sang "What A Wonderful World". It was very strange,' Green says. 'He looked too surreal, too... I don't know – he looked too angelic to be something made up. And you have to figure that the man came out during the Depression, during the hard times. He was from the South, New Orleans, and of course he worked in places where he couldn't even sit down and eat, but he could work there in the band. He couldn't even stay at the same hotel he was singing at. He had to go down the road. And then he sings a song – after all the things he's gone through – "What A Wonderful World".'

I am swept away by the lilting cadence of Green's voice, but when he pounds the table with his fist I am suddenly jolted back into the present moment. 'He got the whole world on that song,' Green says, delighted. 'There's some things you have to endure, but it's a special person who can pull through, like a Satchmo, who can come through and write a song like that. Because he's seen it all! His finishing thought, his consummation, is "What A Wonderful World". That's just nice, there. That's real important to me,' he finishes, his beatific smile lighting up the entire room.

Then Lolita interrupts with a message for Rev Green, and he stands up to shake my hand again. 'Well, I won't take up any more of your time,' he says, gracefully ending our interview. As I turn off my tape recorder and make my way to the front door, I can hear his voice echoing down the hall. 'I see skies of blue,' he sings, 'and clouds of white/The bright blessed day, the dark sacred night/And I think to myself, what a wonderful world…' I pause for a moment inside the church vestibule, and just close my eyes and listen. It's a moment I will not soon forget.

GOSPEL IN MEMPHIS
Mike Evans

Although gospel is frequently acknowledged as being part of the fabric of music in both the white and black communities in the South, it often isn't given the attention it perhaps deserves, as part of the environment that produced not only black soul music but white-dominated rock 'n' roll. The gospel influence in soul music is cited in its very name, and traced back in all histories of the genre to the pioneers such as Ray Charles and Sam Cooke, who first broke taboos and 'mixed the sacred and secular', gospel and the blues. However, when the music of early Elvis and the other rockabilly names at Sun is analysed, it's more often than not simply described as a mixture of blues and hillbilly, almost ignoring the fact that church music was as potent a part of the white musical experience as it was of the black.

When Elvis, already a superstar with RCA Records by December 1956, dropped into the Sun Studio as Carl Perkins was finishing a recording, the jam session that ensued with Elvis, Perkins, Jerry Lee Lewis and Johnny Cash became the stuff of legend. Although Cash never appeared on the actual tapes that survived of that session (but was there for the photo-call), the often-bootlegged material came to be known as The Million Dollar Quartet.

What is clear from the repertoire of the ad hoc session, where they relied on songs that were mutually familiar, is the number of spirituals that they included – like 'I Shall Not Be Moved', 'Just A Little Talk With Jesus', 'When God Dips Love In My Heart' and 'When The Saints Go Marching In'. These were songs that were common to both black and white congregations in local churches and on the airwaves of religious broadcasts, often from those same churches. And it was a real part of their musical life too: Johnny Cash had auditioned at Sun with religious songs before Sam Phillips groomed him as a rockabilly singer, Jerry Lee was famously torn between the hot gospel of his family environment and the 'Devil's music' of rock 'n' roll, and Elvis Presley went on to record a huge amount of religious material throughout his career.

Indeed, from the start Elvis was a fan of local gospel acts like The Statesmen, and the Blackwood Brothers Quartet, who recorded for RCA. The latter often sang at the Assembly of God Church the young Presley attended, and as a teenager Elvis even had ambitions to join a group – The Songfellows – which had been formed by a cousin of the Blackwoods.

But long before Elvis's family had even moved to Memphis, the city had a strong gospel heritage. Two of gospel music's greatest composers, Rev Herbert Brewster and Lucie Campbell, came from Memphis, not to mention the great guitarist-gospel singer Sister Rosetta Tharpe. The Dixie Harmonizers were another legendary gospel name, from the 1920s and

'30s, that emanated from the city and worked across America.

Record-wise, gospel music, like blues, was initially often to be found on specialist labels, particularly in the black market place. So when Stax took off it was almost inevitable they would form a subsidiary gospel label, Gospel Truth, although only The Rance Allen Group, an outfit from Detroit, was to meet with any great commercial success. The longest-surviving gospel name in Memphis has to be The Spirit Of Memphis Quartet, who have been going with a changing line-up since the early 1930s. Of late they have adopted a contemporary electric soul-band sound, a crossover backing arrangement for many church vocal groups and choirs in recent years.

And it's in church, as it should be, that you'll hear the best gospel. As well as Al Green's Full Gospel Tabernacle, the Mississippi Boulevard Baptist Church is another great place to hear sacred music. It's not actually on Mississippi Boulevard any more, but can now be found at the corner of Bellevue and Jefferson, about 2km (1 $^1\!/_2$ miles) from downtown.

The Rev Brewster had a saying: 'When grace is in, race is out.' His attitude exemplified the prevailing atmosphere of the modest-sized church that can still be found at 1189 East Trigg in South Memphis, the East Trigg Baptist Church. It was here that congregations crowded in to hear the wondrous gospel of Queen C Anderson and The Brewsteraires each Sunday morning, which was also broadcast live on WDIA. Many of the songs they sang were Rev Brewster's latest compositions. Brewster is counted among a handful of the great gospel music composers, writing classics like 'How I Got Over' for Clara Ward and 'Moving On Up A Little Higher' for Mahalia Jackson. East Trigg is also where Elvis would sometimes sneak off to during the services at the Assembly of God Church.

And, talking gospel, Aretha Franklin didn't simply appear on the fertile Detroit music scene, where she grew up, without having some roots – deep roots that reach all the way to Memphis, the city of her birth, and into the Mississippi Delta. Her famous minister father, Rev CL Franklin, left Clarksdale, Mississippi, to become the minister at the New Salem Missionary Baptist Church, on South Fourth Street, in the early 1940s. During his tenure there, Aretha was born on Lucy Avenue and christened at New Salem. Since 1955, New Salem has also been the spiritual home of The Pattersonaires, a rousing, passionate gospel ensemble that typifies all that is best about the great Memphis gospel tradition.

Anyone waking up in Memphis who wants to explore the world of gospel music, and Memphis gospel music in particular, should visit the Gospel Shop on South Third Street. They've been selling religious paraphernalia to churchgoers for decades now, including Bibles, inspirational books, but (most importantly to the music lover) a great stock of recorded music. Believer or unbeliever, you can scour their CD section for the very best of gospel past and present and, if you're lucky, see and hear one of the live recordings or all-star jams that take place there.

8 Down Mississippi

HARD TIME KILLING FLOOR BLUES
Andria Lisle

I leave Memphis in search of the real country blues juke joint. A decade ago, there were still hundreds of jukes in Mississippi, their names ringing like poetry in the deep Delta night. The Pink Pony Café in Darling, Junior's Place in Chulahoma, Booba Barnes's Playboy Club and the Flowing Fountain in Greenville: those places are all gone, blown down or burned down or simply padlocked for one reason or another, the juke joint quickly assuming the position of dusty museum relic, another addition to our nation's endangered list. Some nights, I am content to put on a copy of *Heartbroken Man*, Booba Barnes's seminal Rooster Blues album, and browse through the pictures in Birney Imes's *Juke Joint*, a full-blown photographic odyssey into the Playboy Club and other bars. But lately the cumulative effect has made me restless, and I itch to hit the dark, open road.

I know of only three jukes in the Delta that open on a regular basis, and the closest to Memphis is a hard 110km (70 mile) drive down Highway 61. That's Lucille Turner's Grill in Clarksdale, a squat building on Issaquena Street in the town's African-American 'New World' section. Like many urban jukes, Turner's features a decent jukebox and a fine soul-food kitchen, with a host of locals happy to accommodate inquisitive visitors. Just south of Clarksdale in Merigold, a gravel road that cuts through vast farmland will take you to the Poor Monkey Lounge, an oddly situated plywood shack featuring DJs Dr Tissue (who reigns supreme on Thursday nights) and the Candy Man. A sign at the door of the Poor Monkey proclaims the joint to be a 'private club' for members only, but a small cover charge will get anyone inside. On Monday nights, rumour has it, the Poor Monkey hosts a handful of curvaceous strippers from Memphis, brought in to liven up the atmosphere. It's a scene I can hardly imagine…

Both Turner's and the Poor Monkey are 'the real deal', but I want to see some live music in a juke setting, so I press onward, cruising through Greenwood on Highway 49, toward Yazoo County. Bentonia – so small it's not on my map – is my final destination. I'm starved, though, so I pull over in Yazoo City for a hamburger at one of those ubiquitous Chinese food and burger joints, a popular combination in the South. My meal is delicious, grilled onions and sharp cheddar cheese almost burning my mouth as I chew. Good food is plentiful around here – catfish farms have brought renewed economic prosperity to the region, and every town boasts its own variation on the product. Fried, blackened, Cajun-spiced, I have eaten more than a dozen catfish filets this month alone, which makes this hamburger even more appetising in comparison.

I've been to Bentonia before, and there are no restaurants in the town. The only businesses I know of are a farm supply store, a tiny grocery that's more often closed than open, a daytime ice-cream stand and a barber-shop. And, of course, the Blue Front Café, where hungry patrons can purchase a bag of pork rinds or spam and crackers, but no hot food. I finish my burger in Yazoo City, and hit the road for the last 30km (20 miles) of my journey to Bentonia. The sky is low, the horizon vast, and stars are everywhere. Cotton has just been planted, the freshly ploughed fields a loamy, deep-brown colour. Mosquitoes from the nearby Yazoo River are annoyingly persistent, causing me to roll up my windows and turn on the air conditioner. My headlights glance off the sign for the Bentonia exit, and I turn left off 49.

In this rural hamlet (population 300), nestled between Yazoo City and Jackson, the state capital, the blues have taken on a supernatural quality. Bentonia resident Nehemiah 'Skip' James put the town on the map back in 1931, when he first recorded 'Devil Got My Woman Blues', his agonising wail soaring high above the eerie E-minor chords of his guitar. Haunting, lonely and utterly heart-wrenching, 'Devil Got My Woman' sprang back into national prominence when James was rediscovered in the mid-1960s, then again in 2001, when it was featured in the film *Ghost World*.

The scene from the movie is unforgettable: Enid, an overly cynical teenager, has met Seymour, a record-collecting geek more than twice her age, while purchasing a blues album from him at a yard sale. When the first notes of 'Devil Got My Woman' come out of her cheap bedroom stereo, she stands stock-still, as if in a trance. Enid plays the cut over and over again, mesmerised by the loneliness, the longing and the sorrow emanating from the speakers. James's voice transcends time – and all other barriers – as it washes over her weeping form.

It's doubtful that many people who have seen *Ghost World* will ever go to Bentonia, and even more unlikely that any of the town's residents have seen the film. But Skip James is just the tip of the iceberg as far as the local blues scene goes. Of course, 'Skippy' – as the locals call him – is long gone, as are the Stuckey brothers, Henry and Jacob, James's cousins who also played. And a few years ago, the world lost Jack Owens, another guitarist in the Bentonia style, who many – including musicologist Dr David Evans – say played and sang even better than James did. But Bud Spires, Owens' irascible sidekick, still picks up his harmonica on occasion, blowing and wheezing in an odd droning style that perfectly complements the minor guitar chords popular in Bentonia blues.

Bud can oftentimes be found at the Blue Front Café, open an astounding seven nights a week. Located on Railroad Avenue downtown, the Blue Front serves as the nucleus for the local black community, a place to drink beer and listen to music after a long workday out in the fields or in nearby Jackson. With its cinder-block walls and dimly lit interior, the Blue Front beckons like a desert oasis in this steamy-hot (and long ago shuttered) Delta town. Jimmy 'Duck' Holmes, currently the only acoustic guitarist on the local scene, has owned and operated the café for decades.

'Henry Stuckey introduced me to my first guitar,' Duck, a tall man in his 50s, explains. 'The Stuckeys lived next door to us, and I grew up hearing them play the blues.' Despite the gathering dusk, he wears a baseball cap to shield his eyes as we stand outside, leaning on his brand-new pick-up truck. Duck drives a farmer's vehicle and wears a farmer's clothes – denim workshirt and Levis. But the cleanliness of his truck and the carefully starched creases in his jeans make it clear that he works in town, not out in the fields.

'It was Jack Owens who actually taught me to play. Jack had a juke joint in his house out in the country, and we had the Blue Front in town.' Mary Johnson Holmes, Duck's mother, opened her juke in 1947, raising 14 children – ten of her own, and four of her siblings – on the side. Thirteen kids went on to college – 'the last one wanted to be a farmer', Duck ascertains. 'After I graduated from Jackson State University, I came on ship at the café – my mother groomed me into it.' That was 32 years ago.

The set-up is simple – a low-ceilinged, wide, musty place, with a plain wooden bar anchored on one side of the room. A crowd congregates around the cash register, vying for attention from the pretty girl behind the bar, drinking their beers as fast as she can serve them. Duck's cousin Willie Earl, a strapping, handsome man, smiles flirtatiously. Willie Earl is a deaf mute, but the handicap hardly slows him down. He can say more with his eyes than some folks can with a thousand words, and reads lips easily. As long as I'm at the Blue Front, my beers are on him.

Posters advertising Budweiser and Colt 45 malt liquor – a juke joint staple – adorn the walls, alongside photographs of Japanese tourists and, even more incongruous, a Hollywood film crew who shot a Levi's commercial outside the Blue Front a few years ago. Near the bathroom, a velvet portrait of Stevie Wonder sits on a dusty shelf, forgotten. The floor back here is littered with cigarette butts and bottle caps, and the smell from the damp plywood room that hides the commode rises, threateningly, as the door is opened.

Back in the main room, chitlin' soul circuit favourites Mel Waiters and Bobby Rush blare from the jukebox, prompting a couple or two to begin a slow grind on the makeshift dance floor. There's more action outside on the front porch, and at the barber-shop in the back of the building. When he's in the mood, Duck unplugs the jukebox and picks up his battered guitar. 'Skippy used to play here,' he casually remarks. 'We called him that because of that sporty walk he had, you know. Sonny

Boy Williamson used to come through, and Muddy Waters – before he was known, of course.'

Duck plays with some hesitation, and it takes a song or two before he hits his stride. But when the feeling overtakes him, he can let out a powerful moan, broodingly picking his guitar as he summons up an other-worldly blues sound. 'Well, the people are drifting, from door to door,' he sings on an intense rendition of James's 'Hard Time Killing Floor Blues'. 'Can't find no heaven, I don't care where they go…' The song is an appropriate choice, as the city of Bentonia has been giving Duck a hard time of late, trying to shut down the Blue Front. 'The mayor, Tommy Hancock, is a die-hard racist,' Duck says. 'He can't deal with tourists coming by here, so he sends his henchmen to run people off the parking lot. I tell him that the only reason Bentonia is known worldwide is because of the blues, but he's so set in those old ways that it's like a cancer sore just eatin' him up!

'I have to go to court next Friday,' Duck concludes, signalling an end to this interview. 'They cut my water off, and when I called to get it turned back on, I had to call the police department, because they're also the power company. The next day they arrested me, saying I called 911 under false pretenses.

'I am a warrior,' he proclaims on his way to the door. 'I'm determined to stick it out. They might burn me down, but they won't shut me down.' Skip James sang it, and now Duck Holmes lives it: 'Well, you hear me singin' my lonesome song, these hard times can last us so very long.'

I return to the bar for a last round with Willie Earl before making my way to the car. Slamming the door and buckling my seatbelt, I say my goodbyes, then slowly head north toward home, worrying about Duck's hard-time Mississippi blues. It's enough, I realise, to make me weep.

FROM SENEGAL TO SENATOBIA
Andria Lisle

It's unbearably hot in Memphis this August – on the ten o'clock news, the weatherman calls it the 'dog days' of summer, the hottest month on record since the 1930s. Daytime is sweltering, with the temperature climbing up into the hundreds. After the sun goes down, it's still miserably warm, and my dogs and cats lie stretched out on the hardwood floors indoors, too exhausted to chase each other. When I go to the kitchen for a glass of water or another beer, Tishomingo, my black-and-white spotted feist dog, lifts his chin and cocks an ear, then settles back down, unwilling to move any further. In my backyard, only the cicadas are happy. Even in the city, they pleasantly whirr, crowding out most other noises as they provide a rhythmic accompaniment to my typing.

Despite the heat, August is a busy month down here – there's Death Week, the Memphis Music and Heritage Festival, the WLOK Stone Soul Picnic and various other end-of-summer celebrations to attend in town, as well as the Sunflower Blues Festival in Clarksdale, Mississippi. By the last weekend of the month, it all comes to a head – the drinking, the socialising and the good music – at Othar Turner's annual Labor Day picnic in Gravel Springs, Mississippi.

Situated in the heart of the hill country, Gravel Springs is a locale so minute it doesn't even merit a dot on my Mississippi map. New Town and Thyatira, which border Gravel Springs to the east and west, are similar-size communities – blink once while driving through and you're sure to miss them. The closest municipality, Senatobia, which straddles I-55 and Highway 6 just northwest of Gravel Springs, represents town to most folks in the area who work and shop at the truck stops, fast-food restaurants and Wal-Mart clustered at the interstate exit. Still others travel up I-55 to Memphis, over 60km (40 miles) away, for better-paying jobs and a big city future.

Ask anyone at Wal-Mart or one of the convenience stores in Senatobia if they know of any blues musicians in the area, and you're more than likely to get a baleful stare. For the majority of Senatobians, the blues is an antiquated, country tradition, and one they seem hell-bent on distancing themselves from with their Nike shoes, Tommy Hilfiger wardrobes and shiny SUVs (Sport Utility Vehicles). Rap music – from Memphis, New Orleans and beyond – provides the soundtrack for their lives, updated versions of the existence their parents and grandparents eked out, lifestyles sponsored by credit cards rather than extended loans and the hope of a good cotton crop.

Yet in parts of the hill country, the older blues tradition still rings true. Fred McDowell, Blind Sid Hemphill, Napoleon Strickland and Ed, Lonnie and Cag Young are long gone, but others have taken up the slack: Glen Faulkner picks out tunes on the one-stringed diddley bow, Jessie Mae Hemphill (Sid's granddaughter) plays mean, rhythmic guitar chords, and Othar Turner and his Rising Star Fife And Drum Band occasionally get together to recreate a rare and ancient sound.

'I never expected to see this African behavior in the hills of Mississippi,' Alan Lomax would write in *The Land Where The Blues Began*. But that's exactly what Lomax found when – travelling Mississippi in search of indigenous music on the behalf of the Library of Congress in the 1940s – he ran across the fiddle player Blind Sid Hemphill. In 1942, Lomax recorded Hemphill playing the panpipe (or quills) at a picnic in Sledge. 'It was music harsh and crude and vital and as rank as milkweed,' Lomax wrote, 'a tune such as the African Pygmies have played from time immemorial.'

Then, in 1959, when Lomax returned to the hill country, he ran across Ed Young, whose family band played the first Mississippi fife and drum music the musicologist was able to record. The tradition, Lomax deduced, originated in Senegal, was brought to this country by slaves, and has existed as a remote blues form in north Mississippi ever since. As a musical form, it stood in stark contrast to the military fife and drum music Lomax was familiar with. 'Consider first', he wrote, '*the Spirit of '76*, three musicians marching into battle, proud, erect...another thing entirely from the Young brothers, slouching along with their hip twisting, their hot licks, and an occasional Watusi leap. One message was writ large,' Lomax concluded. 'This was Africa come to life in America.'

Inspired, he returned in 1967 to further document the phenomenon: nine years later he filmed a weekend of partying, or 'frolicking' as the locals call it. Folklorist George Mitchell also detailed the musical picnics in his book *Blow My Blues Away* and captured several of the events on audiotape. Both Lomax and Mitchell focused on Othar Turner, a first-generation bluesman who learned to blow the fife in the mid-1920s. For more than half a century, Othar has been the hill country's preeminent fife musician and, consequently, the most recorded.

'The shrill whistle of the fife is sounded,' Mitchell wrote of one of Othar's performances, 'its piercing notes cleaving the heavy afternoon air. Soon the drums add a frenzied rhythm to the fife's wailing. The musicians reel and twist from one end of the field to the other as they play. Without moving from where they are, men and women begin to sway their bodies to the wild rhythm. Laughing kids leap around and in and out between the drums.

'The drunken shouts join with the booming, and the smell of gyrating bodies merges with that of beer and whiskey,' continued Mitchell. 'The drums change hand frequently, but the fife blower, so wrapped up in the sounds of his cane that he is almost oblivious to the revel around him, continues without interruption into the night. A young woman in a tight white dress jumps in front of him and begins to undulate her hips slowly, working until her whole body is quivering and lurching. The men cheer her on. The fife player cocks his head upward, bending his back toward the ground, and blows the same riff again and again until she finally collapses into an onlooker's arms. By this time, most of the crowd is panting, pitching, reeling. For two more days, the frenzy will go on.'

Compare Mitchell's account to footage from this year's picnic, and you'll find that not much has changed. Black men, for the most part neatly dressed and compactly built, lean on shiny cars and dusty pick-up trucks parked in front of Othar's tiny, patchwork house, boasting about their vehicles, their wives, their crops. The women and children are gathered around a picnic area set under a shade tree, where Turner's daughters Betty, Dorothy, Nettie and Bernice sell beer, Coca-Cola, fried fish and barbecued goat.

Copies of Othar's most recent CDs, *Everybody Hollerin' Goat* and *From Senegal To Senatobia*, are listed for sale on a makeshift marquee, along with handmade fifes, which go for $75. Downhill, at an outdoor stage, a guitarist idly strums his instrument, killing time before the big crowd shows up. The drums, two bass drums and a marching snare, sit waiting beside him on the rough plywood.

Behind the concession stand and the stage, Othar's farm sprawls to the south. The smells of fresh manure, hog slop and cut hay mingle – not unpleasantly – with the aroma of cooked fish and goat. Corn liquor, an illegal delicacy, can be purchased if you know the right people. The scene is unique and, despite the inevitable cycles of birth and death and teenage fashion, attending the picnic takes you back in time – to the '50s, the '40s, to the days when slaves' meetings were clandestine affairs that depended on drum signals, then back in boats to West Africa, where the music originated.

While Othar is resting at a picnic table before the party gets rolling, I ask him how he got his start. The short dark man, still spry at 94 years, lifts his baseball cap ('I love my Grandpaw', it reads) to scratch his fluffy white hair. He's been up, working, since 5am, and he has a long evening ahead of him. He sighs, and spits in the dust. Finally, Othar looks out to the road yonder and waves to a passing truck, adjusting his braces before he begins to talk.

'When I was just a boy, I heard an old man called RE Williams blowing the fife,' Othar tells me. 'We were pickin' cotton, and had to come out of the field when it rained. I asked Mr Williams what he was doing, and he showed me the fife. I asked him to make me one of 'em, and he said "If you be a good boy, be smart and listen to your mama, and obey her, I might make you a fife." About four weeks later, he told me to come by, and he made me one. I made my mama mad, but I learned how to play. She'd say, "Put that dadblamed cane down, I'm tired of it!" But I kept on and learned how to blow it.

'One day, I could hear the music at a picnic, and I begged my mama to take me. I heard it – "Boom, boom" – and I said, "Mama, I hear the folks playing them things. Let me go see 'em. Mama, please." The men playing the fife and drums were on the side of a porch so I stood over there lookin'.' Othar is an enigmatic storyteller, and when I close my eyes to imagine the scene he's describing, I'm almost there.

Will Edwards, a tall, brown-skinned man – 'an old man back then', as Turner recalls – noticed the boy. '"Hey, Sonny!" Mr Edwards called. He said, "What are you lookin' at?" "I'm lookin' at you." "You reckon you could do that?" "Yes–" "No, you ain't gonna do that." And I said, "I'm gonna try." And he said, "That's the boldest words you ever said – if you try, you'll probably do it." So he put the drum around my neck. He said, "Now look. Take your time and play that drum, walk right around here, then come on back. And don't hit it hard! Play it in the middle, don't play it on the edge." You can bust a drum playing it on the edge. You have to play it right in the center. So I did it! And he said, "Hey son, go back there and do it again." And I did it again.'

Othar takes a sip from a water bottle pulled from his hip pocket, neatly wipes his face with a faded blue handkerchief, and continues the story. 'Mr Edwards said, "Son, you surprised me. I never thought you could've done that. I'm gonna give you a job." And he gave me one, playing the drum in his band. We'd get up and leave home at five o'clock in the morning. Put two quilts in the wagon – that's to keep the nails from sticking a hole in your drums. We'd hang a lantern in front of the wagon tongue and one behind, and then we'd leave home. I played all down south, over to Sardis and Como. We'd go everywhere. I was a youngster, playing the drum. And they'd all shout, "Look at that boy! Play it, son!"'

Like many of Othar's stories, there's a moral. 'That's what I'm trying to tell you – you just gotta try. If you start something, start it right. Because if you never try to get up, you ain't gonna get it! But if you try to get up, and the Lord'll let you – if you try, then you can do that. And if you don't, you won't. You can't doubt yourself. If you never try, you'll never know. That's something to think about,' he sagely notes, taking another pull off the water bottle.

Othar was born in Rankin County, in the middle of the state, in 1908, but he was raised in north Mississippi, where his mother was from. His parents separated when he was three months old, and he never knew his father. They met once, when Othar was a teenager, in the middle of the road near Gravel Springs. 'He was riding a bay horse,' Othar tells me, 'and he didn't recognize me or my sister Rosie. Mama had to tell him who we were. My daddy, his name was Ollie Evans, asked me to come away with him, but I told him I had to stand by my mama. She raised me up.'

Othar's blue eyes are about the only thing he got from his father. 'Ollie was part Indian,' he says, 'Chickasaw or Choctaw, I don't know which.' When I pursue the matter, he's suddenly cantankerous. 'Hell, I don't know if he was an Indian – for all I know, he was part goat. Hey, now!' Othar slaps his thigh, and steers the conversation back to his mother's side of the family.

Othar helped his mother, Betty Turner, look after his sisters, and worked as a sharecropper in Tate and Panola counties. He's had two wives – his second marriage, to Ada, lasted for six decades, until her death in the mid-1990s. Othar and Ada raised four daughters and a son on their own 0.8 hectare (2 acres) of land, growing corn, peas, sweet potatoes and cotton, while fishing and hunting to supplement the chicken and pigs they slaughtered. It's been a hard life, but a good one, and from what he tells me Othar has no regrets.

'My granddaddy taught me to tend to my business,' Othar says. 'Be careful, and be mindful of how you treat other people. And that will make you successful in life! My mama taught me that there's white people and colored people. There's some good white people, and there's some mean white people. And there's some good colored people, and some mean colored people. So I honor white people and colored people – no matter which you is.'

Othar defers to the older white men in the community, calling them 'boss man', even though he's at least 30 years their senior. And, although we've been friends for more than a decade, he called me 'ma'am' for five years, referring to me as 'that wide-faced girl' when he talked to his daughters in private. But over the last few years we've grown closer, and he finally calls me Andria, although Bernice still gets tickled about my nickname. Yancey Allison, my photographer friend, will be called Nancy for ever – apparently, Othar is getting hard of hearing, and mistook her name for something more recognisable. Our familiarity, however, has forged a bond that would have been impossible in the old days.

'You used to didn't catch a white laughing or talking with no colored people, didn't shake hands with 'em,' Othar told George Mitchell in the 1960s. 'They used to didn't do that. But now, not here, but in town or up in Chicago and all, [they] just laugh and talk, sit down at the table. I've seen the times, you just dare to be sitting up on this porch. You couldn't sit here and talk, and I couldn't either. There's a man come in here quick and tell you, "Don't be caught on my place, around my hands, my niggers, no more." That's what he say. That's why I say it's better. This is my house. Nobody tell you nothing.'

Today, it's the one thing that's noticeably different: folks come from as far away as Europe, Australia and Japan to celebrate Labor Day in Gravel Springs. Car doors slam and trucks drive past on OB McClinton Highway to bring party-goers to the picnic; college kids eager for an authentic blues experience drive down from Memphis for the weekend. The entire world is welcome to dance and drink past midnight and well into the next morning, then rest, and do it all over again. White, black and every shade in between, we all laugh and sweat, shaking off the heat of the summer.

A dark-skinned man in dungarees and a ragged, buttonless shirt beckons to me, wanting a dance. His beard is long and white, and perspiration drips off his body, quickly evaporating in the dust. He gulps from his whisky bottle then recaps it, reaching for me. I try to shrug him off, but my rejection makes him more persistent. 'I'm the best dancer here,' he proclaims, moving his feet in an intricate pattern. I point to the friends I came with, singling out one man as my boyfriend. 'Aw, he don't care if you dance with me,' I'm told, and suddenly I'm yanked into the middle of the quaking, writhing throng.

Othar is taking a break, and RL Boyce, his bass drummer, plays a set of open-tuned bottleneck blues on a beat-up guitar. Luther and Cody Dickinson accompany him, while Kenny Brown, another hill-country guitarist, waits for his turn with the group. I take a sip of whisky, then throw my head back and see the moon, just a shiny sliver in the summer sky. I've been reading Borges, and a poem from *The Iron Coin* enters my mind: 'There is so much loneliness in that gold/The moon of the nights is not the moon/Whom the first Adam saw. The long centuries/Of human vigil have filled her/With ancient lament. Look at her. She is your mirror.'

I look and look, as I whirl around, reaching for my partner's strong hand. We stumble together, and the spell is broken as we laughingly make our way to the sidelines. RL puts down his guitar, just as Othar's granddaughter Sharde Thomas urges the drummers to pick up their instruments. Only 12 years old, Sharde is already a precocious performer, and she calls out songs like 'Shimmy She Wobble' and 'Little Sally Walker' with authority. 'Ride, Sally, ride', she commands, as Othar watches the drummers closely, encouraging them one minute and cajoling them the next.

'Shake it to the east, shake it to the west, shake it to the one that you love the best', Sharde sings, mimicking the older dancers with her risqué movements. Next to her grandfather, she's the best fife blower in Tate County, and her notes carry over the roar of the crowd as she finishes one song and begins another. The youngest member of the Rising Star band, Sharde is indefatigable.

Eventually, Othar takes over, calling for 'Glory, Glory Hallelujah'. The party is wrapping up for the night and, as custom dictates, things must end with a gospel number. Alternating between blowing the tune and rejoicing in the words – 'I'm goin' home, Lord, higher and higher, when I lay my burden down' – Othar marches off into the distance, his music shimmering, then fading as the future approaches.

JUST ASK FOR MR CALDWELL
Mike Evans

The Sunday-morning drive down to Holly Springs, Mississippi, 50km (30 miles) or so south of Memphis on Highway 78, was leisurely enough, and relaxed save for the fire and brimstone warnings of hell and damnation from a Bible-thumping preacherman on the car radio. The mission was to find Mr Caldwell, proprietor of the Akei Pro record store. I'd been told his shop was a treasure trove of blues, and advised that only black folks in those parts would be likely to know where it was.

Cruising round the oven-baked main square, it looked like a ghost town, dusty and deserted. Couldn't see anyone to ask directions from, black or white, till down an even dustier side road I spied a handful of middle-aged black men sitting outside a tumbledown shack, its corrugated tin roof rusting gently in the sunshine. As I approached I realised I need look no further, for 'AKAI PRO RECORDS SHOP' above the door told me this was it, though the darkened interior behind the firmly closed door suggested it wasn't open for business. 'I'm looking for Mr Caldwell.' 'That's Mr Caldwell over there.' They gestured to a man in T-shirt and jeans, clearly in his 70s, who came over at the mention of his name.

I explained I was from London, visiting Memphis, had heard of his shop, was he opening up this morning? 'No, I'm going to church…' (Of course, that's why the town was deserted, everyone was probably on their way to church) '…but I'll be back after lunch if you'd like to come back then.'

A drive across to Oxford, Mississippi, filled in lunchtime, the main square of the college town neat as a new pin compared to Holly Springs. Red, white and blue bunting was hanging from the balconies above the storefronts – it was coming up to Fourth of July – this was small-town America, just like the movies. Lunch at a Mexican restaurant confirmed that some things don't change much in this part of the world, like you can't be served a beer on a Sunday, no matter how hot the sun outside or the chilli inside.

Arriving back in Holly Springs, Mr Caldwell was waiting outside his shop, now dressed in Sunday-best suit right out of church, unlocking the door as I greeted him. 'Come on in… There's not much room.' I'm not sure now what I expected to see: neat rows of CDs, vinyl – 78s even – like in any record store, something like that. I certainly wasn't prepared for a mountain of broken radios, in-car cassette players, old TV sets, piled up in haphazard fashion, at some points touching the low ceiling. 'Just climb over here… I guess this is what you're looking for.'

Risking injury, I picked my way over the metal, wire and plastic scrapheap to find the four walls of the shop lined with row after row of music – jazz, gospel, rock 'n' roll, kitsch pop, country, and (most importantly) blues.

David Caldwell has been famous as a source of facts 'n' info on the North Mississippi blues scene ever since he moved from his native Nebraska to the area and opened the shop back in the 1950s. An Army veteran, he moved to the area before the rise of the Civil Rights Movement. In those tumultuous days in the '50s and '60s, he became an activist, and was to see the black voting rate rise from 14 people to 75 per cent of all the people, the town now having a black sheriff and black mayor.

As he explained to Andria Lisle in *Mojo* magazine, a company called Walker Bros were the previous occupants and somehow the name evolved into Akai Pro's – 'Selling records was the first thing I wanted to do'. At its peak, by the early '60s his enterprise extended to a chain of 11 stores over Mississippi and Arkansas, but now he's back to the original one, where his passion for music is partly subsidised by the radio and TV repairs work that dominates his shop space.

But the music is his first love, and he thumbs speedily through hundreds of brown-paper-sleeved 45s, casette tapes and CDs at my prompting – Johnny Ace, Lucille Bogan, he knows exactly where to find them.

Apparently Mr Caldwell is regularly visited by students from 'Ole Miss', the University of Mississippi in Oxford, honing up on their southern history or preparing their blues thesis. Postcards from Holland, Germany, Japan are pinned to the wall.

After 20 minutes or so I've spent over $60, and now he's laying a freebie on me, someone new I've not heard of, 'but you just gotta hear it'. Giving me a firm farewell handshake, he tells me where there's a juke-joint session later in the week, 'just in case you can make it down'.

PLANTATION MENTALITY?
Andria Lisle

Located some 110km (70 miles) south of Memphis in the Mississippi Delta, Clarksdale (with a population of 20,000) is considered a 'big city'. Regardless of size, Clarksdale does have plenty to boast about – it's the birthplace of Ike Turner, Sam Cooke, Little Junior Parker, Son House, John Lee Hooker and a wealth of less famous, but equally talented, Delta bluesmen. Over the last few decades, the city's fortune has waxed and waned, and as the cotton industry has declined the blues has become a marketable commodity. But much of the white population refuses to acknowledge the primitive sounds emanating from the area, a music that has nevertheless attracted fans and scholars from around the world.

'That's why I organized the first Exile on Sunflower Street festival – it was in reaction to the Coahoma Tourism Commission's refusal to fund the education program at the Sunflower Blues Festival,' Nancy Kossman, the proprietor of Delia's Stackhouse, tells me one lazy fall afternoon. 'Jimmy Walker, the head of the commission, got into my face when we were trying to get John Lee Hooker here – he told us that no one would travel any distance to hear a black man play a guitar! This is the head of the Tourism Commission! So I decided to hold my own little festival – I decided that I could ask the Tourism Commission for money then raise a stink when they turned me down. So I did, and they did, and then I put the festival together anyway. That's the plantation mentality – black folks – let's make money off them, and then not give them any of it!'

Nancy, who reopened the Stackhouse after its owner, musicologist Jim O'Neal, relocated to Kansas City, Missouri, just happens to have white skin. But she's always identified with the underdog, and has been an outspoken advocate for Clarksdale's population of 'black folks' since arriving in the Delta in the late 1970s.

'I came to Mississippi in 1978 to work for Legal Services,' Nancy says, leaning on the counter as she talks. 'I married a man from Greenville, then we moved up to Cleveland in 1979 and went into private practice. In 1987, I went to work for Congressman Mike Espy, and that's how I got to know Clarksdale. He had me working here as a field representative. I was really interested in this city – I knew that the blues were from here, but I didn't know much about it. Then I met people that were really into the music scene, like Jim O'Neal and Patty Johnson. Sid Graves got me interested in the Delta Blues Museum, and I started doing research for them – birth dates and death dates, and birthplaces and stuff like that.'

While Nancy talks, I wander around her one-room store, which is named for O'Neal's 7-year-old daughter. The cardboard boxes full of dusty 78s are a record collector's dream come true, while the plethora of tapes and CDs could amp up even a cursory blues fan's curiosity level. A stack of astrology books – Nancy's own – rest on a wooden bookcase, which, she's quick to tell you, came from William Faulkner's house in Oxford. Postcards, paintings by James 'Super Chikan' Johnson, a guitarist and artist, and drawings by Delia O'Neal and her older brother Louis, cover the walls. The overall effect is 'down-home' – and, true to that sentiment, only about half the items in the Stackhouse are for sale. The rest, of course, are Nancy's personal possessions.

'You can't live in the Delta without feeling really horrible about the poverty and the way black folks are treated here and stuff,' Nancy says, drawing me back into the conversation. 'I saw Sid's idea for the museum as a really good way to bring money into the local economy and help black folks feel better about their culture, because the music started having such a positive effect on people.

'I saw the blues as a tool to boost the economy. The museum was in pretty pitiful shape back then,' Nancy says, shaking her head. 'I started hanging out there, and then I started working at the Stackhouse in 1993. My husband and I had separated, and I was living in Clarksdale year-round. I moved to Kansas City to help Jim O'Neal with his kids, but once they got into school I decided to return to Clarksdale. There's something about the Delta that I love – I really can't articulate it, but it's got something to do with the agricultural rhythms.'

'Clarksdale is so far behind the times,' Nancy says. 'It's been a real loss of innocence, trying to make the museum nicer and keep tourists coming into town. But the city doesn't want to fuel the income it gets from the blues back into the culture it comes from. There's a real danger that if the political people have their way we'll have a little version of Beale Street. But, then again,' she sighs, 'things might continue to stumble along in their own weird, funky way. That's what I think people are coming here looking for.'

'I guess I'm a contrarian', Nancy admits, 'because I don't want to see Clarksdale get too organized. We're moving from the Piscean age into the Aquarian age, and there's a real paradigm shift going on. People are moving away from corporate cookie-cutter stuff, and looking for the real deal. Now whether Clarksdale will stay this way, or if the people who run things will get it their way, all fixed-up and shiny, remains to be seen. It could go either way...'

Our conversation is interrupted when the bell on the Stackhouse front door chimes, signalling a visitor. It's Mae Smith, an employee of the Delta Blues Museum, stopping in on her way home from work to commiserate with Nancy about the current state of the blues.

'A man from South Africa came into the museum today, and he said "Didn't I see you last night?" I had to think about it for a minute, but then I said, "Oh yeah, you came through my line at Kroger's,"' Mae laughs, her voice a deep, throaty tickle. It's true that she has to hold down two jobs to make a living in Clarksdale, but she's quick to find humour in the situation.

'When I was a student at the University of Mississippi, I worked in the Blues Archives there,' Mae tells me. 'I used to brag about how, after I graduated from Ole Miss, I was going to go somewhere else – I would never come back to Clarksdale! But of course I ended up coming home… My mom was diagnosed with cancer, and I'm an only child, so I came back to take care of her. I began working at the Delta Blues Museum, and I began to feel like this was something I *needed* to do – I am from this area, and this is part of my culture, too. I felt like I could make an impact, and help to change things.'

The museum, formerly located in the town's Carnegie Library, is now in its own building downtown. 'We have more space,' Mae says of the move, which took place seven years ago. 'We can spread our exhibits out, and we have classrooms for our educational program. The kids who are in Dr Mike's guitar class can practice without people complaining about the volume. I redid the Robert Johnson exhibit, and last week I put back up the Son House exhibit,' Mae says, running down the grocery list of changes that have occurred.

At the Delta Blues Museum, Mae has found her calling. 'I started out as part of the staff, then got promoted to Gift Shop Manager. I started doing tours, too. It wasn't like I went through any training; they were basically like, "You're all we've got, and we need you to do this!" I remember being so nervous when I first started conducting the tours. I was afraid I didn't know enough to tell people about the blues – I guess I didn't realize how much I already knew. One day I took a group of Germans on a tour. They spoke very little English, and they had a translator with them. So I would talk a little while, and then the translator would tell them what I said, then translate their questions back to me. At that point, I realized that I did have a gift for this, because these people really seemed to understand – even through the translator – what I was saying. I got a lot of confidence from that, and suddenly I knew that this was what I wanted to do.

'I feel that where we are now, we have the potential for real growth,' Mae says forcefully. 'There is progress – but some people have negative feelings and opinions that can get in the way of that progress. I think that instead of just including a certain group of people, there should be community involvement with everybody from both sides – no matter what side of the tracks you're from, you should be allowed to contribute to the city.'

Mae is just getting warmed up. 'You know, the musicians aren't even involved most of the time – just a certain group makes all the decisions, and I don't think it should be like that,' she says. 'There are a few blacks involved, but not many. Clarksdale is like a melting pot, and there are so many different people here with ideas that could help the city grow. But so many people don't feel like they're part of the community. They need to be allowed to get involved, to feel the growth, and really *see* the progress, instead of just a few leading citizens running the whole show. They fight and bicker against each other when they should be trying to find common ground.

'I go through a lot of trials and tribulations – these last few years have been a little rough,' Mae admits, 'but I always come back to work. I like people. One lady at the museum said that when I start doing tours, I really light up and become a whole new person. I'm known as a dependable person, so everybody comes to me with their problems. They say, "I never see you unhappy", but I tell 'em that looks can be deceiving. But, you know, you get more wrinkles when you frown.

'People create false personas for themselves – they say that we're one big happy family, and that we all get along. They go to places they normally wouldn't go to, trying to show that they're down with the blues,' Mae claims. 'But it's a front – they hang out at the country club, or someplace upscale like Ground Zero. They'd rather be caught dead than be seen at Sarah's Kitchen or Smitty's – one of these juke joints. They want to make the world to think that we're all great, but once the tourists go home, things go back to the old way, which is "I work with you, but I don't want to hang out with you." Now, they have a select few they hang out with, so they can say, "I have black friends – I'm not racist."

'When I moved back to town, and I was looking for a place to live, some people told me, "Now, Mae, you don't want to live over there – you need to live over here." They were saying that now I am above the ghetto, and I don't need to associate with those people now that I work at the blues museum. I'm a house nigger, and I don't need to associate with those field niggers.' Mae's laughing while she tells me this, but then her big brown eyes get even bigger, and she falls silent as she realises the enormity of her words. She glances at her watch, and exclaims, 'I'm gonna be late for my shift at the grocery store. Gotta run,' she cries, and with that she's gone.

I leave, too, headed for Roger and Jennifer Stolle's new store, Cat Head, located just a few hundred metres from Delia's Stackhouse, in a Delta Avenue storefront. Cat Head opened its doors during last year's Sunflower Blues Festival, a regular destination for blues fans since its début in 1988. Just a few months ago, I made my day down a crowded sidewalk, intent on catching bluesman T-Model Ford's free set at Cat Head in between acts at the festival. The store was packed – blues fans stood shoulder to shoulder amidst paintings, pottery and wooden carvings, enjoying the cool air as much as the hypnotic music. I poked my head in the door, looked around and then settled down on the hot pavement out front, content to avoid the crowd.

Today, Cat Head is much quieter. A couple from nearby Cleveland stop in to buy a miniature replica of Clarksdale's much-touted 'crossroads' sculpture, which stands at the intersection of highways 61 and 49, but after they leave I am the only customer. The Stolles greet me from the back of the store, a rustic building that once housed a jewellery shop. As newcomers to the community, I hope they can shed light on the hotly contested disparity between the tourism council and area businesspeople.

'I'm originally from Dayton, Ohio,' Roger, a lanky 35-year-old with a Midwestern drawl, tells me. 'I have a Journalism degree, went into marketing and advertising, and ended up in St Louis, Missouri. So this move for us was like a night-and-day thing.'

'We met after college,' Jennifer explains. 'About ten months after we got married, we moved to St Louis. I worked in the marketing department at Anheuser-Busch. I'm a print buyer; I know how to work with designers. Roger and I both come from a creative field, but we've got the business side of it down, too. After awhile, we were creatively dead in St Louis – we were both working around the clock, and were really stressed out about our jobs. We would work and work to be able to come down here on vacation – we'd recently discovered folk art, and were already really into music.'

'The real turning point for us, with music and Mississippi, was going to Junior Kimbrough's juke joint,' Roger interjects. 'That was in early 1996.

'We went down to Junior's on a Sunday afternoon,' he says. 'There was a little bit of activity going on outside, and we got out of the car kinda sheepishly. We'd never been in that kind of place before! It was bright outside, that end of the afternoon sunlight, and I tried to look in, but the windows were so dark I couldn't see what was going on inside. Somebody said, "You can come on in," and there was Junior sitting in his recliner. People started showing up – RL Burnside came in, David Kimbrough, and tons of locals. Of course nobody knew anybody's names, so we were called "St Louis". And we'd been into Chicago blues and old Delta blues for quite a while, but it was so exciting to see these young people play it.'

'And in the back of my mind, I was thinking that Roger married a good woman, because not too many girls would be willing to come to a place like this,' Jennifer adds, with a laugh. 'We had been told, and had read, that the blues were dead, and new blues didn't exist anymore. So going to Junior's place was one of those life experiences, a real revelation.'

'To see people alive today, making their own sound, was incredible,' Roger says. 'Junior opened the door for us, and then we met T-Model Ford and Pat Thomas. And, of course, all the juke joints were decorated with folk art, and that really opened something up for us.'

'I would tell people stories when I got back to work in St Louis, and no one believed what I told them,' Jennifer claims. 'The metropolitan St Louis area has more people than the entire state of Mississippi. There are also true dividing lines in St Louis – the races are really split geographically. And so it's hard to believe that, six hours away from where we lived, could be a world that's so different and so amazing.'

But neither of them was ready to get further involved. 'I had a bee in my bonnet about galleries,' Roger tells me. 'I felt like so many galleries were taking advantage of their artists, and that a lot of outsider artists weren't getting their fair share of the take. Of course, there is overhead, and all the work that's involved with selling something, it's a fairer situation than I initially thought. I'm a big believer in perception being reality – and I don't want to be perceived as someone taking advantage of the artists, which is why I wasn't sure I wanted to open a gallery. But we'd reached a saturation point,' Roger says, naming artists they'd collected from all over the South, like John Henry Toney, Butch Anthony, Buddy Snipes, Lonnie Holley, and Joe and Rosalie Light, 'and we couldn't buy any more art for our home.'

'We'd been coming down to Clarksdale for seven years, and one night we sat around talking, just thinking out loud and wondering "what if",' Jennifer says. 'I think we'd been drinking too much! We'd talked about coming down here when we retired, but it became a point of defiance – why do we have to wait until we retire to start this new life?'

'In the end,' Roger adds, 'it came down to me wondering if I wanted to spend time hanging around with the CEO of a really big company, or with somebody like Pat Thomas or T-Model Ford. I wasn't into golfing, or boating, and I didn't really care about the corporate lifestyle. We started looking for a place to live in Clarksdale, and there were about 30 houses for sale in the neighborhood we ended up settling in.

'We didn't want to compete with the Stackhouse – we wanted to help make Clarksdale a destination, to form symbiotic relationships that could help the whole area,' Roger says, careful to point out that none of the objects for sale at Cat Head can be found at Delia's Stackhouse, or at the Delta Blues Museum, or any of the other small businesses that dot downtown Clarksdale. Even the albums and CDs for sale vary from Nancy Kossman's eclectic selection down the street.

'Some people are waiting to see who we're gonna side with: the tourism council or the blues fans,' Roger says. 'But we don't feel like we have to choose a side. At the mayor's meeting a few weeks ago, people thought the town has spent too much on blues. But nothing is going to bring money to this town like tourism!'

'We are former tourists,' Jennifer says. 'We know why people want to come down here. So we're trying to promote the whole area. We're becoming a clearinghouse for the entire area, directing people to Delta Amusement or Big Terry's club, Blues Station, or to Ground Zero or Hopson.'

While, as the Stolles point out, there are hardly any incentives for small businesses, 'Bubba' Kinchen O'Keefe plans to change that. 'I feel like Gary Cooper in *The Fountainhead*,' Bubba, a building contractor, tells me. He's in his truck, with the window rolled down, and I'm on my way back to my car on Sunflower Avenue. 'This town has screwed up too many opportunities!'

A native of the city, Bubba has grand plans for downtown Clarksdale, including book stores and coffee shops, and a rock 'n' roll museum in the old WROX radio station, where a teenaged Ike Turner DJed and often performed. 'We can do it or screw it,' Bubba says. 'We are a dysfunctional town – there's no environment here for people of different races to interact and, as a result, there are so many fine people I will never get to know, unless we can change things.' Bubba plans to use the Main Street USA programme, a non-profit foundation, to help revitalise downtown and generate an interchange between the city's black and white residents. But today, he's too busy to exchange more than a few words, so I head on down the road.

My head is swirling at this point, so I bypass stops at John Ruskey's house and at Ground Zero, actor Morgan Freeman's latest venture. I do drop in at the Riverside Hotel, better known in its previous incarnation as the GT Thomas Afro-American Hospital, where blues singer Bessie Smith bled to death after a car wreck in the fall of 1937. But Frank Ratliff, the hotel's proprietor, is out mowing lawns, so I make my way to the crossroads on the edge of town.

There's certainly no argument that legendary bluesman Robert Johnson sold his soul to the Devil at some Mississippi crossroads – the confusion, it seems, surrounds which crossroads he sang about. Standing outside Abe's Bar-B-Q with one hand shielding my eyes from the bright sunlight, I peer up at the blue metal guitar and shiny Highway 61 sign, hoisted some 6m (20ft) above the ground. Cars and trucks whiz past, headed to Tutwiler, Greenwood, Grenada and Yazoo City. Looking around, I tend to agree with the blues purists who insist that Johnson was singing about a more desolate crossroads than this busy, well-lit setting. I go into Abe's for a quick pork shoulder sandwich ($2 including tax), then head down 49.

My last stop before the sun sets is the Shack Up Inn at the Hopson Plantation. With shotgun shacks renting from just $50 a night, this is one of the most economic – and coolest – ways to get a dose of Delta life. The first mechanised cotton-picker was introduced at Hopson; Pinetop Perkins (who lived and worked at Hopson during World War II) said of his time there, 'I would do everything with a cotton machine but make it talk.' Today, five shacks – including one named for Pinetop – have been moved onto the plantation (its own were torn down long ago) and upgraded with 21st-century amenities like air conditioning and indoor plumbing.

James Butler owns the Hopson Plantation with his wife, Cathy, whose family founded the farm in 1852. James and four other self-described 'shackmeisters' (Guy Malvezzi, Bill Talbot, Jim Field and Tommy Polk) run the 'beer and breakfast' inn, a concept they came up with by accident. Nashville songwriter Tommy Polk wanted a country retreat, so he turned to his cousin James, who also serves as Clarksdale's director of public works. James purchased a shack on the nearby LaFlore Plantation for $600, relocated it to Hopson and, as he's quick to tell with a smile, 'things just grew from there'.

Blues fans clamour to the Shack Up Inn and the Hopson Commissary for a dose of 'the real deal', but the majority of Clarksdale is in an uproar over the concept. 'They think we're running some kind of hippie commune,' Guy once told me with a smile. 'That, or some kind of nudist colony.'

Even the politically correct don't quite know what to think of the goings-on out at Hopson. They're concerned about the racist implications of people paying to sleep in a two-room sharecropper's shack, and tout the cotton plantation's place in Mississippi history as a reason to shun the Shack Up Inn. But when it comes down to it, many of the very people they worry about offending have embraced the shacks.

When Pinetop Perkins plays at the Sunflower Blues Festival, or the King Biscuit Blues Festival across the river in Helena, Arkansas, he stays in his shack at Hopson, and other bluesmen are clamouring for shacks to be dedicated in their honour. But local resident RJ McGill puts it best. After a recent headline in Clarksdale's *Clarion-Ledger* newspaper raged, 'Shack Up Inn attracts celebrities, distorts truth', McGill wrote in to say his piece.

'It is a crying shame to see so many still live in the past,' he wrote. 'My great grandfather was a sharecropper and he took pride in what he did. I cannot see how we can hold that against anyone today. We have learned from our mistakes and it is better if we keep those opinions to ourselves.

'It is that kind of talk that keeps the whole south in the past. Forget and forgive. Truly James Butler has made Hopson more than it would have been if it were allowed to rot to the ground. Get out of the past and make Clarksdale a place we may all say we like to live. I give [James Butler] a hand in his attempt to make Clarksdale a better place. Congratulations, James.'

And congratulations to RJ McGill and Nancy Kossman, and the Stolles and Bubba O'Keefe. Hopefully, their visions will persevere, and Clarksdale will continue to prosper, to, as Nancy put it, 'stumble on' in its 'own weird, funky way'. It could, she often reminds me, go either way.

9 So It Goes: The Rock 'n' Roll Backbone

BIG STAR OVER MEMPHIS
Mike Evans

Because, no doubt, of its preeminence in the history of blues, early rock 'n' roll and soul, there's a danger of the history of mainstream rock in Memphis being overlooked, certainly by the outsider looking in. But it would be a big mistake – if only for ignoring the contribution of Alex Chilton to the musical legacy of the city over the past four decades.

One of the best-remembered chart-topping singles of the of the mid-1960s was the 1967 smash 'The Letter', by The Boxtops. With a searing lead vocal by singer Alex Chilton, the track was truly innovative, with its dramatic arrangement, cool horn parts and even some aeroplane sound effects. It went on to sell over four million copies worldwide, which was not bad for Memphis's nearest thing to a garage band, fronted by a 16-year-old who'd never been inside a studio before.

Alex Chilton had grown up with music in the household – his father Sidney played jazz piano, though not for a living – and while still a child he was initially inspired to sing by the vocals of Chet Baker, rather than what was going on in the pop charts in the mid-to-late '50s. As he told Robert Gordon in *It Came From Memphis*, 'I was aware of Elvis and Jerry Lee, I was given a copy of "Great Balls of Fire" for my seventh or eighth birthday, but I really wasn't much of a fan of all that. And by 1959, Elvis was syrup and Jerry Lee was pretty much gone, and the rockabilly thing was sort of over.' Like thousands upon thousands of American kids of his age, it took the British Invasion to motivate him in the direction of rock 'n' roll music – 'I didn't get really caught up in the rock scene until the Beatles came along.'

He was recruited into the embryo Boxtops, then calling themselves The DeVilles, a high-school group at Central High who were undergoing personnel changes. He rehearsed briefly with guitar/organist John Evans, guitarist Gary Talley, bass player Billy Cunningham and Danny Smythe on drums before the group found themselves in the American Sound studios run by Chips Moman. Here, guided by Dan Penn, who was to produce all their major sides, The Boxtops emerged after 30 takes one Saturday morning with 'The Letter', which they had culled from a demo by an unknown singer, Wayne Carson. A local – and influential – DJ, Roy Mack, was managing them, and he promoted the record enough to make it a hit in Memphis. Word of mouth from Mack was enough for others like him to follow suit around the South, and the domino effect that one-time-in-a-million catapults a record from regional success to international smash came into play.

A follow-up, 'Neon Rainbow', didn't even make the *Billboard* Top 20, but their third, 'Cry Like A Baby', with topical psychedelic guitar and Chilton's blue-eyed soul vocals made the Number Two spot with ease. By this time, however, the group – who were being touted as Memphis's answer to New York's Young Rascals – became more and more the studio creation of Chilton and Penn, Evans and Smythe having being replaced by Rick Allen and Tom Boggs after the disappointing performance of the second single.

In fact, after the sensational début release Chilton was the only member of the original line-up actually to appear on the records, with subsequent singles and long-players usually featuring the studio's house band – Reggie Young, Bobby Wood, Bobby Emmons, Tommy Cogbill and Gene Chrisman. They were to have one last (minor) hit in 1969, 'Soul Deep', and despite their albums being briefly afforded cult status in Britain's influential *Melody Maker* the band was on the point of disintegration, with Alex Chilton quitting just when they were about to embark on a UK tour.

Still only 19 years old, Chilton headed for New York City, where he struggled to make it as a folk artist for a year or so. Disappointed with his lack of success, he headed back to Memphis and found work at Ardent Studios, where he also tried unsuccessfully to record the solo album that was in his head. Here, he met another guitarist, Chris Bell, who had a band called Ice Water. Chilton had soon joined the band and they renamed themselves Big Star after a supermarket chain.

Going very much against the trends of the day, which in Memphis were very blues- and soul-based, and in rock generally self-consciously 'progressive', Big Star crafted a version of pop-driven Brit-rock that was very much to do with their avowed admiration for groups like The Beatles, The Kinks, The Who and The Byrds.

The band recorded two seminal masterpieces, *#1 Record* (1972) and *Radio City* (1973), that were characterised by crisp melodies and complex harmonies, but both albums suffered from poor distribution and the critical assessment that the time was not right for such Beatle-tinged excursions. Chilton, who already felt he had been short-changed in his eventual earnings from The Box Tops, was now convinced that his songs were not reaching their natural public because of Stax Records' distribution problems. These frustrations had already manifested themselves in inner tensions in the band, Chris Bell quitting after the first album's release. But the others (Chilton, bass player Andy Hummel and drummer Jody Stephens) were to stick it out for their third long-player.

Recognised generally as more of a Chilton solo project than Big Star teamwork, the album – referred to as *Big Star's 3rd Album* or *Sister Lovers* (because Chilton and Stephens were dating a pair of sisters) – was to achieve genuine cult status. Its sparse production and the down-side aspect of most of Chilton's songs (reflecting his growing disillusionment with the music business) didn't grab record buyers by the million at the time, but has a resonance that was felt later, not unlike the fate of The Velvet Underground's records, which found their fullest acclaim long after the band's demise. Like the later music of The Smiths, it struck a chord with disaffected youth with what the respected *Trouser Press* guide to alternative rock described as 'alternately depressing and uplifting, ugly and beautiful'.

On completing the album in 1974, Chilton made another foray into New York, again to no avail. He returned to Memphis, recording what eventually became *The Singer Not The Song* EP with producer Jon Tiven, the whole period being one in which Chilton seemed on a doomed self-destruct mission, moving from one casual band to another. This was confirmed in vinyl with the 1979 recording *Like Flies On Sherbet*, *Trouser Press* describing it as 'a bunch of drunken louts running amok in a studio with no producer to restrain or guide them'. At the time it was seen as a once-great talent's final spiral into a drink- and drug-fuelled oblivion, but in retrospect it can be viewed in the context of Chilton's struggle with those self-induced problems, his final raised finger at the music biz he felt had exploited him and a coming-to-terms with the death of former colleague Chris Bell, who had died in a car crash not long before.

The therapeutic aspect of *Like Flies On Sherbet* was confirmed with Alex's next move, to New Orleans, to drop out of music altogether for a time. He had a variety of jobs, during which time he managed to clean up his act before returning to Memphis and his music roots, where he recorded a couple of albums with the rockabilly outfit The Panther Burns.

So he was back on the music scene, a new cleaned-up Chilton who startled everybody with his next album venture, 1985's *Feudalist Tarts*, in which he emulated a classic Memphis R&B bar band. Bearing in mind this was just when his Big Star output was being reassessed as seminal rock. His cache was also improved no end by the attention he was getting from contemporary outfits like the all-girl LA band The Bangles by covering one of his songs ('September Gurls'), The Cramps (whom he produced) and The Replacements, who named him as a major influence and even named a single after him.

Chilton continued in the R&B/soul vein of *Feudalist Tart* with 1987's *High Priest* and *Black List* in 1990, before embarking on a re-formation of Big Star, prompted by the re-release of their now-legendary material in the CD era. He recruited two members of The Posies – Jonathan Auer and Ken Stringfellow – to replace Andy Hummel and Chris Bell, and their 1993 concerts and live album further substantiated his final acceptance as an important though oft-neglected voice.

But, with his career more successful than it had ever been, Chilton wasn't going to capitulate to critics and record labels – or fans for that matter – who merely wanted a replay of the Big Star phenomenon most of them had ignored, or neglected, first time round. He could easily have been a 'rediscovered legend' wheeled out to perform his (now) old classics. Instead he traced the whole circle back to his personal musical roots, one the public weren't in the main aware of, and brought out a solo acoustic collection of jazz-tinged standards entitled *Clichés*, the kind of material that had first attracted him when delivered by the smoky-voiced Chet Baker.

In 1996, he released what has been described as his most commercial record for years, *A Man Called Destruction*, followed by another 'full circle' in 1997 when he re-formed The Box Tops for a series of concerts that would be their first in 28 years.

Then, in 2000 he released *Set*. Described by one critic as 'Sounding a lot like the best lounge act anyone has ever heard…much like a late-night set Chilton might perform in some nearly empty cocktail dive', it was reminiscent of 1994's *Clichés* more than anything else in his recording output. More than one review of *Set* (which was titled the more reckless *Loose Shoes And Tight Pussy* on non-US versions) drew attention to Chilton's fine, and often underrated, guitar playing.

Now in his early 50s, and a name since the age of 16 – when he was thrust into (albeit brief) superstardom – he is now the stuff of legend. Alex Chilton's continued defiance of the record business dictum that any success should define what you do for the rest of your life is particularly appropriate to Memphis, where over the years much sound judgement tempered with good taste has often been voiced in the face of accepted (so-called) wisdom.

OUT OF THE GARAGE
Mike Evans

After Sun, Ardent is one of the longest-surviving studio names in Memphis, and its history – which began, hitwise, back in 1966 with Eddie Floyd's 'Knock On Wood' – has spanned decades and styles, taking in artists as varied as REM, Led Zeppelin, Al Green, Big Star, Soundgarden, Robert Cray, BB King, Travis Tritt, Isaac Hayes and Primal Scream on the way.

Located in midtown Memphis since 1971, at 2000 Madison Avenue, its founder John Fry has often been quoted as saying that he got into the recording business because 'I was unable to find honest employment'. Like thousands of American kids, he was caught up in the buzz of the British group invasion, but soon realised The Beatles, the Stones and such were importing a modified version of American music, as he told an interviewer in *Mix* magazine: 'As a kid, I had a big interest in music and in electronics. I was brought up on the great rhythm and blues music of the late '50s and mid-'60s, and especially the English rock bands. I remember thinking, "Boy, that's great, this is something really important. This is too cool to miss." I later realised that what the English bands were doing was taking a lot of our R&B music and feeding it back to us in an Anglicised form.'

Although Ardent's official beginning as a commercial studio is dated as 1966, Fry actually began recording as early as 1960, when he and two schoolfriends, John King and Fred Smith, set up their own studio. It was located, according to Robert Gordon, in his grandmother's sewing room when she wasn't using it. Fry has described it as a garage studio – maybe grandma did her sewing in the garage. 'In this business, everything starts out either in a garage or a basement,' says Fry. 'It's a garage band or basement band. When I was still in high school, I had a garage studio.' Predictably, they recorded garage bands there.

With a two-track and full-track mono machine, overdubbing from one to the other, they actually put out records on their own Ardent label, the first being 'At The Rock House' by a Jacksonville, Florida, singer called Freddie Cadell. Four more singles followed, including archetypal garage outfit The Shades, and 'the guy with a studio in his house' became something of a talking point among the aspiring young rock fraternity of Memphis.

After a brief hiatus, during which John Fry gave up the studio activity for a while, in 1964 he returned to the sewing room (that wouldn't have been a bad name for the studio!) to record a teenage band called Lawson And Four More, with a new associate, Jim Dickinson, producing. One of the group, Terry Manning, was to become part of the Ardent set-up – as in-house producer – for the next 20 years.

Fortuitously, as it turned out, Fry's family decided to move out of the house in 1966, so Fry had to find new premises, which he did on National Street, just around the time that Stax Records were really taking off. He was now running a four-track facility, which was as much as anyone had, so when Stax realised their own studio couldn't accommodate the increasing capacity required, nearby Ardent was a natural choice.

Over the next couple of years Fry's studio became, in effect, Stax's B studio. Ardent's first big hit for Stax was 'Knock On Wood' by Eddie Floyd, followed by 'Soul Man' by Sam And Dave, then singles and albums for Isaac Hayes, The Staple Singers and many more.

Ardent moved to its current midtown location in 1971, adding several elements to the complex since then. In 1980, Studio C was added, making the three-recording-studios-plus- mixing-suite facility that exists today.

The business now also includes a very successful contemporary Christian record label, which is distributed by Forefront Records, and a youth-oriented gospel label that is a booming part of EMI Christian Music. Nor should we forget Ardent's well-established role as music publisher for many of its artists and writers.

But it's as part of the very backbone of the Memphis recording scene, which in the last decade continued with albums from Gin Blossoms REM, Soundgarden, Afghan Whigs, Primal Scream, BB King, Jimmie Vaughan, Robert Cray and many, many more, that Ardent has survived from its 1960s garage embryo into the 21st century.

CHIPS MOMAN AND THE AMERICAN WAY
Mike Evans

In the story of recorded music coming out of Memphis, when it comes to actual studios the name 'American' ranks along those of Sun, Stax and Ardent. Like Ardent, American Sound Studios was just that, a working studio with no label tie-in (unlike both Sun and Stax), even though its founder Chips Moman had cut his teeth at Stax.

Moman's association with Jim Stewart and Estelle Axton at Stax began right back in the earliest days , when the operation was still being conducted from Estelle's uncle's garage. A guitar player from LaGrange, Georgia, he'd drifted into Memphis after gigging on the road with the likes of Gene Vincent and Johnny Burnette, and paying some dues as a session man on the West Coast. He soon got in on the fledgling recording enterprise, producing, playing sessions, whatever was required, and the first hit – Carla Thomas's 'Gee Whiz' – was produced by Chips, while the label was still called Satellite. He went on to be a prime architect of the Stax sound, producing all the label's big hits up to the time of Booker T And The MGs' 'Green Onions' smash. Moman didn't happen to be in the studio for the 'Green Onions' session, but that wasn't why he left – it was through a more fundamental disagreement with Jim Stewart over money.

Both parties have since proffered different versions of the dispute, though, as Wayne Jackson put it to Peter Guralnick in *Sweet Soul Music*, it was 'just a matter of the placing of a decimal point'. Whatever, the net result as far as Chips was concerned was the $3,000 settlement he got with the help of Memphis music lawyer Seymour Rosenberg, enabling the two to set up the American Studio as a partnership.

Chips Moman found a suitable building in North Memphis with a barber shop on one side and a restaurant on the other. He moved in and set up with some modest equipment, for what would be a slowish start to one of the biggest success stories in studio history, on a par with that of Stax or even the mighty Motown in Detroit.

Right from the start, Moman was potentially his own worst enemy, his drinking in the first couple of years after its 1962 inception taking priority over much that was going on. He even managed to stand aside as another partner moved in with a $300 investment and picked up Chip's share for the same kind of money. He still engineered occasional sessions there, paying for his whisky habit from that, pool-hall gambling and painting gas stations!

Then, late in 1964, his fortunes changed. He agreed to produce a disc, and quoted $5,000 instead of his usual $20 or so – just for the hell of it really, as he'd nothing to lose, except maybe $20. To his amazement, it paid off, and he got the gig for $5,000. At last Moman was getting his act together, and the next chapter was to be a hit record.

In terms of pure pop, as opposed to the soul-infected sounds coming out on Stax, Atlantic and the Tamla Motown axis, America was reeling from the impact of The Beatles. Suddenly, thousands of high-school groups, usually rehearsing in the garage at home, were growing their hair mop-top style, donning neat little Italianate suits and coming up with chart-aimed 'catchy' songs – the latter, as often as not, anodyne covers of black R&B records (in rock 'n' roll, there are some things that never seem to change).

One such Memphis outfit were The Gentrys, who had, according to Robert Gordon, changed their name from The Gents to give it a more 'British' ring. Chips Moman ran into the seven-piece late in 1964, and early in 1965 had them in the studio. Among tracks they laid down was their own version of a record by a local black vocal group, The Avantis, called 'Keep On Dancing'. By September 1965 the single (on the MGM label) had reached the Number Four spot in *Billboard* and sold more than a million copies.

It was around this time Moman also managed to buy back control of American with the help of a farmer from Arkansas, Don Crews. Now he had the studio back in his hands, he put together a house band comprising a rhythm section he'd worked with on sessions for the Goldwax label during his 'lost' two-year spell after Stax. The band – guitarist Reggie Young, Bobby Wood and/or Bobby Emmons on keyboards, bass player Tommy Cogbill and Gene Chrisman on drums – had even had a hit together at the beginning of 1965, the much-remembered 'Wooly Bully' by Sam The Sham And The Pharaohs.

With The Gentrys, Chips Moman had tasted pure pop success, and it tasted sweet (as did the rewards), and there was more to follow. Summer 1966 saw another huge seller, 'Born A Woman', this time for an ex-secretary and session singer at American, Sandy Posey. She went on to score with three more charting singles, all produced for MGM, through 1966 and 1967.

It was at this time that Dan Penn came into the picture. Penn had been working in a studio in Muscle Shoals, Alabama, as a house guitar player. Chips came over as a country boy, but Penn… 'Redneck' was the word Guralnick uses. Anyway, when singer, songwriter and proto-producer Dan Penn started in partnership with Chips Moman, it was clear that the two hit it off from the start. They worked together with an understanding and feel that seemed intuitive and, with The Box Tops' smash 'The Letter', Penn put the seal on his growing reputation as a producer.

As well as both being superlative guitarists in their own right, they collaborated on songs, including hits for James Carr ('Dark End Of The Street') and Aretha Franklin (with 'Do Right Woman').

The advantage a studio like American had over its label-linked rivals was that the opportunities were endless: as long as they kept up their commercial and artistic standard, they had the industry's top record companies as potential clients. Like when they were approached by Atlantic's Jerry Wexler to produce the next Wilson Pickett sessions in 1967.

So down-home was the soul feeling of the American studio players, many listeners assumed they were black, and some of the greatest singers on the scene now wanted to use them. The Atlantic connection came into play again when Moman was chosen for some guitar work on Aretha Franklin's memorable soul hits in the late '60s – the actual session took place in New York and the FAME studios in Muscle Shoals rather than Memphis. But when Wexler had a falling out with FAME owner Rick Hall, Moman's studio was the obvious next choice.

The formula of a singer going to a studio 'down South' to achieve a more 'authentic' sound became something of a trend, with Neil Diamond and (oddly) the British singer Petula Clark making the trip to American. But one such collaboration that did pay off artistically was when UK songstress Dusty Springfield cut her rightfully acclaimed *Dusty In Memphis* album (produced by Jerry Wexler) at American in 1968, a magnificent collection highlighted by the Top Ten single 'Son Of A Preacher Man'.

American's credibility was finally confirmed at every level when Elvis Presley, staging his 1969 'comeback' to recording in Memphis, chose American – with Chips Moman producing, and the house musicians backing – for the sessions that were to include hit tracks like 'Suspicious Minds' and 'In The Ghetto'.

Between November 1967 and January 1971, the studio was responsible for no fewer than 120 hits. At one point, Moman's success was such that during one particular week, over a quarter of *Billboard*'s Hot 100 hits were generated at American.

The American story as far as Moman was concerned, however, was to come to an end the following year, when he closed the studio, first to move with the rhythm section to Atlanta, and then to Nashville. There, he wrote 'Luckenbach, Texas' for Waylon Jennings, helping *Ol' Waylon* become the second ever platinum country record. Moman stayed in Nashville throughout the late '70s and '80s, producing and playing on records by Willie Nelson, Merle Haggard and Tammy Wynette, among other artists.

He was to return to Memphis in the mid-1980s after pleas, from the mayor and local bankers, to help rebuild the city's declining music industry. In this context he was to produce the *Class Of '55* album, a Sun reunion featuring Jerry Lee Lewis, Roy Orbison, Johnny Cash and Carl Perkins recorded at the Sun Studio. The album didn't do particularly well over the counter, and an abortive project with Ringo Starr cost Moman even more in both time and money. Chips Moman returned to Nashville in the early '90s, where he is still active in various studios, producing younger country acts as well as movie soundtracks.

MEMPHIS ROCK IN THE '90S: TWO CASE HISTORIES
Mike Evans

It's tempting for the visitor to Memphis to bemoan the passing of the great days of the city when it was hub of the blues, hotbed of rockabilly, melting pot of soul or whatever. But, come on – all that was 40, 50, 60 and more years ago. There's been, and always will be, a contemporary music scene, particularly an 'alternative' rock scene, which like the bands themselves is constantly changing.

One of the long-term leading voices in this process has been Jim Dickinson, as session player, producer, general enthusiast and promoter of other's talents, and frontman with his own much-regarded outfit Mud Boy And The Neutrons. Similarly, singer and guitarist Alex Chilton has moved in and out of the Memphis underground music mafia over the years, his seminal influence far greater than his (lack of) solid gold successes would imply.

Among several bands with whom both Dickinson and Chilton were involved in various capacities in the '80s and '90s, The Panther Burns were akin to a rockabilly-revival band gone punk, a vehicle for their off-the-wall frontman, Tav Falco.

Singer, songwriter, guitarist, performing artist, dancer, photographer and filmmaker, Gustavo 'Tav' Falco Nelson grew up in the backwoods of rural Arkansas, his family having their roots in southern Italy.

He moved to Memphis in 1973 after various jobs that ranged from railroad 'brake man' to gas station attendant, and immediately got involved in the city's avant-garde. He became involved with Big Dixie, an alternative performance group, and Televista, an experimental film and video cooperative. Falco also worked with the legendary photographer William J Eggleston and, via Eggleston's work featuring blues musicians across the rural South, became more and more fascinated by their music, to the point where he was playing blues guitar and singing himself.

Once he began taking his musical performance seriously, however, Falco soon exhibited a much broader attitude, one that reflected not just the influence of blues and rockabilly but also his continuing awareness of what was happening at the avant-garde end of things. This was made spectacularly apparent when, during his début solo performance alongside Mud Boy And The Neutrons, at the Orpheum Theater in Memphis, he sang Leadbelly's 'Bourgeois Blues' while destroying an electric guitar with a chainsaw.

In 1979, Tav put together his band, The Panther Burns, named after a legendary plantation located (still) off 61 Highway in the lower Delta. From the start it would serve as a vehicle for Falco's musical and conceptual ambitions, as he is quoted on the band's website: 'Here was an art form I could participate in by just picking up the instrument, like a Kodak Instamatic camera. It was the feeling and aesthetic that mattered, more than musicianship or virtuosity. I didn't feel hindered by my lack of conventional guitar knowledge. I just went into it full tilt.'

The most important thing about The Panther Burns, historically at least, was the fact that they managed to revive the careers of more than one hitherto-neglected 'legend', by covering their numbers, promoting their back catalogue and even arranging for them to share the stage with them on dates. In this way the fortunes of RL Burnside, Charlie Feathers, Cordell Jackson and Sonny Burgess were changed for the better.

And the eclectic spirit of Falco's inspiration guaranteed a weird and wonderful repertoire outside the confines of blues, R&B, rock, or even North American music generally, with mambos, tangos and sambas regularly thrown into the heady brew.

As well as occasional appearances in the line-up of founding members Dickinson and Chilton, other regulars have included, over the years, co-founders Eric Hill on keyboards and drummer Ross Johnson, and a number of 'revolving' members, including Michael Lo on bass, guitarist Peter Dark and Tall Cash on drums.

Never losing touch with the avant-garde scene that spawned his artistic enthusiasms as much as his love for music, Tav Falco spent some time in the early '80s in New York, playing and making friends with such bands as DNA, Walter Stedding and James White on the so-called No Wave scene, dedicated to musical freedom and experimentation. This made for his critical acceptance, and that of his still-continuing musical project, in periodicals such as *New York Times*, *Village Voice* and Andy Warhol's *Interview*. Cult status, to be sure.

The most recent studio release by The Panther Burns was *Panther Phobia* in late 2000, followed in 2001 and 2002 by tours that took in the US and countries across Europe.

As always, Tav Falco is his own best publicist, with tongue-in-cheek press statements that echo the left-field approach of one of the most original talents to come out of Memphis: 'The Panther Burns are the missing link between the earlier forms of swamp blues' unbridled howl and the psychological onslaught of the new millennium. We are, essentially, the ditch diggers in American music. You may have heard of the commedia del'arte, the peripatetic theater troupe of the 15th century, well the more rustic American version is The Panther Burns' staging of what we term antler del'arte. In other words, The Panther

Burns are the last steam engine train on the track that don't do nothing but run and blow.'

The Grifters emerged out of the 1990s musical milieu that was Memphis rock, first to appear fiercely independent with their home-tape sound challenging any preconceptions; then to settle into a 'safer' groove that earned more widespread acceptance; then, effectively, to break up.

Formed by David Shouse in 1989, they consisted of Shouse on drums, Tripp Lamkins on bass, and guitarist Scott Taylor. Shouse, who was about ten years older than the rest of band, initially called the outfit A Band Called Bud, then changed it to The Grifters in 1990 with the addition of drummer Stan Gallimore, and Shouse moving to guitar. They immediately started putting out seven-inch singles on their own Doink label, and making a mark on the Memphis underground network, for what it was.

Their short career was a template for indie rock bands all over the States in the early '90s, and in Memphis it was little different, except that, almost as part of the history of the music business there, indie was the norm rather than the alternative. Unlike Nashville, its nearest neighbour in terms of music centres of America, it never saw the majors really set up shop in a permanent way. The big companies – Atlantic, MGM, whoever – came as clients to the increasingly prestigious recording facilities, while their A&R folk targeted new bands, as A&Rs always did, and always will.

So with The Grifters. After a 1992 début album, *So Happy Together*, on the short-lived Chicago label Sonic Noise, they had their first full-length *One Sock Missing* out in 1993, to rave reviews. It was recorded on a four-track mostly in the flower shop where Shouse and Gallimore worked (and where the band practised at night), and mixed at the rather more sophisticated Easley Recording. Another album, *Crappin' You Negative*, followed in 1994, this one getting a four-star review in *Rolling Stone*. After various singles, EPs and such, including the previous two albums, all released on the Memphis Shangri-La label , they were signed to the mighty (though still indie in the greater scheme of things) Sub Pop label in 1995. The result, like the first two recorded with Doug Easley at Easley, was their third full-lengther, *Ain't My Lookout*, and immediately it became apparent that some smoothing down had taken place in the process. Sub Pop even mentioned it in their press matter, quoting a gushing (and blushing?)-sounding Scott Taylor: 'We were totally surprised we came up with such a poppy record this time. We didn't expect it to turn out that way, but we're really pleased and excited about it at the same time.'

Crunch time came for The Grifters when Shouse – despite the fact that the band were busier than they could have possible imagined a year or two before, with a tour of Australia as well as the US – began cutting tracks for a solo project he called Those Bastard Souls. Not to put too fine a point on it, this parallel activity soon became to all intents and purposes the rival activity, Shouse paying more and more attention to the 'Bastards' than the 'Grifters'.

Grifter Tripp Lamkins confirmed what many fans had suspected concerning the band's feelings on the subject: 'We really felt him leaving and pulling away. Resentment started building up and it stopped being as much fun. We used to all have pretty good, impassioned fights about songs, about where they needed to go. But on the last record we didn't fight as much about stuff because there was this larger fight brimming under the surface.'

Sadly, Robert Gordon's assessment (in *It Came From Memphis*) of The Grifters' positively independent stance to the major record labels was not to reflect the picture for very long: 'The band has so far declined all [offers], opting for a tiny local label where they know their integrity will not be compromised, as sure as they know the same assurances from the majors were bullshit.'

'So it goes' – to quote the words of Kurt Vonnegut Jr – and, in terms of rock 'n' roll, that can be as appropriate a response in Memphis as anywhere else.

10 A Modern Mix

DIGGIN' THE MEMPHIX BREAKDOWN
Andria Lisle

Kneeling on the floor of my record room, I carefully drop the 45rpm single on my turntable and watch the black wax spin. 'I'm in Memphis, Tennessee', croons a soulful voice. 'Now c'mon and breakdown!' And the music does just that, dropping straight into a heavy hip-hop groove. The voice belongs to Oliver Sain, one of the underrated giants of southern soul, but the beats are courtesy of the Red Eye Jedi, aka 27-year-old Luke Sexton of Memphix Records.

The red and black Memphix label goes round and round as loops from Rufus Thomas and Howlin' Wolf hit the speakers. 'You know,' Luke says, moments after the track is over, 'I have newfound respect for this city. When I started getting into samples, I realized that half of the music I loved was Memphis music.'

Luke, a lanky and affable guy with dark hair, has been listening to music all his life. 'I grew up in Missouri, the same town Sheryl Crow is from. My mother is a music teacher there, and my grandfather is a piano tuner. They bought me a drum kit when I was five, and it just went on from there.' He grins, remembering those early days. 'Music was in my face ever since I was born. I finally traded my drum kit for turntables when I was 19,' he says. 'It just seemed the natural way to go.'

Across the room, 24-year-old Chad 'Chase One' Weekley speaks up. 'I grew up right here in town,' he says in a soft drawl. 'I've been a music fan', he tells me, pausing for effect, 'always.' As Chad's accent is so thick that his words are occasionally difficult to decipher, I lean in close to listen. 'My mom used to take me to rap concerts and to movies like *Breakin'*. One time she bought me a Whodini tape, and that was it. I was hooked.'

Luke and Chad are both white, but they have launched their careers DJing urban black hip-hop records. Their audiences are also predominantly Caucasian, 90–95 per cent white, according to Chad. 'I think blacks see the music as outdated,' he says, taking a moment to ponder the question. 'They think it's old – even if I play a hip-hop track from 1992, they'll scoff at it.' Yet, musically at least, the two have crossed the colour barrier.

They started the Memphix hip-hop label in 1999. 'It just happened,' Chad explains. 'Nobody was doing hip-hop 45s at the time. We decided to cut a split single with a Chicago-based DJ, a friend of ours named Dante Carfagna. He came up with the Memphix logo, and things kept rolling from there.

'Our friend DJ Klever started winning European competitions right after we put out his record,' says Chad. 'So we headed overseas for two weeks. It was a good experience – we made excellent contacts. When we went back a year later we had 13 shows set up.'

That second visit was wild – Dante was on tour with DJ Shadow and Cut Chemist, huge stars on the international hip-hop scene. 'They were like The Beatles,' Chad recalls. 'I've never been involved with anything like that – walking off the bus and seeing a street loaded with kids. I thought "what the hell?" That ain't happening in Memphis!'

In Europe, Chad learned, 'a thousand kids will dance for six hours straight. Eighteen-year-old kids all the way up to 45-year-old dudes are on it – they're dancing and having a good time. So we educated ourselves, spending our own money to get around and learn from people over there, stuff we couldn't do in Memphis.'

According to Chad, the local hip-hop scene suffers from a lack of organisation. 'I can't walk down the street and sell 100 Memphix records locally. I need to go out of town to handle my business. You just can't do it here.'

'Nobody here travels, and that holds people back,' Luke adds. 'Even the guys that consider themselves hardcore hip-hop are behind the times.'

Chad, meanwhile, points to local rappers Triple 6 Mafia. 'Why are they the biggest group from here?' he asks rhetorically. 'They're pitiful! I mean, they might work hard, but they're not any good. They've done the same thing since 1992,' he says disgustedly.

'The clubs here don't treat the music well – whether it's local or from out of town,' Luke tells me, recalling a few Memphix gigs that have been poorly attended or – worse yet – cancelled. And, as Chad points out, 'even in Nashville, you can go to a party and see 200 kids dancing to funk music. Here you can't get five people on the dance floor!'

But Memphis remains their home base for now. 'I do love it here,' says Luke, who continues to draw inspiration from the local music scene. 'Right now, I'm taking a lot of Willie Hall breaks and working 'em into my new record.' Willie, a session drummer who backed Isaac Hayes on all of his Stax-era albums and provided the back-beat for The Bar-Keys and The Blues Brothers, currently plays with The Bo-Keys, a Stax-influenced instrumental group led by bassist Scott Bomar.

Both Luke and Chad are big fans. 'I'd like to see The Bo-Keys on Memphix,' Chad says. 'It would help them open some doors in Europe, where people want to hear original players like Willie Hall. I was just over there', he continues, 'and there were plenty of decent bands, but none as good as The Bo-Keys.' Our conversation moves to an upcoming show headlining Bomar's group and the Memphix crew, which will feature DJ loops intertwined with live music, a first-time experiment for Chad and Luke.

Yet, as far as they are concerned, The Bo-Keys are just the tip of the musical iceberg. 'I've got about 1,500 hip hop records,' Luke says, '500 jazz records, some blues, high-school marching bands, and movie soundtracks. I'm trying to thin stuff out, but unfortunately…' His voice trails off just thinking about it.

Chad is quick to add his two cents. 'We're just getting started collecting,' he claims, though he's been digging for vinyl for a decade now. Both cite River Records on South Highland Street as one of their preferred haunts. 'I got the Memphians' single on Bluff City Records there,' Chad says, referring to a rare instrumental track from the early 1970s. 'It's so hard to find! Once I found an Ike Turner 45 on the Pompeii label – that shit is hot! He's backed by the Soul Seven band, who are so on-point that they sound like a DJ mixing records, doing some James Brown and then busting right into Bobby Byrd.'

'I found a record from Forrest City, Arkansas, that's one of a kind,' Luke says, naming an obscurity by a group called Abraham And The Metronomes. The 45, released on Lee Anthony's True Soul label in the 1970s, prompted Luke and Chad to take a road trip last year. After a few wrong turns, they met Lee Anthony himself.

Hip-hop scribe Egon Alapatt captured the details of their visit in *Big Daddy #9*. 'Betcha [Lee] didn't know', Alapatt writes, 'that those little pieces of black plastic would come to be a commodity amongst DJs and collectors fiending for fresh-sounding funk music.' Lee, apparently, had no idea – according to Chad, he was more than a little surprised to find out that two white boys had rediscovered his True Soul catalogue and cared enough to track him down.

'There's so much good stuff in this region, it's not even funny,' Chad says today. 'We take portable battery-powered record players with us wherever we go. It's a serious thing, because if you don't know your shit when you walk into a record store, you're screwed.'

His favourite Memphis record is an obscure piece of wax by Ricky Calloway called 'Get It Right', relesed on the Camaro label. It was recorded by amateur musicologist Style Wooten, who, Chad explains, 'ran an ad in the newspaper saying, "come on in and cut a record". He'd press up 100 copies on anything. You could walk in and scream, and he'd record you!

'Camaro's deep,' Chad continues. 'Artists like The Fabulous Verbs, The Fabulous Caprices, The Fabulous Fugitives – there's some sick stuff on that label!' A single by Gran Am, on Style's J'Ace imprint, was another lucky find. 'It sounds like the mikes were in one room and the drums were out on the street,' Luke laughs. 'Very funky – and very low budget.'

With only dozens of copies originally pressed, 45s on J'Ace and Camaro are rare finds today – and, thanks to exposure from fans such as Chad and Luke, they might go for hundreds of dollars on the collectors' market. 'That makes it hard to find fresh stuff,' says Luke, somewhat frustrated. 'But that's how it goes – keep the supply low, so there will be a demand.'

It's an ongoing tradition: all five Memphix singles, released in pressings of 500 or fewer, have quickly sold out. 'We sold out of our last record in one day,' Chad says proudly. Two hundred copies were shipped to Europe and Japan, half of which went straight to New York. Dusty Groove, a mail-order company in Chicago, took the rest. 'I held onto 25 copies,' says Chad. 'I only had 15 left to sell in Memphis.'

MAFIA RAPPERS
Mike Evans

In a world that has been dominated by acts coming out of New York, Chicago and Los Angeles, for a rap act from Memphis to break through nationally as big as Triple 6 Mafia have is nothing short of phenomenal.

Because of the violence that has tainted some large rap concerts, with very few clubs booking rap acts, Memphis rap has become genuinely 'underground'. In this context, Triple 6 Mafia's national success is even more of an achievement. It's a success story that can be traced to the early '90s and Memphis hip-hop names like Eightball, MJG and DJ Jimmy, who made their early sales out of car stereo shops, before taking the record industry by storm in the more traditional record store outlets.

DJ Paul began his musical career as a DJ in Memphis around 1990, initially making mix tapes at home, with his brother Lord Infamous, and gaining a small following. He soon met up with another local DJ who was making sonic waves around the local underground, DJ Juicy J, and (as with the genesis of much rap across the land) things just developed from there. J was a big fan of Paul's mixes, and the two began producing tapes rapping over beats, and eventually – after developing something approaching a trademark sound – integrating local MCs into their music.

For a short time they went under the name of Backyard Posse, before settling for 'Triple 6 Mafia' because, their publicity later claimed, of their 'demonic content and evil references'. It was under the former title that they released their début underground tape, *Smoked Out, Loced Out*, which got a good response across the South.

This initial success enabled them to bankroll their first official album release in 1995 – *Mystic Stylez*. To this day many of their fans, particularly those who've followed the group right through since those early releases, feel this is Triple 6's best piece of work. It was certainly sensational, laced with demonic overtones, horror-filled beats, hypnotic vocal samples and no shortage of implied street fighting in the lyrics. As with many emergent rap groups at the time, it firmed up a self-styled image of being as raw-edged as possible with tough (albeit posturing) lyrics dwelling on sex, drugs and violence. And what it did do, in establishing the group as a credible act across the South, was to shine a spotlight on the Memphis underground – a genuine first.

Next came their much-publicised musical spat with Bone Thugs-N-Harmony. The Cleveland-based million-sellers had angered DJ Paul and co (and many mid-South fans) with their description of Memphis as a 'bunk ass town', and in response the Triple 6 crew released an EP *Live By Yo Rep (BONE Dis)*, in which they bad-mouthed the Ohio rappers big time.

Up to now, the group's output had been on their own independently run Prophet Entertainment label, as was their second album in early 1997, *Da End*, which was marked by something of a toning down of the 'satanic' references and certainly more sophisticated production. Triple 6 Mafia, with the same core members (DJ Paul, Juicy J, Lord Infamous and Crunchy Black), and after very favourable sales for *Da End*, was now being courted by major names in the industry. Relativity Records final signed them, under a deal that would allow them to record under their newly launched Hypnotize Minds label.

Significantly, as more widespread popularity became a very real possibility, they started to tone down their act, lyrics-wise. A new album (the first with the major label), *Chapter 2: World Domination*, contained substantially fewer satanic references – in fact, virtually none at all. The raunch and power was still there, though, and it looked like, commercially at least, they could do no wrong.

As something of a master-stroke, they also released a re-recorded and rewritten version of one of their old club hits from *Mystic Stylez*, 'Tear The Club Up', renamed 'Tear The Club Up '97'. The single took off in a big way, not just in the South, and was followed in charts all over by the album, which eventually went gold.

With these successes under their belts, Juicy J and DJ Paul weren't going to let the grass grow. The group name now became a general branding for a number of solo projects by group members (Gangsta Boo, Koopsta, Knicca), non-group members (Project Pat, the Kaze) and some compilation albums, including *Tear The Club Up Thugs* and *Hypnotize Camp Posse*. Suddenly Triple 6 Mafia was in danger of suffering the backlash effect of too many records in the marketplace.

What it did do, however, was raise the profile of Memphis in the wider world of hip-hop, which stood the group in good stead when they finally released their first 'official' album in three years, *When The Smoke Clears*, in the summer of 2000. The album – hailed as their most commercial yet, with sing-along lines and a bass-heavy sound – was trailed by a single release of one of the tracks, 'Sippin' On Some Syrup', which broke through nationally. Things were really moving now, and the album débuted at the Number Six spot in the *Billboard* album charts.

They followed with the critically applauded *Kings Of Memphis Vol. 3*, which included previously unreleased material, and also started work on a direct-to-video film, *Choices*, plus more solo albums. Triple 6 Mafia have emerged as one of the greatest southern acts in rap history, and the most talked-about in recent years. *When The Smoke Clears* was selling half a million units in a week at its peak, quite an achievement for an outfit whose first LP cleared less than 100,000 in a year. Especially one from such a 'bunk ass town' as Memphis…

EAST MEMPHIS'S PERSIAN PRINCESS
Andria Lisle

Memphis jazz virtuoso Calvin Newborn says that she is 'one of Memphis's best-kept secrets', while local classical guitarist Mark Allen calls her 'a perfectionist', but the late Andrés Segovia put it best. After hearing Lily Afshar perform in 1986, the master simply said, '[It is] my prediction that she will be a beautiful celebrity.'

A decade and a half later, Segovia's prophecy rings true, for Lily Afshar is beautiful, both in the traditional sense and in a deeply spiritual manner. She is also at the top of her craft, a classical guitarist of world renown. 'A Persian princess', the Memphis transplant laughingly calls herself, but the title fits. Dark-haired and dark-eyed, she is luminous, a brightly burning star in the velvet-black night.

One lazy Sunday, I drive down Poplar Avenue to spend the afternoon at Lily's East Memphis town house. She lives in a neighbourhood that is connected to the city's exclusive Racquet Club, and in the shadow of Clarke Tower her place blends into the busy suburban atmosphere.

With the Mississippi River blocking westward growth, citizens have had no choice other than to look east when it came time for expansion. So the realisation that the city's epicentre has shifted over the years should come as no surprise – even famed producers Sam Phillips and Willie Mitchell live a few blocks from each other, less than 1.5km (1 mile) from Lily's home. It is a popular area for up-and-coming Memphians, as well as a trendy destination for well-to-do shoppers, and I battle traffic as I head east down Poplar Avenue, doing my best to avoid the oversized SUVs and mini-vans that seem to dominate the narrow lanes.

By the time I pull into Lily's driveway, I am frazzled, and a few minutes late for our date. Nonplussed, she greets me at the front door holding her guitar, eager to serenade me with a song while I take off my jacket. Her house is quite elegant inside. Colourful paintings and photographs of musicians – mostly guitarists, of course – cover the walls, while books and more photos crowd the built-in bookshelves. A beautiful, intricately woven Persian rug covers the floor, and I have to fight to resist taking my shoes off and sinking my toes into the faded tapestry.

Lily guides me to a comfy seat in her living room, before disappearing into the kitchen for refreshments. She has some tea brewing, and a delicious, delicately spicy aroma wafts from the open door, transporting me to a world far beyond the confines of East Memphis. I breathe in deeply, so allowing the scent to fill my lungs, then I close my eyes and relax, feeling pleased to find myself in such a serene environment.

'In my family, everyone played an instrument – violin, piano, guitar,' Lily tells me over a mug of piping-hot tea a few minutes later. She's settled into her living-room couch, reminiscing about her youth in Tehran, Iran. 'My father was an electrical engineer, educated in England and America, and an excellent musician. He loved the arts – he was a very broad-minded man. The way he brought me up was very contrary to how people bring up their kids in Iran. In that house I could do anything – there were no limits.

'When I was ten years old, I heard a cousin take a classical guitar lesson,' Lily says, her voice growing warm from the memory. 'She couldn't do the things the teacher wanted her to do, and I was frustrated: I wanted to grab the guitar from her and do it myself. I understood it all and I felt it. It was so strong.' Within a day, the instrument was hers. 'It was love at first sight', she declares passionately, adding, 'and it's been like that ever since.'

The youngest of four girls, Lily longed for something to set her apart from her sisters. 'The guitar gave me a voice – that's mine,' she points out today. 'As soon as I picked up the guitar and had my father's support, nothing else mattered. I put all my attention on the guitar. I gave up skiing and many other things – but because I wanted to,' she insists. 'I used to take my guitar to school, and during free periods I would practice. When we'd have guests in the house, my father would have me come play for them. When I had my guitar in my hand, I knew I could do anything,' Lily says. It's a credo that has taken her around the world many times over.

At age 17, Lily left Iran to attend college in the United States. 'At the time, I had no idea that I could continue my guitar studies and get a degree,' she says, amused at her own naïvety. After two weeks at Boston University, Lily withdrew from her classes, determined to devote all her energies to classical guitar.

By sheer coincidence, she saw a class catalogue for the nearby Boston Conservatory of Music. 'I went to the guitar professor's house in Cambridge the next day and played for him in his kitchen,' Lily says, still somewhat awed by her own resolve. 'He accepted me, and the next day I transferred. I had music there, and that's all I wanted.' Lily moved to the New England Conservatory of Music for her master's degree, and then Florida State University, where she became the first woman in the world to gain a doctorate of music in guitar performance. 'I couldn't go back to Iran – the revolution had happened,' Lily explains. 'My father said to continue my studies, so I became a professional student!'

Determined to maintain her visa, Lily became a model scholar, scooping up accolades at international classical guitar competitions near and far. Summers were spent competing against equal-minded young musicians in Banff (Canada), Aspen (Colorado) and Siena (Italy), where Lily often took home the top prizes. 'They used me a lot in advertising for my school,' Lily says with a grin. 'And competitions really opened up my career.' Yet an incident after one competition in Siena nearly ended Lily's dream before it had really begun…

'It was 1983, a very bad time in Iran, shortly after the Islamic Revolution,' Lily recalls. 'Most Iranians didn't travel because they were afraid of getting deported. But me, I was fearless,' she says. 'At the American Embassy in Rome, I was told, "You have been in America long enough. I am not going to send you back." And bang! He stamped my passport.'

Enrolled at Florida State University at the time, Lily continued on to the United States. 'I'd heard that you could ask for asylum once you landed on American soil,' she says, 'so that's what I did. I got a green card from an agency in New York that sent me around the country as an artist-in-residence. I played in libraries, senior citizen homes, schools, all over. It was a big responsibility,' she says with a sigh, crediting all the travelling and performing to her deep inner strength. 'No one's ever heard you or seen you,' Lily explains. 'All they have is that program in their hand, and by the time you leave that stage, everybody knows you. You have friends and fans, and you've touched their hearts.'

While that thought sinks in, Lily tunes her guitar. It's a gleaming, delicate instrument, made of gently curving cedar and Brazilian rosewood. The machine heads that tighten the nylon strings are handmade from shiny mother-of-pearl, and they glow in her grasp as if they were still awash with salt water on some sandy ocean floor. 'I like performing for people but I have to play for myself, so I can understand the message,' Lily explains, considering her guitar. She calls it an extension of her being and, looking at the curving slopes of the instrument, it's impossible to disagree. 'There's no two of us, just one,' Lily murmurs.

And then she begins to play. The piece, a gently lilting waltz by the South American composer Agustin Barrios Mangore, is on Lily's latest album, *Possession*, recently released on the local label Archer Records. The notes ring like bells in a country church, Lily ably coaxing subtle nuances from the six strings. I sit, rapt, as she demonstrates her flexibility. Her hands are the same size as mine, but limber in ways I can only imagine. 'I can stretch one fret past an octave,' she says, easily reaching from the first fret to the seventh. 'It's pretty good – some men can't do that,' Lily laughs, showing me how the little finger on her left hand has grown longer than the one on her right because of the constant stretching.

She moves onto another work, a piece by Mario Castelnuovo-Tedesco called 'Dios La Perdone: Y Era Su Madre'. Composed as one of 24 *Caprichos De Goya*, the music is meant to accompany an etching by the 18th-century painter Francisco Goya. 'Each piece has a story,' Lily explains patiently. 'You have to understand the rhythmic structure, the melody and the articulations.' She begins playing the opening movement, which consists of a deep, pleading line followed by a few measures that are higher-pitched and, I could swear, argumentative.

'Here we have a conversation between two characters,' Lily clarifies, showing me the picture of an old woman begging for alms from a younger woman. 'Begging/go away,' she sings, echoing her voice with the guitar. 'Next, we get this sweet section that's like a tango.' Lily's fingers dance across the strings, as she reveals an emotional shift in the piece. A strong chord comes next and, I learn, 'the young one turns back and sees that the old woman is her mother. That's the climax.' It's like magic – I see the story, and simultaneously hear it, in a language that knows no words.

The music continues, softer now. 'The whole thing is basically hopeless,' Lily says with a shrug, translating the title of the song as 'God Forgive Her: It Was Her Mother'. 'It's tragic, no?' asks Lily. 'The story behind the picture is about a young woman who left home and went to

Cadiz. She's all fashionable-looking walking around the Prada, and her mother sees her.' Goya, it seems, was making a stand against prostitution.

When she first came to America, Lily had purchased a copy of the *Caprichos*, but the music was too difficult for her to follow. Then, when it came time to complete her doctorate, she remembered the work and chose it as the subject of her dissertation. 'The music was originally composed in 1961,' she tells me, 'but all I could find on it was a two-page article in a German guitar journal. Segovia told Tedesco they'd be the most important pieces in the history of the guitar – but he never got around to playing them. The *Caprichos* ended up ignored by guitarists everywhere. So I became a detective – I thought this piece was made for me because of my love of art and the guitar.'

Lily relished the challenge. She researched Goya's history – the politics, social climate and personal events in the artist's life. She took art lessons, and analysed every single etching. Then she contacted Tedesco's son, the architect Lorenzo Tedesco, in California. 'He gave me so much material,' Lily remembers. Next, she journeyed to Italy, where she studied with Angelo Gilardino, the musician who edited Tedesco's compositions. Along the way, she picked up a grant from the government-funded National Endowment of the Arts to finance her own recording of the *Caprichos*. 'It was monumental work,' Lily tells me, 'but my dissertation was immediately published. It was translated into Italian and German, and it quickly became my stamp on the guitar world. I am', she proudly reveals, 'the world authority on this topic!

'I did my doctoral hearing, then came to Memphis the next day,' Lily says. 'I couldn't go back home, so I applied for a teaching job at the University of Memphis. When I arrived here in 1989, I did not know a thing about the city,' she laughs. 'But I am very adventurous, and I am lucky that I have been able to stay here and take advantage of all the sacrifices my father made for me.'

The newly minted US citizen transformed the classical guitar programme at the University of Memphis. 'I like to teach all levels,' she says, pointing out one student who studied here for his bachelor's, then went to Yale for his master's degree. 'He came back here for his doctorate,' Lily notes delightedly. In 2000, she won the Orville H Gibson Award for Best Female

Classical Guitarist and became the first member of the music department to receive the Board of Visitors' Eminent Faculty Award. But she's most proud of the classical guitar society she founded at the university in 1991.

'Artists come from all over the world, to play concerts and hold master classes for my students. It energizes all of us,' Lily says excitedly. 'My students really have to work hard – I have high standards,' she laughs, her eyes gleaming. 'I have learned that when you go on stage you have a responsibility to your audience – and I have prepared my students the best I can. In the music world, you have to be tough all the time,' she says, punctuating her words with a sharp arpeggio. 'School is no time to sleep – if you snooze, you lose!'

In the last few years, Lily has returned to Iran for similar workshops. 'In the time of the Shah, it was customary to give concerts all the time – it was like Europe,' Lily explains. 'As an international performer, it was always my dream to go back and teach master classes there, even after the Islamic Revolution. Since then, the demand for lessons has grown – music and art are in the Iranian nature. And even under the regime,' she clarifies, 'a lot of women play guitar.

'Next February, I will perform with the Tehran Symphony Orchestra,' Lily tells me. 'That was always my big dream – and sure enough, I'm going to be doing it in a big symphony hall. Under the Islamic regime, the concert halls are always packed – people are thirsty for anything new.' Today, Lily has such a following in Iran that she is constantly emailed for instruction from devoted students. 'There was no Persian music written for the guitar,' she says, 'so I arranged five traditional pieces and published them in a Mel Bay music book. The tar, a traditional Persian stringed instrument, was the forerunner of the modern guitar. Even the word *tar* means "string" in Persian.'

Glancing around the room, I notice her neatly stacked suitcases near the front door. 'Oh,' Lily exclaims, 'I traveled all summer and haven't had time to unpack.' She performed in Africa, Australia and New Zealand, and will fly to England for a series of concerts featuring the *Caprichos* before the year is out. 'If you want to hear me play, come out to the Memphis airport.' Lily laughs. 'I play at the gate while waiting for my flight – why waste time? I've got to practice,' she giggles. 'And I have an audience – what's better than that?'

But, for now, talk returns to Memphis. 'Here, it doesn't matter what style you play, as long as you play it well,' Lily remarks. 'People in Memphis are very open-minded. Three years in a row, I was given the Memphis Premier Player Award for Best Guitarist, and here I am competing with jazz musicians and blues players who are so different.'

Then she jumps up to play me a recording of 'Working Man', a blues song she cut with singer Brenda Patterson and organist Charlie Wood for Archer Records. 'I play my Gibson EC-30 on this,' Lily says, putting a glass slide on her pinkie for a demo. 'Who would have imagined me playing a blues song! But Ward Archer has a vision – he has ambition and a lot of guts. You know, it's funny that we even met. He heard me play one night, and asked me to come by his studio. I didn't take him seriously, but almost before I knew it I had this CD out! Thanks to him, my new album is very modern and innovative.'

I think back to something Mark Allen told me earlier in the week. 'I have known Lily since she came to town,' Allen said. 'She is such a perfectionist, but she loves the influence that Memphis has – the spirit of blues and rock 'n' roll. Style and show means so much more than hitting the right notes. At first I think it bothered her classical way of thinking, but she didn't run away – she has chosen to stay.'

As if she is reading my mind, Lily picks out a jaunty version of Carl Perkins's rockabilly classic 'Matchbox', then easily returns to 'Afro-Cuban Lullaby', a Leo Brouwer composition from *Possession*. 'I had to be rigid for a long time to focus on my practicing,' she says, 'but now that I have my own voice, I am always asking people to teach me music!' She smiles elatedly, then plays a spirited blues lick, perfectly content to shine for her audience of one.

SHAKE IT AND BREAK IT
Mike Evans

Even for the visitor newly acquainted with the city, there's plenty in Memphis beyond Beale, particularly on the music front, including some funky establishments that give just a taste of what downtown must have been like in its glory days.

Now a lot of the action is to be found elsewhere on the map, top of most people's list being Wild Bill's on Vollentine, which Andria Lisle covered in depth in Chapter 1. Suffice to say that those rows of classic-looking autos outside are a regular testimony to the fact that the place is as popular as ever, and will remain so just as long as the music rocks and Wild Bill keeps serving the drinks.

Almost as well-known as Bill's, the Hard Luck Café on musically historic East McLemore is a low-key joint which, as Andria Lisle pointed out, lives up to its name, having certainly seen better days. The faded '70s décor says it all appearance-wise, but once the music starts, who's looking at the wallpaper? Like Wild Bill's, it's a place to hear some of the best blues bands in town, in an authentic 'no-frills' atmosphere that likewise make no concessions in their music.

Down on South Main Street, a jazz and blues joint with a real history still survives. After starting life as a drugstore through the '30s and '40s, what is now, and has been for many years, Earnestine and Hazel's, developed into a bar-cum-hotel-cum-brothel in the early 1950s, catering for musicians who would socialise and do business downstairs, while others used the more exotic facilities upstairs.

Earnestine, wife of the nightclub operator and Beale Street hotel proprietor Sunbeam Mitchell, bought the place in the late '50s with business partner Hazel, converting it into a hotel for railroad passengers using the train station opposite. But it was still favoured by musicians as a hangout, even if they weren't travelling, and a virtual who's who of famous blues, rock 'n' roll and soul people socialised or stayed there through the '60s, including Steve Cropper, Otis Redding, Howlin' Wolf and (so the legend goes) Elvis.

In latter years Earnestine and Hazel's underwent a much-needed refurbishment, but you'd hardly guess. Despite a tidy bar and sometimes well-heeled clientele from the new downtown professional classes, the joint has an unmistakable atmosphere of dilapidated grandeur, not to mention just about the best jukebox in town if it's golden Memphis oldies you're talking about. And there's still a handwritten sign on the door declaring 'No dope smokin', No cursin', No freeloadin'', which gives just a hint of the somewhat rowdier customers that you were likely to rub shoulders with in days gone by.

Earnestine and Hazel's stands at 531 South Main, at the intersection with Calhoun, which was the site until not long ago of the wonderful

Wolf's Corner. Considered by many, until its demise, to actually have that much-vaunted 'best jukebox in Memphis'. I was lucky enough to visit Wolf's in 1995, four years before it finally closed its doors, and the joint, as they say, was jumping. Formica-topped tables were strewn with beer bottles (no draught!), in front of which was a small space full of swaying dancers, most of whom, I got the impression, were well into middle age or even older – R&B fans from first time round, shakin' it and breakin' it till the small hours. That night the records were being played by a house DJ who seemed to go by the name of Cowboy – probably on account of the large stetson he wore – who spun a non-stop segue of contemporary soul, '60s Stax and rock 'n' roll classics. Most of the 45s sounded like original releases, certainly if the scratches evident on the Fats Domino and Johnny Otis sides were anything to go by.

Right next to Wolf's, which was once a voodoo supply store and is now, by contrast, a fancy accessory shop, stood the Arcade Hotel; it was the one used in the Jim Jarmusch movie *Mystery Train*, in which Screamin' Jay Hawkins played the reception desk clerk. That too has fallen to the redevelopers' plans, like much of downtown of yore. Like the spectre of Elvis in the movie – there one minute, gone the next – the ghosts of the music makers of old are all that's left on many a street corner or once-buzzing thoroughfare. Nevertheless, as long as Wild Bill's, the Hard Luck, Earnestine's and the like continue to shake and break it into the new millennium, the final disappearance of such places is hopefully a long way away.

ROCKIN' AROUND THE CLOCK WITH LUTHER DICKINSON
Andria Lisle

I am nearing the end of this book, and my head is swirling with the complications of race relations and music. Everything I thought I knew when I began interviewing these musicians has been compounded by their own personal histories and stories of Memphis, good, bad or as indifferent as the city may be.

During the decade and a half I've lived here, the city has taken on a mythic quality, and in more recent years I have seen reality and fiction combine into a new fabric as strong as the old tapestries of Sun and Stax. For the first time in a long while, I don't wish that I were old enough to witness Fred McDowell playing in Como, Mississippi, or to see Rufus Thomas and Gatemouth Moore in a travelling tent show. I am fortunate enough to get those memories secondhand, and young enough to create my own.

Luther Dickinson, Jim's number one son, agrees with me. 'I always wanted to play guitar, and I always looked to the guitar players that my dad played with,' Luther tells me. It's summer, and we're at my house, resting on the couch drinking beer. I am lying on my back, watching Luther talk, his scruffy beard outlining his boyish mouth as he shapes the words.

'Ry Cooder, Lee Baker and Charlie Freeman – I always thought those were the cool guys,' Luther says. 'Their whole scene was from coming up in the '60s with the beatniks and the folk houses, and the early blues festivals. They all had a connection with Furry Lewis, who was the spiritual godfather of the whole scene. Bukka White, Sleepy John Estes, Fred McDowell, Rev Robert Wilkins, Nathan Beauregard.' When I tell Luther that Nathan Beauregard once lived across the street, he jumps up to take a look out the window. 'He was a real inspiration to my old man – a 100-year-old man singing about 12-year-old pussy,' Luther laughs, momentarily distracted. 'And it's true, you can rock – no matter whether you play jazz, blues or rock, you can do it all your life.

'For a long time I never thought that I could be in a situation where I could hang out with someone like Furry Lewis or Fred McDowell,' Luther says. 'When I was a kid, I always wanted to be grown. Now I'm just glad that we were cool enough kids to realize what was going on. 'I was born right in the middle of that crazy '70s Memphis scene,' Luther tells me. 'My brother Cody and I grew up in this awesome community of artists and musicians. When I was six and Cody was three, we got guitars for Christmas. Mine was electric, and Cody's was acoustic. Dad tuned mine to an open "E" and taught me a Bo Diddley chord. I remember doing that with as much distortion as I could muster up. Cody was extremely talented from the jump – he learned "KC Jones" first.

'I remember one time my brother and I were down in a ditch beating on the dirt with some sticks, singing "Rock Around The Clock",' Luther says, as he rolls an American Spirit cigarette. 'Dad came along and said, "The rhythm is good, but you don't have the words right!"' Luther shakes his head and laughs. 'Dad always knew that we wanted to be musicians. He only discouraged us by saying that it's a hard life. He'd say, "Don't do it because I'm a musician – just do it if you have to."

'I knew all my life that I wanted to be a guitar player, but it's a weird ambition to have, because there's no set way to go about becoming one,' Luther explains. 'You just gotta take it day by day, practicing and learning and hanging out with new people, jamming and studying some more. So I was always working toward that. I thought it was my responsibility, coming up in Memphis, to know all the local styles. So I honed up on my Roland Janes, my Charlie Freeman, Teenie Hodges, Steve Cropper. I knew I had to be familiar with the language.'

From the beginning, there were no distinctions between black and white in the Dickinson household. 'We lived out in Rossville, Tennessee, for a long time,' Luther tells me. 'We were right on the state line – our next-door neighbors lived in Mississippi. Our street was a gravel road with fields and farms and houses on it. There was a juke joint about half a mile [800m] down the road, and a big farm across the street where they would have baptisms in the summertime.

'Tape machines also fascinated me. You know, I destroyed Dad's collection,' Luther says with a laugh. 'I remember when they were working on *Big Star's 3rd*, my mom and I would listen to those songs all day. I love the memory of how music sounded when I was a kid. It was like hearing these abstract, amorphous vibrations. I wasn't thinking, "Oh, that's a cool overdub." I was just falling into this world.

'When I was five I was watching *Mr Rogers's Neighborhood* with my dad, and we saw Othar Turner on there with Jessie Mae Hemphill. Dad said, "Check this out – he lives just down the road." Then through the Center for Southern Folklore's Music And Heritage Festival, I met Othar. We'd play with Dad every year, and Othar and his family would play every year. I'd always remembered the *Mr Rogers* show, and I would try to go hang out with Othar. He'd be in the craft tent making fifes, and I met Bernice, his daughter. So the next year Bernice talked to me, and by the third year we were friends.'

In the meantime, Jim Dickinson formed Mud Boy And The Neutrons with Jimmie Crosthwait, Lee Baker and Sid Selvidge. 'We'd go to these concerts and festivals and just rock out,' Luther remembers. 'And I learned songs like "KC Jones" and "Going To Brownsville", blues songs, country songs, early rock 'n' roll songs. By the early '90s, we got to play with Mud Boy – the band never had a rhythm section, so we got to fill in. They showed us the ropes – Cody says that's where he learned how to make the girls shake their asses.

'If you make a family tree of the blues, garage and punk rock scene, it all goes back to The Panther Burns, and then further back to Mud Boy,' Luther explains. 'It's just a weird Memphis hybrid of what happens when you mix crazy hillbillies and crazy black guys together. Back in the '60s, when Bobby Ray Watson would bring RL Burnside up to Roland Jane's studio, he'd have a duffel bag of homegrown Mississippi reefer, and RL would have the corn liquor and, man, it's just a crazy combination! Look at RL and his guitar player Kenny Brown – they're family. People just don't understand how well we can get along in the South…'

When Luther was 12, the Dickinsons relocated to Hernando, a north Mississippi town that straddles the tip of the Delta and the hill country. 'Somewhere in there I realized that there was a very alive blues scene in Mississippi, right where we were living. I guess that I started hearing rumors of Junior Kimbrough's juke joint when I was in my teens, but it wasn't until I got a car and started exploring that I could experience it firsthand.

'Before that, I was listening to Robert Johnson, Charley Patton, early Bo Diddley, Chuck Berry and Howlin' Wolf, but I just thought that it was music from the past,' Luther says. 'I couldn't imagine modern-day primitive country blues was taking place in my own backyard! Thank God for Robert Palmer and Fat Possum Records – they not only captured what was going on, they pushed everybody into the future, by having Junior tour with Iggy Pop, and making RL a worldwide phenomenon. Of course, it was going on everywhere – Beck came out with a very folky, very bluesy album, and G Love, who had an entirely different take on the kind of blues-soul music he grew up with, and Jon Spencer and The Gories. I loved anything that had a bluesy twist.

'Eventually, we got to know these other musical families, like the Burnsides and the Kimbroughs. The hill-country families were more farm-based, and they stayed at home with their families. It was much more of a community-based thing,' Luther explains. 'So when Cody and I hooked up with these guys, they had a juke joint and all the talent in the world, and we had a studio set up in Dad's barn. With the older cats like RL, we have common ground as musicians. But with the younger guys, we're hanging out, smoking blunts and drinking beer and just jamming.'

Of course, the Dickinson boys were listening to more than just blues music at the time. Cody moved on to drums (he played a kit his dad brought home from the Stax studio) and, as Luther recalls, 'we had a basement band, a garage band, a house party band, all these little-kid teenage kind of bands, but once I got that car, we were driving up to Memphis and hanging out in town. We started the band DDT with Paul Taylor. I listened to everything from Black Flag to JFA and spent time hanging out at Rare Records and trying to get into the Antenna Club,' he says with a snort.

'When I first got into Black Flag, I got a copy of the "Six Pack" 7-inch. I felt like "Alright, I finally found music from my planet." Later on, I tried to get Dad to help me learn how to play it, and he said, "What is this shit?" He didn't get into it for a while. Dad couldn't believe that I found music that he hated, but then he said it gave him confidence in rock 'n' roll, that it could still create music that the parents hated!'

But there was no real need to rebel in this family. 'I always knew that my parents were different,' Luther admits. 'I still don't have a good perspective on it because its just natural to me. I always felt lucky – I always felt like it was cool.' I remind him of the days when his mother, Mary Lindsay, would let the boys sleep until three or four in the afternoon because they'd have a big gig that night. Luther giggles, remembering. 'We were brought up in an alternative creative way out in the country. My folks kept us out of school till third grade. My mom taught me math and ABCs and all that. Local artists like Tom Foster and Jim Blake would come down and teach me how to draw. They taught me the joys of the copy machine, which was a key to the do-it-yourself punk rock aesthetic.

There was such a community of musicians and artists and outlaws and criminals and freaks. Not freaks, but just real people,' Luther says. And they were pioneers of a lifestyle – those were different times.

'When I was in high school, Dad worked with The Replacements, who were a big influence on me,' Luther says. 'I would go through his demo tapes, and I think I learned a lot about songwriting that way.' He played guitar on their album, 1987's *Pleased To Meet Me*. Locally, it was a big deal, but Luther claims that he felt like a geeky high-school kid who 'never really fit in anywhere'.

'I would go down to Senatobia all the time and help Othar do chores,' Luther says, laughing. 'He didn't really need help – I would just follow him around and bother him. Then we decided to do a single, and I went down there and paid him to record him. From that point on, our relationship changed. But it was good – he became a recording star.

'Once I played guitar for him, our friendship really cemented. I didn't know that he and Fred McDowell were neighbors and best friends, and one day I was sitting on his porch playing guitar, and he said, "What are you doing? Can't nobody run the strings like Fred McDowell!", but I could tell that he liked what I was playing.'

Meanwhile, Luther and Cody's band, DDT, morphed from a three-man punk rock group into The DDT Big Band, an ensemble featuring vocalist Kelley Hurt, a horn section and various percussion instruments.'After a certain time, I couldn't play or couldn't write in that style anymore,' Luther says. He pauses for a few minutes, but can't really articulate his reasons for dissolving the band. 'Our band got to be too big, and my heart wasn't in it,' he says. 'A few months later, I was hanging out in a friend's trailer down in Water Valley, Mississippi, and taking mushrooms. I was lying on the dirty shag carpet trying to go to sleep, and listening to this Fred McDowell song, "Crazy 'Bout You", and it came to me: This is what I want to do, to form a band called The North Mississippi Allstars.'

Of course, Cody stayed on as drummer. The Dickinson brothers brought in bassist Chris Chew, a hulking man who towers over the stage like a chocolate Buddha. Then Dwayne Burnside came on board, part of what Luther sees as the beginning of a great southern travelling band. To date, The North Mississippi Allstars have cut three albums, toured to great acclaim worldwide, and been nominated for a pair of Grammies. Their version of Fred's hill-country boogie takes fans far beyond the traditional blues world, an amalgamation of black and white, blues and rock 'n' roll.

'I am just loving this life,' Luther exclaims to me as he gets up for another beer. We've been talking for hours, a rare treat in these busy days of sound checks, interviews and practice sessions. Then Luther stops and shakes his head as his cellphone rings, signalling his return to the real world. He checks the number, then turns the phone off and puts it back into his pocket. 'It's weird, too,' he says. 'It feels like the more time that passes and the more we do our thing, the further we get from where we come from.' And like that he's out the door, on his way home, then back on the road.

THE NEW GARAGE ROCK
Mike Evans

Like the names of Dickinson and Chilton before them, three names have emerged as leading lights in Memphis grassroots rock over the past few years – Jack Yarber, Greg Cartwright and Jeffrey Evans.

At the latter end of the 1990s, Jack Yarber featured in two bands that made their mark on the Memphis alternative scene, The Compulsive Gamblers and The Oblivians. The Compulsive Gamblers were originally an early '90s band featuring Yarber and Cartwright, both on guitar and vocals, making three singles and an EP between 1991 and 1993 before morphing into The Oblivians, a name that was to become synonymous with Memphis garage rock.

The three-piece featured Yarber and Cartwright, both of whom had added drums to their repertoire of instruments, while taking on the surname Oblivian as a *nom de guerre*. The third member, Eric Friedl – likewise billed as playing drums, guitars and vocals – now became Eric Oblivian. The band was a seminal influence on the local scene, with its blues-based punk pop being likened to Jon Spencer, Beck and – going back further into the rock 'n' roll heritage – even Johnny Thunders.

Their albums, seven between 1994 and 1997, garnered rave notices across the South, most of them on the local indie Sympathy for the Record Industry label.

Jack and Greg Oblivian couldn't keep still, however, and a variety of side-projects (including '68 Comeback in which Greg appeared with its leader Jeffrey Evans) were the prelude to The Compulsive Gamblers' reforming. If all this sounds like the branching-out of an increasingly incestuous rock family tree, that's exactly what it was, and it's fair to say that Yarber, Cartwright and Evans have been in and out of each other's various projects with bewildering frequency ever since.

Once described as the godfather of Memphis punk, Jeffrey Evans – or Monsieur Jeffrey Evans as he prefers to be billed – originally hit Memphis back in 1989, and began making his presence felt with appearances with local line-ups including The Oblivians, The Workdogs and La Fong. At the same time, he was making an indelible impression with his own bands, first The Gibson Brothers and then the seminal trash-rock heroes '68 Comeback, both of which, according to local critic Chris Davis (the *Memphis Flyer*) 'are so universally influential that people in France have his Cadillac tattooed on their backs'.

As well as his bands, plus innumerable guest appearances on other people's records and on other people's gigs, guitar-vocalist and harmonica player Evans has made solo albums, not least of which was his (outdoor) live album *I've Lived A Rich Life* in 2001. Other recent Evans excursions have included his collaborations with Jack Oblivian in The Tearjerkers, South Filthy and The Cool Jerks, plus a production role on the début album by The Porch Ghouls.

Formed in 2001, The Porch Ghouls, comprise the fabulously named Eldorado Del Ray on guitar and lead vocals, Slim Electro on guitar, drummer Duke Baltimore and Randy Valentine on harmonica. There is some considerable pedigree in there, however, for 'Duke Baltimore' is actually Bruce Saltmarsh (who had been with '68 Comeback), while 'Slim Electro' is an alias for Scott Taylor, whose credentials go back through Hot Monkey to '90s favourites The Grifters.

Wearing their local blues roots firmly on their sleeves, they describe their music as 'ruckus', which they claim was a 1920s slang term for the music of Memphis jug bands. Whatever, their modern take on country blues-blowin' was well represented on their eponymous Evans-produced ten-inch début album, which included numbers by Hound Dog Taylor, Willie Dixon and RL Burnside among others, prompting *Memphis Flyer* writer Mark Jordan to enthuse about them: '[a] group that mixes white and black blues and rock in a way that Memphis has done to unique effect, whether it be Elvis or more recent, less-celebrated bands'.

Greg Cartwright, meanwhile, had been putting together Reigning Sound, launched in 1991 (with a début album, *Break Up, Break Down*) with Alex Greene on keyboards and guitar, Greg Roberson on drums, and bassist Jeremy Scott, to form an explosive line-up fusing the spirit of Memphis soul with a '60s pop dynamic and country-boogie edge. Talking to the Memphis media, Cartwright was anxious to distance the new band from what he'd done previously, without dismissing past achievements: 'I didn't want to be in another band that sounds like The Oblivians or The Compulsive Gamblers, I just wanted to do something different. And I've always been a big fan of folk rock.'

A few months after the début of Reigning Sound, Cartwright's fellow Oblivian and Compulsive Gambler Jack Yarber emerged with yet another musical manifestation, this time called The Tearjerkers. And, while Carwright's latest line-up had served to mark a move into more soft-focus territory than those previous punk-oriented ventures, Yarber's new thing was confirmation of his position at the cutting edge of tough garage rock 'n' roll. With guitarist John Whittemore, bassist Scott Bomar and Bubba Bonds on drums, The Tearjerkers' début full-length offering, *Bad Moon Rising*, epitomised much of what contemporary Memphis rock 'n' roll is all about. As a review in *Cyclops* magazine confirmed, 'The Tearjerkers are a rock 'n' roll band with a few funky and country twists thrown in for good measure. In a blind taste test, I could tell the band is from Memphis. There's just something about the Bluff City that seems to infuse that city's music.'

However, Yarber and Cartwright were to get together again soon after, as The Knaughty Knights, followed by Evans and Yarber (that family tree must be looking pretty complicated by now!), with the cream of the Austin, Texas scene, as South Filthy. The latter was a down-home evocation of bar-room blues *You Can Name It Yo' Mammy If You Wanna* (again on the influential Sympathy for the Record Industry label) with Austin heavyweights that included harmonica man Walter Daniels and drummer Mike Buck.

Jack 'Oblivian' Yarber's most recent project has been what one magazine called 'the latest installment of the Memphis/North Mississippi musician exchange program.' It saw Yarber collaborating with three denizens of Oxford, Mississippi – David Boyer on guitar and vocals, drummer Forrest Hewes and bass player Scott Rogers, who had been together for some years as The Neckbones.

Heavy on riffs quite a lot of the time, their début LP nevertheless avoids the sins of 'heavy' blues bands of the late '60s to which guitar riffing can often allude, reflecting more the local influences of North Mississippi players like Junior Kimbrough and RL Burnside. *Cleaned A Lot Of Plates In Memphis* was actually recorded in Nashville, where Boyer had moved to, with Hewes and Rogers now resident in Memphis.

In the case of bands like The Cool Jerks and players of the calibre of Yarber, Cartwright and Evans – seasoned musicians all – 'garage' has become something of a misnomer, redolent of a healthy but amateur dynamic that characterised their earlier musical adventures. But whatever term is used, it's clear that rock 'n' roll – as a living music, not just a museum piece – is alive and well in Memphis.

Appendix 1

TEN VENUES FOR THE SOUND OF MEMPHIS

ALFRED'S
A barn of a bar, but worth checking out when the 17-piece Memphis
Jazz Orchestra are playing.
197 Beale St
(901)525-3711

BB KING'S BLUES CLUB
Tourist-oriented, but with decent blues bands and soul acts – and BB
from time to time.
147 Beale St
(901) 524-5464

BLUES HALL
Low-key atmosphere, mostly local acoustic blues.
180 Beale St
(901) 528-0150

EARNESTINE AND HAZEL'S
Faded grandeur with live bands and a great jukebox.
531 South Main St
(901) 523-9754

GAY HAWK BAR
Things can get pretty wild on the DJ-driven dance floor.
685 Danny Thomas Blvd
(901) 947-1464

HARD LUCK CAFÉ
'No-frills' juke joint with straight-ahead blues acts.
216 East McLemore
(901) 942-6092

HI-TONE CAFÉ
Lively roots-rock hangout with a good bar.
1913 Poplar Ave
(901) 278-8663

NEW DAISY THEATER
Concert venue features everything from rock to jazz.
330 Beale St
(901) 525-8979

WILD BILL'S
If you want the real blues experience, it doesn't come more authentic than this.
1580 Vollantine Drive
(901) 726-5473

ZANZIBAR
Trendy-ish restaurant with some of the best local jazz musicians in an informal 'jamming' atmosphere.
412 South Main Street
(901) 543-9646

TEN RESTAURANTS FOR THE TASTE OF MEMPHIS

ANDERTON'S STEAK & SEAFOOD RESTAURANT
One of the very best – a favourite eating place for discerning Memphians since the 1950s, and it hasn't changed a bit.
1901 Madison Ave
(901) 726-4010

ALCENIA'S DESSERTS & PRESERVES SHOP
Famous for its desserts, and one of the few soul-food places open late.
317 North Main
(901) 523-0200

AUTOMATIC SLIM'S TONGA CLUB
Upmarket eating place with a Caribbean slant, plus an exotic range of cocktails.
83 South Second St
(901) 525-7948

BLUES CITY CAFÉ
Famous for its steaks – sold by the pound – BBQ ribs, southern-fried catfish, chilli and other home-town favourites.
138 Beale St
(901) 526-3637

BIG S GRILL
Juicy rib tips, succulent chopped BBQ sandwich, fabulous French fries and great jukebox – need we say more?
1179 Dunnavant St
(901) 775-9127

DYER'S BURGERS
They've been serving their speciality deep-fried burgers since 1912, and apparently the secret's in the grease!
205 Beale St
(901) 527-3937

FELICIA SUZANNE'S
Southern States cuisine with a Creole emphasis at this elegant eatery located inside Brinkley Plaza.
80 Monroe Ave
(901) 523-0877

McEWEN'S ON MONROE
Eclectic bistro serving a variety of four-star dishes.
122 Monroe Ave
(901) 527-7085

MOLLY'S LA CASITA
A great Tex-Mex institution, but watch out for the revellers on Margarita Mondays.
2006 Madison Ave
(901) 726-1873

STEIN'S FAMILY RESTAURANT
Down-home cooking – try fried chicken and collard greens with cornbread stuffing – at down-home prices.
2248 South Lauderdale
(901) 775-9203

TEN PLACES FOR THE MEMPHIS EXPERIENCE

A SCHWAB'S DRY GOODS STORE
Step back into old Memphis.
163 Beale Street
(901) 523-9782

CENTER FOR SOUTHERN FOLKLORE
Not as appropriate a location as previously in Beale Street, but worth
supporting with a visit.
119 South Main Street in Pembroke Square at Peabody Place
(901) 525-3655

THE FULL GOSPEL TABERNACLE
Where you can see and hear the Rev Al Green sing and preach –
unmissable.
787 Hale Road
(901) 396-9192

GIBSON GUITAR PLANT/MEMPHIS ROCK 'N' SOUL MUSEUM
Including the Smithsonian Institution's *Rock 'n' Soul: Social Crossroads*
exhibition. On the first floor, tour the Gibson factory where they make
the world-famous guitars.
145 George W Lee
Memphis, TN 38103
(901) 544-7998 / (901) 543-0800

GRACELAND
Call it cool or call it kitsch, no visit to Memphis is complete without a
trip to the house where the King lived and died.
3734 Elvis Presley Blvd
(901) 332-3322

NATIONAL CIVIL RIGHTS MUSEUM
The building was previously the motel where Dr Martin Luther King
was shot. Despite some local misgivings, go see for yourself.
450 Mulberry St
(901) 521-9699

THE PYRAMID
Only in America… A stainless-steel 21,000-seat basketball stadium that's
a full-size replica of the Great Pyramid in Egypt. A must-see.
1 Auction Ave
(901) 521-7909

SOULSVILLE: STAX MUSEUM OF AMERICAN SOUL MUSIC
Opening in spring 2003 in the heart of the district traditionally known
as Soulsville.
926 East McLemore Ave
(901) 946-2535

SUN STUDIO
If rock 'n' roll has a birthplace, this is it.
706 Union Ave
(901) 521-0664

WC HANDY HOUSE MUSEUM
Moved from its original location, the small wood-frame house is now a
museum dedicated to the 'Father of the Blues'.
352 Beale St
(901) 527-3427

Appendix 2

SOME HOTELS IN MEMPHIS

COMFORT INN DOWNTOWN
Inexpensive with no frills, near Mud Island and trolley line to downtown nightlife.
100 North Front St
(901) 526-0583

FRENCH QUARTER INN
Next to Overton Square in midtown, with a good bar and restaurant in the lobby.
2144 Madison Ave
(901) 728-4000

HAMPTON INN
A midtown hotel that's fairly inexpensive, close to downtown and near the Interstate.
1180 Union Ave.
(901) 276-1175

PEABODY HOTEL
Smartest hotel in town, for Old South luxury at a price.
149 Union Ave
(901) 529-4000

RADISSON HOTEL
Regular chain, clean and functional.
185 Union Ave.
(901)528-1800

SLEEP INN AT COURT SQUARE
Inexpensive, and convenient to the trolley and downtown; gets busy
during peak tourist times.
40 North Front Street
(901) 522-9700

TALBOT HEIRS GUESTHOUSE
Elegant rival to the Peabody, just across the street, with a more intimate
atmosphere.
99 South Second Street
(901) 527-9772

GETTING THERE

BY AIR
Memphis International Airport (MIA) is served by AirTran,
American/TWA, ComAir, Continental, Delta, Midway, Northwest,
United, US Airways, KLM Royal Dutch, and Northwest Airlines.

The airport is approximately 14km (9 miles) south of downtown, it
takes 15–20 minutes to get downtown by taxi, which costs $23–25.
Taxi companies: Checker Cab ((901) 577-7700) and Yellow Cab ((800)
796-7750)

Car rental companies at the airport are Alamo, Avis, Budget, Dollar,
Hertz and National. If you're driving, for the scenic route into downtown
exit Airways Blvd north to I-240 west, keep straight as the freeway name
changes to I-55 and bends northward. At the US 61 intersection, one
exit will take you to Riverside Drive—and a great view of the downtown
riverfront and Pyramid.

BY ROAD

Getting there by car is via Interstates 40 or 55: I-40 from eastern Tennessee North Memphis & DeSoto Bridge, I-55 from Mississippi to St Louis. Plus major highways into town: 51 US Route North to South Memphis (Danny Thomas and Elvis Presley Blvd), 61 US Route from Arkansas to South Memphis (Netters Blvd) and 78 US Route southeast (Mississippi) to downtown Memphis.

BY RAIL

Amtrak (www.amtrak.com) features a once-daily City of New Orleans train that travels on a Chicago–Memphis–Jackson–New Orleans route. You can catch the train at the newly refurbished Central Station at 545 South Main Street at Calhoun Ave (also named Patterson Ave).

GETTING AROUND

TROLLEY

The Main Street Trolley service, refurbished in recent years, runs every ten minutes on each block of Main Street and several locations along Riverside Drive. Fares: $.60 regular, $.30 for seniors and people with disabilities. The all-day passes are a steal at $2.50. Mon-Thurs 6am–midnight, Fri 6am–1am, Sat 9:30am–1am and Sun 10am–6pm.

Main Street Trolley Service Office
547 North Main St
(901) 274-6282

TAXI

Taxis are few and far between compared to cities like London or New York, and can rarely be hailed on the street, so you need to carry their phone numbers with you.
Checker Cab (901) 577-7700) and Yellow Cab ((800) 796-7750)

DRIVING
Parking downtown is fine except during major events, where you need to arrive early. Use secured parking lots with guards, and check for ID badges of the parking lot attendant, even around Beale Street.

WALKING
All the downtown area is relatively compact and walkable, but (assuming that's where you're staying) you need a car or taxi for anything further afield, even a midtown location can be further than you think.

Bibliography

BOOTH, Stanley: *Rythm Oil* (Random House, US, 1991)

ESCOTT, Colin: *Good Rockin' Tonight* (St Martins, US, 1991)

GEORGE, Nelson: *The Death Of Rhythm And Blues* (Random House, US, 1988)

GORDON, Robert: *It Came From Memphis* (Faber & Faber, US, 1995)

GURALNICK, Peter: *Careless Love: The Unmaking of Elvis Presley* (Little, Brown, US, 1999)

GURALNICK, Peter: *Last Train To Memphis: The Rise of Elvis Presley* (Little, Brown, US, 1994)

GURALNICK, Peter: *Sweet Soul Music* (Harper & Row, US, 1986)

LOMAX, Alan: *The Land Where The Blues Began* (Random House, US, 1993)

MITCHELL, George: *Blow My Blues Away* (DaCapo, US, 1983)

RODMAN, Gilbert B: *Elvis After Elvis* (Routledge, US, 1996)

TOSCHES, Nick: *Unsung Heroes Of Rock 'n' Roll* (Secker & Warburg, UK, 1991)

Index

Streets and venues are in Memphis, unless otherwise stated.